HATE CRIMES
revisited

HATE CRIMES
revisited:

America's War Against Those Who Are Different

Jack Levin and Jack McDevitt

NORTHEASTERN UNIVERSITY

Westview
PRESS

A Member of the Perseus Books Group

Copyright © 2002 by Westview Press, a Member of the Perseus Books Group

Westview Press books are available at special discounts for bulk purchases in the United States by corporations, institutions, and other organizations. For more information, please contact the Special Markets Department at the Perseus Books Group, 11 Cambridge Center, Cambridge MA 02142, or call (617) 252–5298.

Published in 2002 in the United States of America by Westview Press, 5500 Central Avenue, Boulder, Colorado 80301–2877, and in the United Kingdom by Westview Press, 12 Hid's Copse Road, Cumnor Hill, Oxford OX2 9JJ

Find us on the World Wide Web at www.westviewpress.com

Library of Congress Cataloging-in-Publication Data
Levin, Jack, 1941–
   Hate crimes revisited : America's war against those who are different / Jack Levin and Jack McDevitt.
      p. cm.
   Includes bibliographical references and index.
   ISBN-10: 0-8133-3922-7   ISBN-13: 978-0-8133-3922-1 (alk. paper)
   1. Hate crimes United States. 2. Prejudices United States. I. McDevitt, Jack, 1953
II. Title.
HV6773.52 .L48 2002
364.15 dc21   2002007109

To victims of hate crimes
everywhere whose pain is too
often minimized or ignored

CONTENTS

ACKNOWLEDGMENTS

We acknowledge a number of individuals who have assisted us through the development and preparation of this book. First, we want to thank Deputy Superintendent William Johnston, former Commander of the Boston Police Department's Community Disorders Unit, who has dedicated his career to fighting hate crimes and has taught thousands of police and public officials (as well as the authors of this book) that hate crimes are among the most serious of all offenses. We also acknowledge the important activities of advocacy groups across the country, particularly the Anti-Defamation League of B'nai B'rith; the Southern Poverty Law Center; the National Gay and Lesbian Task Force; the Prejudice Institute; and the National Hate Crime Prevention Center, whose members have worked for years, with little public encouragement, to document and address the suffering of hate crime victims.

In conducting the research for this book, we depended on the assistance of a number of individuals. We are particularly grateful to Michael Levin of the New York Institute of Technology, whose research assistance for this book was indispensable. We also thank Gordana Rabrenovic, Amy Farrell, Debbie Ramirez, Shea Cronin, Jen Balboni, Suzy Bennett, Glenn Pierce, and Robyn Miliano of Northeastern University's Institute for Race and Justice. Thanks to Janese Free, Colleen Keaney, Jason Mazaik, and Stas Vysotsky of Northeastern's Brudnick Center on Violence and Conflict for their support in developing and refining many of our ideas about hate crimes.

Other colleagues and associates who contributed important suggestions include Jim Nolan of the University of West Virginia, Nancy Kaufman of the Jewish Community Relations Council of Greater Boston, Brian Levin of the Center on Hate and Extremism at California State University, Michael Lieberman of the Anti-Defamation League, Steve Wessler of the Center for the Prevention of Hate Violence at the University of Southern Maine, Joan Weiss and Stan Orchowski of the Judicial Research and Statistics Association, Karen McLaughlin of the Educational Development Center, and Chip Berlet of Political Action Associates. Our thanks to James Alan Fox, Arnold Arluke, Michael Brown, Morris Jenkins, Leonard Brown, Mervin Lynch, Debra Kaufman, Robert Hall, Will Holton, Tony Jones, Harlan Lane, Richard Lapchick, Bill Miles, Jeff O'Brien, Donnie Perkins, Dan Givelber, Robert Fuller, Robert Croatti, Skip McCullough, Robin Chandler, Peter Murrell, and Patricia Golden (who died unexpectedly as we completed this book, but whose memory continues to inspire optimism about the future of race relations) of Northeastern University; Paul Bookbinder, Richard Robbins, and Albert Cardarelli of the University of Massachusetts, Boston; William Levin of Bridgewater State College; Dan Bibel of the Massachusetts Crime Reporting Unit; Larry Greenfeld, Jan Chaiken, Paul White, Charlie Kinderman, and Matt Hickman of the Bureau of Justice Statistics; Yoshio Akiyama, Bob McFall, John Jarvis, and Tony Pinnozotto of the FBI Uniform Crime Reporting Program; Rob Leikand, Andrew Tarsey, Marvin Nathan, Lenny Zakim, and Barry Morrison of the Anti-Defamation League of B'nai B'rith; Mark Potok, Morris Dees, Richard Cohen, and Danny Welch of the Southern Poverty Law Center; Brian Flynn and Dan O'Niel of the Boston Police Community Disorders Unit; Richard Cole of the Civil Rights Division of the Massachusetts Attorney General's Office; Christina Bouras, Pricilla Douglass, and Don Gorton, co-chairs of the Massachusetts Governor's Hate Crime Advisory Committee; Sheri Liebowitz of Suffolk University; Kevin Berrill of the National Gay and Lesbian Task Force; Maty Walsh of the Community Relations Service; Hank Tischler of Framingham State College; Diana Brensilber of the Massachusetts Executive Office of Public Safety; Phil Lamy of Castleton State College; Deena Weinstein of De Paul University; Philip

Jenkins of Penn State University; Bruce McCabe, Bill Porter, Francie Latorre, Larry Harmon, and Marjorie Pritchard of the *Boston Globe*; Shelly Cohen of the *Boston Herald*; Daniel Goleman of *The New York Times*; Sharon Shaw Johnson of *USA Today*; Gary Field of the Wall Street Journal; and Scott Wolfman, Greg Bura, and Jordan Miller of Wolfman Productions. In addition, we owe a debt of gratitude to the Bureau of Justice Statistics, US Department of Education Safe and Drug Free Schools, and the Boston Foundation for providing funding for some of the research cited in this book.

We also acknowledge the valuable input and insights of Irving and Betty Brudnick, Robert Agnew, Ed Dunbar, Howard Ehrlich, Raphael Ezekiel, Mark Hamm, Range Hutson, Paul Iganski, Valerie Jenness, Fred Lawrence, Meredith Watts, Bill Stone, Alan Rosen, Heather Walcutt, Daniel Weiss, Eric Silverman, Paul Maas, Paula McCabe, Jason Landau, Deborah Baiano, Louis Kontos, Karen Lischinsky, Kevin Borgeson, Kim McInnis, Michele Eayrs, Michael Kozack, Gail Pessas, Bizhan Monavarian, George Parangamilil, Lewis Chow, Monica Cantwell, Louise Lafontaine, Deb Ross, Kim McCarthy, Samantha Bouchard, Rich Sparaco, Steve Ostervitz, Shana Baxter, Lisa Bailey, Nancy Tierney, Chrisie Halkett, Anna Bouteneff, Tracy Johniken, Lisa Sanbonmatsu, Paul Phillips, Josh Shafran, Myron Lench, Lin Dawson, and all of the students who have participated in the prejudice panel for Sociology of Prejudice.

In addition to our students and colleagues at Northeastern University, we are indebted to President Richard Freeland, former President Jack Curry, Provost David Hall, Vice Provost Ron Hedland, Pat Meserve, Daryl Hellman, Dean James Stellar in the College of Arts and Sciences, and Dean Jack Greene in the College of Criminal Justice for their generous support of the research for this book; the Office of University Communications with special thanks to Terry Yanulavich and Laura Schmidt; William Frohlich of Northeastern University Press; Linda Regan of Prometheus Books; members of the Society Organized Against Racism, particularly Pat Venter; and Vice President John O'Bryant, whose untimely death ended a brilliant career. We would also like to thank Marion Sullivan at Northeastern University and Katharine Chandler of Westview Press for their skillful assistance in preparing this manuscript and our competent and creative editor at Westview Press, Jill Rothenberg, whose feedback was responsible for many improvements in the final version of the book.

Finally, we thank our children—Michael Levin, Bonnie and Brian Bryson, Andrea and Michael Segal, and Sean and Brian McDevitt—and most of all, our wives, Flea and Jan, who have endured our absences, untimely phone calls, and more importantly, whose insights and values have helped us keep the voice of victims foremost in our research and recommendations.

Jack Levin
Jack McDevitt

INTRODUCTION:
HATE CRIMES RECONSIDERED

Ten years have passed since the publication of *Hate Crimes: The Rising Tide of Bigotry and Bloodshed*. In conducting research for our 1993 book, we were struck by the large number of brutal and grisly cases of hate-motivated murder and assault that occurred during the 1980s and early 1990s. Of course, the level of hate violence paled by comparison with the hideous acts associated with institutionalized slavery of the antebellum South, the Ku Klux Klan (KKK) during the 1920s, or the Holocaust of the 1940s. Yet the hate crimes we examined in our first book were, at the same time, surprisingly prevalent and vicious, especially given the fact that they had occurred after the elimination of Jim Crow, the massive civil rights struggle of the 1960s, and the effective activism of the women's movement.

In fact, at the very time we might have expected a decline in bias crimes, they seemed to be sharply on the rise. Apparently, many Americans felt personally threatened by the rapid—in some cases, unprecedented—growth of interfaith and interracial marriages; immigration from Latin America, Asia, and eastern Europe; and movement of people of color into previously all-White neighborhoods, schools, and workplaces. In response to increasing competition for scarce resources—jobs, housing, money, and education—bigoted behavior apparently represented a sort of violent backlash perpetrated by anxious individuals who resented the substantial progress made by traditionally oppressed groups and were willing to go outside the law to prevent any more of it.

1

Since the early 1990s and into the new millennium, hate crimes have become increasingly complex. Some ten years ago, it appeared that hate attacks based on religion and race were finally on the decline, perhaps reflecting a more general drop in violent and property crimes—particularly those committed by young people. Thanks to a combination of targeted law enforcement and community-based preventive measures that worked to reduce serious crime, fewer young people resorted to gang warfare and other forms of criminal behavior in order to solve their personal problems. Indeed, these youngsters turned away from all forms of violence, including hate violence. In addition, many Americans who initially felt challenged by the promise of equality may have resigned themselves to the new reality of cultural and racial diversity becoming part of their everyday lives. Recognizing that we were experiencing the longest period of uninterrupted economic growth in this country's history, they may have concluded that their economic future was bright regardless of the increasing diversity. In the long run, they may have reasoned, "If we can't beat them, can't get rid of them, we'll just ignore them."

But then, essentially without warning, everything changed. By 1998, as the crime rate began to level off and, in some cases, to reverse direction, advocacy groups once again reported growing numbers of hate incidents around the country. After an unparalleled period of prosperity, the national economy took an unexpected nosedive, causing income inequality to continue its long-term ascent and individual economic anxiety to reemerge. In addition to the more commonplace incidents of vandalism and assault, individual hatemongers seemed to be committing more serious and dangerous criminal acts, resulting in multiple injuries and deaths. Moreover, after an extended period of decline, White supremacist groups grew not only in numbers but—thanks to clever manipulation of the Internet—in their ability to reach alienated young people around the world.

At the same time, bullied, harassed, and hate-filled students in public schools across the country decided to get even with their classmates, teachers, and parents—sometimes with an AK–47. In April 1999, two young men at Columbine High School in Littleton, Colorado, who identified with the Nazi movement, selected Hitler's birthday to shoot to death twelve of their schoolmates and a teacher. Reflecting their antipathy for those who are different, the two shooters sought out a Black student who was a popular athlete, but some victims were killed simply because they happened to be in the line of fire. The shooters' plan included much more than a killing spree at school. As indicated in a suicide note, they had also planned to hijack a plane and crash it into the New York City skyline!

On September 11, 2001, Americans witnessed the most violent single incident of hate-motivated violence in this country's history. The attacks on the Pentagon and the World Trade Center were inspired by an intense hatred of Americans and a desire to eliminate as many American citizens as possible. This horrendous incident demonstrated the power and devastation that hate is capable of generating. Of course, we have seen similar incidents perpetrated in other countries; but until September 11, Americans felt immune from the tragedies that occurred elsewhere. One of the lessons learned from the attack on America was that to ignore hate is to risk the potential for unimaginable tragedy. We will be forever changed by that realization.

If we were ever unsure, the September 11 attack on America provided indisputable evidence that a single situation can precipitate major changes in the ways that we behave toward the groups in our midst. In the aftermath of the devastation created by Middle Eastern terrorists, Americans of Arab descent or Islamic religious beliefs who had previously lived in relative peace and tranquility abruptly found themselves at great personal risk. Prejudiced feelings and beliefs about Arabs and Muslims, long hidden from view, suddenly were expressed in a generalized suspicion of anyone of Middle Eastern heritage. This suspicion was played out in violent acts across the country ranging from simple assault to murder.

At the same time, in response to an interdisciplinary campaign of research concluding that racial profiling by the police had been ineffective in waging the war against drugs, many Americans by the year 2001 were just beginning to recognize the futility of profiling individuals based only on the fact that they were Latinos or Blacks. In polls of citizens around the nation, a majority of Americans reported believing that racial profiling was wrong. The same Americans, however, in the aftermath of 9/11, were also eager to protect themselves from terrorism and were furious about the thousands of innocent lives lost at the

World Trade Center and the Pentagon. In response to what might be considered the largest hate crime in American history, they were now willing to profile millions of innocent people—most of them American citizens—based only on the fact that they had a "Middle Eastern look." At the more benign end of the continuum, anyone in an airport who had a dark complexion and spoke with a foreign accent was likely to be detained and searched. In some cases, travelers refused to fly because one of their fellow passengers appeared to be from a Middle Eastern country. More destructively, hundreds of hate crimes were perpetrated against immigrants who had absolutely no connection with terrorism but were mistakenly perceived to be "the enemy." Some were victims of arson, vandalism, or assault. Others were murdered simply because they wore a turban or spoke with an accent.

In addition, rumors were circulated by White supremacist organizations that thousands of Jews who reportedly worked at the World Trade Center in New York City had received a mysterious phone call in the early morning hours of September 11, urging them not to report for work. When published lists of victims of 9/11 included many Jewish names, organized hate groups (e.g., the National Alliance) and anti-Semitic figures in the hate movement (e.g., David Duke) changed their story so that it named Israelis rather than Jews as having received a warning call. Only a few Israelis died at the World Trade Center, they proclaimed. Could White supremacists have thought that the terrorists bombed Tel Aviv rather than New York City?

Scapegoating Arabs, Muslims, and Jews for the attack on America is just the most recent example of a long-term phenomenon. During World War II, thousands of innocent immigrants of Italian, German, and Japanese descent were rounded up, arrested, detained, and interrogated. Thousands more loyal American citizens of Japanese origin, many of whom were able to trace their American ancestry back several generations, were sent to internment camps for the duration of the war.

The college campus has never been immune from hate violence. During the Iranian hostage crisis in the late 1970s, international students on campuses around the nation were victimized by American students who were looking for someone to blame. In the early 1990s, during the Persian Gulf war, international students on campuses around the country were attacked by American students who were looking for someone to blame. And in the aftermath of the September 11 attack on America, international students on campuses around the nation were shunned, harassed, and in some cases beaten by American students who were looking for someone to blame.

After 9/11, what made it especially tempting to target college students who spoke with an accent and had a dark complexion was the ambiguity in identifying the real enemy. President Bush blamed Osama bin Laden, a shadowy figure who resided in a far-off land and had been seen only a few times on videotape. For most Americans, bin Laden, even if he was completely responsible for the terrorist attack—was an abstraction, little more than a caricature of a terrorist. It was therefore far more satisfying psychologically to target flesh-and-blood human beings in proximity—international students on campus. Hundreds of them decided to withdraw from classes and return to their homelands, rather than risk being assaulted by anxious and angry Americans.

Many early cases of hate crimes continue to provide valuable lessons for those who seek to reduce bigotry, and we have included such examples in this volume. Thus we review the murder of a Black young man whose only crime was to walk through a White working-class suburb of New York City, the beating death of a gay man in Jackson Heights, New York, an episode of "wilding"(the mob behavior in youth gangs) in Central Park that resulted in the brutal assault of a female jogger, and the videotaped beating of a Black motorist by police officers in Los Angeles.

At the same time, we have sought to update our illustrations to take account of the changing face of hate attacks during the last several years. In Jasper, Texas, James Byrd was viciously dragged behind a pickup truck to his death, simply because he was Black; outside Laramie, Wyoming, gay college student Matthew Shepard was beaten and then tied to a fence in the desert and left to die; in suburban Pittsburgh, out-of-work lawyer Richard Baumhammers, who despised immigrants from Third World countries, drove from location to location, shooting at people based only on their skin color or religion; on the campus of Indiana University, Benjamin Smith killed a Korean graduate student and then drove to Northwestern University, where he shot to death a Black basketball coach; at a Jewish Community Center in Los Angeles, Buford Furrow injured five people and then murdered an

Asian-American postal worker who just happened to be in the wrong place at the wrong time; in New York City, a Black immigrant from Haiti was sodomized with a broomstick by a police officer.

Every year, hundreds of thousands of serious crimes are motivated not by hate but by profit, protection, uncontrolled anger, or revenge. In fact, there are relatively few hate offenses—by most estimates, somewhere between eight thousand and twenty-five thousand—committed on an annual basis. Yet it takes only a small number of hate attacks to make life miserable for the large number of decent citizens. As we saw after September 11, a single incident of hate violence can spark a series of retaliatory attacks that can easily escalate into even more violence. A police officer shot to death on the streets of Derry inspires another round of violence between Protestants and Catholics in Northern Ireland; one suicide bomber in Jerusalem causes a retaliatory attack against Palestinians and a new cycle of bloodshed. Under the appropriate conditions, hate crimes can easily escalate into large-scale intergroup conflict, even warfare.

We believe that hate crimes are offenses against society. They target not only a primary victim but everyone in the victim's group—in fact, everyone perceived as different. They impact not only the victim's group but society as a whole, eroding the bond that holds its members together. A growing body of research conducted since we wrote *Hate Crimes* in 1993 has accumulated to suggest that hate offenses are more likely than comparable crimes to leave their victims in psychological and physical distress and to motivate them to retaliate against someone (in most cases, anyone) from the other side.

In another development since the early 1990s, hate crime laws have been challenged by legal scholars, social scientists, politicians, and journalists. Some have questioned the constitutionality of hate crime legislation, suggesting that it violates the First Amendment by punishing speech. Yet hate crime laws do not punish constitutionally protected hate speech. Most of them increase the penalty for behaviors that are already illegal, such as vandalism or harassment. Moreover, using the words of a perpetrator to establish motivation is nothing new or irregular in criminal law. Indeed, the difference between killing someone in self-defense versus committing first-degree murder may rest largely on what a defendant has said. The criminal law has always taken into account the motivation of the offender.

Another argument against hate crime laws suggests that they apply only to "special groups." In truth, however, according to every state hate crime statute, each and every American potentially receives protection. Such statutes criminalize acts that are motivated by the fact that victims are targeted because they are perceived to be different from the perpetrator. Thus Christians who are attacked are as likely as Jews and Muslims to be protected by the law. Whites are as likely to be protected as Blacks, Asians, and Latinos. Straights are as likely as gays and lesbians. Of all the racially motivated incidents reported to the FBI in a year, some 20 percent involve White victims targeted by members of another racial group. In *Todd Mitchell v. the State of Wisconsin,* the U.S. Supreme Court upheld the constitutionality of hate crime statutes in a case involving an attack on a White victim by a group of African-American youngsters.

We emphasize that hate crime laws send messages to both victims and perpetrators. They tell the victims that we encourage and support them in their efforts to exercise their constitutional rights. Hate crime legislation signals victims that law enforcement authorities will aggressively attempt to catch the perpetrators who have tormented them. To the offenders, moreover, hate crime laws say loud and clear that Americans reject hatemongering in all of its forms and that they will no longer tolerate bigotry. In today's world, this is a message of mutual respect and unity that we simply cannot afford to ignore.

one

REIGN OF TERROR: THE ROOT OF ALL EVIL

I t was after midnight on June 7, 1998. Bill King, Russell Brewer, and Shawn Berry rode in their gray pickup truck up and down Martin Luther King Drive in Jasper, Texas, drinking beer, hunting for women, and singing along with tunes on the radio. Just as the three White supremacist buddies were beginning to feel no pain, they spotted a man staggering along the road. At the wheel, Shawn Berry pulled the truck to the side and offered the hitchhiker a ride.

For James Byrd, it was a relief to get off his tired feet and climb into the cab of the truck, even in the company of three drunken White guys. The forty-nine-year-old Black resident of this east Texas timber community was on his way home from a family party, where he had stayed too long and had belted down a few too many. The long walk home would have been difficult enough even for someone in good health, but Byrd had little choice. Predisposed to seizures and other physical ailments, he didn't own a car, lived alone in a small apartment, and had no friends to drive him around. To Byrd, the appearance of three White guys in a pickup seemed like a lifesaver.

Even if he hadn't been drinking, Byrd couldn't have known at the time that he was more a prisoner than a passenger. His three kidnappers were small-time criminals and high school dropouts who loudly proclaimed the superiority of the White race and their contempt for Blacks and Jews. King and Brewer had met behind bars where they shared a cell, membership in a prison gang, and a tattoo artist. Both men's arms were heavily tattooed to their wrists. King also had drawings on his chest and scalp and under one arm—his favorite was a Black man being lynched. One of Brewer's tattoos spelled out "Aryan Pride"; another formed the name of the "Confederate Knights of America," the KKK hate group that he and King had joined together in prison.

Earlier in the week, King had talked with Brewer about starting a local chapter of the Confederate Knights. To this end, King had already drafted a constitution, bylaws, and membership applications. He had decided to name his group the Texas Rebel Soldiers. All that was missing now, King thought, was to instigate some sensational and dramatic incident that would get lots of publicity and attract new members to the cause.

The appearance of James Byrd presented just such an opportunity. Rather than drop their hitchhiker at his home along the way, the White supremacists continued for a few miles into a pine forest east of the town of Jasper. It was now 3:00 A.M. Berry stopped his pickup on a lonely country road in a secluded area, where the three buddies joked and laughed as they attempted to pull their reluctant victim from the truck. For a few moments, Byrd clung desperately to the truck door and then fell to the ground. Exhorting his companions, "Let's scare the hell out of him; let's kick his ass," King stomped his victim with the bottom of his shoe and spray-painted his face Black. Then the White suprema-cists forced Byrd behind the truck, placed a heavy logging chain around his ankles, and connected his chained body to the back of their pickup.

For more than two miles, Byrd was alive and conscious as he was unmercifully dragged on his back behind the truck and down the mid-dle of the road, at first in the dirt, and then on a stretch of solid pave-ment. Moving his elbows and body from side to side, Byrd attempted frantically to keep his head and shoulders from hitting the paved sur-face. But he couldn't avoid the fatal blow that occurred when his body hit the edge of a concrete culvert, ripping off his head, right shoulder, and right arm. The next day, when the police discovered what was left of his headless and bloody body, they found that Byrd's heels, elbows, and buttocks had been ground to the bone. His shredded White cotton briefs were bunched around the lower part of his legs.

The three White supremacists never got a chance to establish a local chapter of their hate group in Jasper. Bill King and Russell Brewer were convicted of capital murder and sentenced to death. Shawn Berry, who testified against his friends, also was convicted but received a life sentence.

Unlike Byrd's murder, most hate crimes do not involve organized hate groups, whose members are dedicated to the goal of achieving racial purity. Perpetrators usually are not card-carrying members of racist organizations; they do not wear racist tattoos, and most have never even heard of the Confederate Knights of America.

Hate crimes are more often committed under ordinary circumstances by otherwise unremarkable types—neighbors, a coworker at the next desk, or groups of youngsters looking for "bragging rights" with their friends. In the aftermath of the September 11 terrorist attack, numerous Muslim- and Arab-Americans were attacked, harassed, threatened, or vandalized simply because they were Muslim- or Arab-Americans. Virtually none of these hate crimes involved a conspiracy on the part of White supremacist organizations such as the White Aryan Resistance, National Alliance, World Church of the Creator, or the Klan. More typically, the perpetrators turned out to be angry and frustrated individuals who had decided on their own, absent a shred of evidence, that anybody with a dark complexion and a foreign accent was unpatriotic enough to be in league with the terrorists who blew up the Twin Towers.

In order to put recent hate attacks into perspective, it is instructive to examine a classic example such as the Howard Beach case, an incident from 1986 that raised the consciousness of Americans, White and Black alike, on how hate crimes develop. Long before terrorists flew jetliners into the Twin Towers, the Howard Beach case showed that brutal attacks can take place spontaneously without the help of organized groups.

It was December 19. "There's Niggers on the Boulevard. Let's kill them," shouted an enraged Jon Lester as he raced through a birthday party of White teenagers in Howard Beach, New York. It was six days before Christmas, shortly after midnight on a cold winter's night; Lester was ready to attack. Earlier that evening, he had exchanged racial insults with three young Black men whose 1976 Buick had broken down on Cross Bay Boulevard and who were searching without luck for a train to carry them back to Brooklyn. Making the best of a bad situation, the hungry trio agreed to stop at the New Park pizzeria at 157th Avenue, one of many Howard Beach pizza shops. That turned out to be a fatal decision.

A largely Italian-American working-class community, Howard Beach is set apart from the rest of New York City by Kennedy Airport and Spring Creek Park. Its unpretentious row houses are distinguished from one another by tidy gardens but little more. The residents of Howard Beach are fiercely loyal to the area that they call home.

The slender and gentle-looking Jon Lester, a junior at John Adams High School, had a more pernicious side to him than would appear at first glance. The only one among his friends in Howard Beach to have a criminal record, Lester had been previously arrested for possessing a loaded .32-caliber handgun.

When he found out that night that the Black men hadn't left *his* neighborhood, Lester was livid. His immediate response was to organize his friends at the party into a posse and run these strangers out of town. Armed with baseball bats, a tire iron, and a tree stump, the twelve teenagers jumped into three automobiles and sped in the direction of the pizza shop.

It was now 12:40 A.M. Spotting their assailants moving toward them, the three Blacks attempted to escape. One managed to elude the hunting party by brandishing a small knife and then, in the confusion of the moment, ran into the darkness northward on Cross Bay Boulevard.

But twenty-three-year old Michael Griffith wasn't so lucky. After being chased through the deserted streets of Howard Beach by his White pursuers, he was beaten severely. Then, in a desperate effort to escape, Griffith scrambled over a concrete barricade bordering the Belt Parkway and darted across its three eastbound lanes, where he was immediately struck head-on by a car in a westbound lane. Griffith's mangled body shot fifteen feet into the air before hitting the cold asphalt of the Belt Parkway. He died instantly.

The Howard Beach teenagers then spotted the third Black, Michael Griffith's stepfather, Cedric Sandiford, as he ran up 156th Avenue. Surrounding their prey, the angry mob assaulted him again and again, beating him unmercifully with the bats, the tire iron, the tree stump, and their fists, until his battered body slumped to the ground. The tall Black man survived by pretending to fall unconscious but sustained serious injuries.[1]

On December 21, 1987, one day after a memorial service for Michael Griffith on the first anniversary of his death, a jury consisting of one Black, two Asian-Americans, six Whites, and three Latinos, after deliberating for twelve days, arrived at a verdict in the Howard Beach incident.

In a decision that left many New Yorkers astonished by its leniency, Jon Lester and Scott Kern, both eighteen, and Jason Ladone, seventeen, avoided a murder conviction and instead were found guilty of having "recklessly caused the death of another," a lesser offense. A fourth defendant was cleared of all charges. In a plea bargain with one of the teenagers who admitted his participation in the Howard Beach attack, Robert D. Riley was permitted to plead guilty to assault rather than murder in exchange for his testimony against his fellow defendants. Seven other White teenagers accused of having participating in the Howard Beach attack have been indicted and await trial.

It is often easy enough to determine whether or not a particular criminal act is a hate crime. In the brutal murder of James Byrd, the motivation was obvious and clear-cut, the bigotry blatant. In the Howard Beach attack, the hate-inspired violence was so intense that it was impossible to overlook.

In some cases, the hatred may be spelled out, literally, for everyone in a community to view. During the Persian Gulf war, for example, a Los Angeles delicatessen owned by an Arab-American was set ablaze. Before igniting the fire, the arsonists scribbled a message on the wall: "You Fuckin' Arab, go home."[2] Similarly, in the aftermath of the September 11, 2001, attack on America, a Missouri University medical student of Arab descent received an e-mail message threatening to kill him and "all the Arab pigs of the world."[3]

In assaultive hate crimes, the attack is often excessively violent. In Bangor, Maine, for example, three teenage boys beat senseless a twenty-three-year-old man whom they believed to be gay. Then they threw him off a bridge to his death on the rocks below. The three youths later boasted to their friends that they had "jumped a fag and kicked the shit out of him and threw him in the stream."[4]

In October 1998, two young men similarly murdered Matthew Shepard, a gay twenty-one-year-old freshman at the University of Wyoming. The two perpetrators, Russell Henderson and Aaron McKinney, both in their early twenties, lured Shepard from the Fireside Lounge in Laramie by pretending to be friendly and gay. They drove their victim to a secluded area in the desert east of Laramie, tied him to a fence, beat him repeatedly with the butt of a .357 Magnum, and then left him for dead. Henderson pled guilty in order to avoid the death penalty and got a life sentence. McKinney's attorney argued at trial a version of the so-called gay panic defense, according to which the murder was triggered by a combination of the defendant's drug and alcohol history, his latent homosexual tendencies, and unwanted sexual advances by the victim. As a result, according to defendant's attorney, McKinney was caused to have an uncontrollable and violent response when he was propositioned by Matthew Shepard. The "gay panic" defense was disallowed by the judge. Like his partner in murder, McKinney received a life sentence from the jury.

Some hatemongers make a career of attacking people who are different. On the night of August 20, 1980, Joseph Paul Franklin, a thirty-nine-year-old former member of the KKK and American Nazi Party, gunned down two young Black men as they jogged alongside two White women in a Salt Lake City park. Ten years later, when asked from his prison cell to explain why he had committed the murders, Franklin replied, "I'll say that it was just because they were race mixing." Franklin was later connected to thirteen killings across the United States. In 1984 he was convicted of bombing a synagogue in Chattanooga, Tennessee,[5] and in 1986 was sentenced to two more life terms for killing an interracial couple in Madison, Wisconsin.[6]

James Byrd was slain by members of an organized group whose raison d'être was to eliminate Blacks and other "subhumans." In Michael Griffith's death, teenagers translated their racism into brutal violence. The incident would in all likelihood never have happened had the three "intruders" been Whites. But hate crimes aren't always easily labeled as such. When violence is perpetrated by youngsters in the neighborhood, motivation can be difficult to determine. Was it a bias crime—an act of hate-inspired violence? Or was it an indiscriminate attack that could have been directed against anyone, regardless of race, religion, or gender? The Central Park jogger assault is a case in point. Although the crime happened more than a decade ago, the sad reality is that sexual assaults against women committed by strangers are just as prevalent today.

It was an unseasonably warm, moonlit April evening; New Yorkers took advantage of the weather by remaining outside after dark. Some made small talk with neighbors while passing time on their front stoops. Others strolled the streets of the city, window-shopping for luxurious items beyond their means or simply mingling with the wide range of humanity. Still others jogged.

A young blond woman of slight build was taking her nightly exercise. At 10:00 P.M., she ran at a brisk pace along a secluded extension of 102nd Street, in the direction of the brightly lit and busy pathways surrounding the central park reservoir in the heart of Manhattan. The lush greenery and winding paths attracted joggers throughout the city, and she would soon have plenty of company—but not the kind the young woman expected.

Without warning, she found herself completely surrounded by a pack of snarling, angry young men, apparently in their teens, who dragged her two hundred feet down the side of a muddy ravine and flung her to the ground on the edge of an isolated pond. She screamed and struggled in vain as her attackers unmercifully ripped off her clothes, bound her hands, and gagged her with her own sweatshirt. For almost thirty minutes, some of the teenagers held her down while others savagely raped her. They silenced her muffled screams by smashing her face and head, first with their fists and then with rocks, a brick, and a metal pipe. They slashed both of her legs with knives and wrapped her shirt around her neck like a rope. Then they left her for dead.

Brutally disfigured and bleeding profusely, the young woman lay unconscious for three hours on a pathway by the side of the pond. When passersby finally discovered her, it was 1:30 A.M. She was close to death, having lost three-quarters of her blood. Her body temperature had plummeted to eighty degrees.

❖ ❖ ❖

The police initially suspected that the Central Park jogger assault was a crime motivated by racial hatred. All of the attackers were of minority status—Black or Latino youths from surrounding neighborhoods—and the victim was a White, relatively well-to-do Wall Street executive. Yet the Central Park jogger was not the only person victimized in the park on the evening of April 19. One hour before they encountered her, the pack of teenagers had joined forces with dozens of other youthful delinquents to engage in a reign of terror. They had pelted rocks and bottles at cars and cyclists and had assaulted joggers and homeless people.

The only explicitly racial incident occurred when the gang taunted a couple on a tandem bicycle with racial slurs: "Whitey" and "fucking White people." But several dark-skinned Latinos were also harassed. Indeed, one Latino victim, after being robbed, was punched and kicked into unconsciousness. Then the pack of teens decided to "get a woman jogger." As more was learned about the case, it became increasingly clear that the basis of the hate crime against the Central Park jogger was the fact that she was a woman. Her female gender, even more than her race, had been a reason for choosing her as a victim. The perpetrators were looking for someone they could sexually assault.

If there was doubt as to why the Central Park jogger had been attacked, there was no disputing the basis for a thirty-five-minute episode of mob "wilding" directed against women in New York City's Central Park on Sunday evening, June 13, 2000. The first assault occurred at 6:14 P.M. Walking into the park, two unsuspecting teenage girls from Long Island were immediately surrounded and charged by a pack of some twenty laughing and shouting men, who sprayed their victims with water bottles and squirt guns and groped them over their clothing. One of the girls was pushed to the ground, her pocketbook ripped from her hands.

Within a few minutes, the group moved on to attack a couple from France who had been honeymooning in the United States. Shouting "Soak her! Soak her!" members of the mob doused their twenty-eight-year-old female victim with water. Then they pulled off her skirt and underpants and jerked two gold necklaces from her neck. The victim's husband tried to protect his bride, but the crowd backed off only when they were confronted by officers from New York's Traffic Control Division.

At approximately the same time as the attack on the French honeymooners was taking place, a young woman on roller blades wearing a backpack turned into Central Park and immediately encountered a mob that threw her to the grass and attempted in vain to pull down her shorts. In frustration, the men finally decided to leave, but only after stealing the cell phone from their victim's backpack.

The last assault occurred moments later, when three tourists from England were confronted by a large group of men. Attempting to get away, the women ran in different directions. One of them was unable to escape. Groping her breasts and genitals, the mob ripped off her blouse and pulled down her shorts. Then they grabbed her purse and ran.

Overall, twenty-two women testified in court that they had been dragged, beaten, groped, or penetrated by their attackers' fingers. Thirty-three men were arrested after the mass assault, which was videotaped by several passersby who turned the tapes over to the police. Out of the men arrested, thirty were indicted, sixteen pleaded guilty, three were tried, and two were convicted. One defendant was acquitted. The charges against eleven of those arrested were ultimately dismissed.

Recent research strongly suggests that hate crimes reported to the police have certain characteristics that distinguish them from other types of offenses, whether committed at the turn of the twentieth century, in the early 1990s, or at the turn of the millennium.

First, hate crimes tend to be *excessively brutal*. In a study of 452 hate crimes reported to the Boston police,[7] fully half were assaults. The others were acts of vandalism or destruction of property (for example, painting a swastika on a synagogue or throwing a rock through a window). Thus one of every two hate crimes reported to the Boston police was a personal attack, whereas nationally, only 7 percent of all crimes reported to the police are assaults.[8] Hate offenses are much more likely to entail personal violence.

The *hatred* in such crimes gets expressed when force is exercised beyond what may be necessary to subdue victims, make them comply, disarm them, or take their worldly goods. Almost three-quarters of all assaultive hate crimes—unlawful personal attacks against an individual—result in at least some physical injury to the victim. The relative viciousness of such attacks can be seen by comparing them to the national figures for all crimes, in which only 29 percent of assault victims generally receive some physical injury. By contrast, many victims of hate crime assaults—fully 30 percent—because of the severity of their injuries wind up requiring treatment at a hospital. For assaults of all kinds, this figure is only 7 percent. Once again, it appears that hate crimes are particularly violent.

The brutality of the attack against the Central Park jogger alerts us to the possibility that extreme hatred was being channeled into vicious behavior. For thirteen days, the twenty-eight-year-old woman lay in

Metropolitan Hospital in a comatose state, precariously clinging to life, so disfigured that even close friends were unable to identify her. She suffered from brain damage, multiple skull fractures, and countless cuts and bruises over most of her body, including her face. According to one physician who observed her at the time, "She received a blow so severe that . . . her eyeball had exploded back through the rear of its socket."[9]

In the case of James Byrd, the degree of viciousness displayed by his attackers similarly suggests that hate played a major role. Rather than kill Byrd in a timely manner, his tormentors apparently sought to maximize his pain and suffering. They chained him to the back of their pickup and dragged him for almost three miles, while he struggled in vain to keep his head from hitting the concrete road. They enjoyed the sight of Byrd's body being buffeted from side to side as their truck continued down the road. They laughed as their victim was decapitated.

It should be noted, in addition, that even where the level of brutality does not vary between hate crimes and similar offenses committed for other reasons, the victims of hate attacks are more likely to suffer psychological distress and for longer periods of time. In a recent study comparing assaults, for example, it was determined that the victims of hate-motivated assaults were significantly more likely to feel unsafe, nervous, and depressed than their counterparts who were attacked for other reasons.

A second characteristic of hate crimes reported to the police is that they are often apparently senseless or irrational crimes *perpetrated at random on total strangers.* As a society, we fear random violence against strangers even more than violence that has a logical basis. For example, if it is reported on the evening news that a drug deal "went bad" and one of the participants killed the other, we react with little fear or even concern. After all, criminals are killing criminals over territorial disputes. And because *we* are not criminals, and therefore not competing with them in business, *we* feel perfectly safe and secure.

In sharp contrast, a story about random violence such as unexplained attacks against innocent bystanders in a public place (e.g., a public park or a post office) engenders widespread fear and anxiety. The reason for this is complex, but one element is that the violence is committed by a stranger against someone he has never met before. This makes all of us feel vulnerable as potential victims. Any one of us could be next.

The September 11 attack on America makes this point more painfully than perhaps any hate crime in our history. The terrorists who targeted the Twin Towers were not interested in distinguishing one American from another. Their purpose was apparently to gain the eyes and the ears of the world. In order to do so, they sought only to maximize the body count, eliminating as many Americans as possible. From their perspective, one American was as good (or bad) as any other. Knowing this made American citizens feel very uneasy. They might be able to avoid high-crime areas of a city in order to reduce their risk of being targeted by car thieves and muggers. But where do they run to stave off terrorists? Should they avoid professional football games? The Olympics? High-rise buildings? Airports and airplanes? Federal buildings? Power plants? Wall Street? Congested highways? And would it make a difference if they did?

In the Boston study, approximately 85 percent of all hate crimes involved offenders whose identity was unknown to their victims. In a few cases, the offenders remained unidentified and so might have been an acquaintance, but the vast majority attacked total strangers. A comparative statistic reported by the Department of Justice's *2000 National Crime Survey* is that 47 percent of all crimes of violence were committed by strangers.

When it comes to hate crimes, a potential victim cannot rationalize his or her future safety by saying, for example, "I don't use drugs, so I won't ever be hurt in a situation like that." Rather, for all members of a group under attack, the mere decision to leave home automatically puts them at risk of being victimized. This threat infuses all daily activities, both inside and outside of an individual's home, and is extremely difficult to eliminate. Even the arrest and conviction of an offender may not necessarily relieve this fear. Because the victims never did anything personally to precipitate the previous incident and never knew why they were chosen as victims, how can they feel sure that the same thing won't happen again? Wherever they go, they carry the reason for their victimization with them. They might be attacked again, whether in the office, at a restaurant, or on a bus stop. Even home is not a safe haven. At any moment, a rock might come smashing through the window, flung by an irate neighbor who despises gays, Blacks, Asians, or Jews and simply cannot tolerate their presence on his block.

Where a crime occurs because a victim's behavior—for example, moving into a neighborhood or attending a particular school—offends the perpetrator, then the victim has recourse. He or she might be able to retreat, conceding defeat in the face of harassment and persecution. However, the cost in both psychological and economic terms may well be prohibitive. In a larger sense, we all lose when victims are frightened away by the acts of hatemongers. To assure our own rights, we must also be able and willing to protect the constitutional rights of all citizens, including even groups that we as individuals may dislike.

Psychologists suggest that rape is a crime of violence; men who feel belittled and powerless use it to express their need for control and dominance. Given the brutality of the assault, this interpretation seems clearly to fit the rape of the Central Park jogger. In one sense, it might be argued that all rapes are hate offenses because they are invariably linked with the gender of the victim. Yet not all rapes are directed against women in general. In date or acquaintance rape, where two people know each other at least on a casual basis, for example, a particular victim may be chosen because of her particular characteristics, which the perpetrator finds repulsive or appealing, or both. He might not have chosen just any woman for his sexual offense.

In stranger rape, however, the victims are often *interchangeable*, their individual characteristics being irrelevant or at best secondary in determining why they were chosen for victimization. Being female is frequently primary, even if the rapist targets only prostitutes, teenage girls, socialites, brunettes, or the like. Under such conditions, then, rape may indeed qualify as a hate crime.

James Byrd was probably chosen as a murder victim not because in the past he had caused his White supremacist perpetrators some problem or difficulty; not because he had offended his killers in any way. Indeed, until he got into their pickup for a ride home, Byrd had been invisible to the three men who ended up taking his life. They treated every Black as they would any other Black—as totally expendable.

Similarly, the Central Park jogger was probably selected *not* because she liked to exercise, *not* because she was five foot five in height, *not* because she was an investment banker on Wall Street, and *not* because she had graduated from Wellesley College. The anger of her assailants could not have resulted from anything that she said to them because no personal conversation took place before the attack. Their anger could not have been a result of their prior relationship because they had none.

It is possible, of course, that the Central Park jogger's race and presumed economic status were also factors in her selection as a victim. Joggers are often upper middle class and White; the perpetrators were neither. Consequently, a poor Black woman may not have been attacked. Still, the Central Park jogger was an interchangeable victim, one who just happened to be at the wrong place at the wrong time. Almost any other female jogger—and especially any other White female jogger—would probably have been similarly at risk. The interchangeability of victims became blatantly obvious in the subsequent episodes of mob wilding directed indiscriminately against women in New York City's Central Park on Sunday evening, June 13, 2000.

Many states are presently in the process of deciding whether or not to include gender as a basis for determining hate motivation. Indeed, twenty-five states now consider as hate crimes any attack against a woman that is motivated primarily by her gender. The controversy revolves around exactly which crimes against women qualify. Should, for example, all sexual assaults be counted as hate offenses?

The fact that hate crime victims are interchangeable may help focus the debate. With respect to race, *any* Black family that moves into certain neighborhoods will likely be attacked. With respect to sexual orientation, *any* man thought to be gay who happens to walk down a particular street will in all likelihood be assaulted. Similarly, gender-motivated hate crimes should include those attacks in which the offender is looking for *any* woman. By this criterion, acquaintance rape and acts of domestic violence, no matter how despicable, would be excluded from consideration as hate offenses. Only random attacks against women would be counted.

In the Commonwealth of Massachusetts, the attorney general has instituted a policy whereby gender-based hate crimes require at least two previous restraining orders issued to protect two different domestic partners. Over the past ten years of its existence, there have been fewer than ten cases in which the criteria for a gender-based hate offense have been met.

The state of California has attempted to apply the interchangeability criterion by specifying that to be considered a hate offense, any crime against women must include an articulated threat by the offender against women in general. Therefore, the offender must say something to the effect that "I am beating you because you are just like all other women and I hate all other women."

Though well-intentioned, the California criterion for establishing interchangeability in crimes against women places too restrictive a burden on the police, who during the course of their investigation must uncover a threat against women in general. Just like other criminals, hatemongers don't always state the motivation for their crimes in the presence of their victims. In place of this rigid standard, victim interchangeability should probably be determined by offender statements not only to the victim, but also in the presence of friends, relatives, or even the police while being interrogated.

Another characteristic of hate crimes is that they are usually *perpetrated by multiple offenders.* This is a group crime frequently carried out by youthful perpetrators operating together for the purpose of attacking the members of another group.

In most situations, violent crimes are perpetrated by individuals acting alone. According to the *2000 National Crime Survey* published by the Department of Justice, only about 20 percent of all crimes of violence are committed by more than one offender. By contrast, 64 percent of hate crimes reported to the police involve two or more perpetrators. Indeed, most are carried out by a group of four or more offenders who attack their victims in a gang or pack. In contrast to gang warfare, in which teenagers fight teenagers, however, the targets of hate crimes are not necessarily in their teens or early twenties. Many victims are over thirty, and some are young children.

James Byrd was forty-nine years old when he was murdered in Jasper, Texas. Two of his killers were dedicated racists with a history of criminal behavior and jail time. Shawn Berry, who testified against his friends, also was convicted but received a life sentence. But many residents of Jasper, including some who were Black, simply couldn't believe that Berry had committed a hate crime based on race. He had Black friends; he interacted with Black residents; he was not known around town as a racist.

Like so many other young men and women, however, Berry craved acceptance from his friends. He might have prevented a murder if he had been able to pull himself from the prevailing groupthink. It would have meant rejecting his friends, being rejected by his friends, acting as a deviant in the presence of social pressure and conformity. If only Berry had had the courage!

In the Central Park jogger episode, dozens of teenage boys had congregated on the evening of April 19 to go "wilding," that is, they got together strictly for the "hell of it" to harass and attack strangers for sport because they had nothing better to do. Early in the evening, the entire pack of youths roamed the park taunting and harassing victims at random. Then, while most of the boys left the park, at least six of them, ranging in age from fourteen to seventeen, splintered off from the others and continued to look for victims. These are the boys who assaulted the twenty-eight-year-old Central Park jogger.

Lieutenant William Johnston, who for years investigated hate crimes for the Boston police, suggests that most hatemongers act in groups because "they are basically cowards." He believes that the experience of being in a group offers the encouragement that may be necessary for offenders to attack a wholly innocent victim.[10]

Johnston is correct when he emphasizes the importance of groups in perpetrating hate offenses. Clearly, there is safety in numbers. In a group, the hatemongers who instigate an altercation believe that they are less likely to be hurt because they have their friends to protect them. The group also grants a certain degree of anonymity. If everyone participated, then no one person can easily be singled out as bearing primary responsibility for the attack. Because they share the blame, it is diluted or weakened. Finally, the group gives its members a dose of psychological support for their blatant bigotry. Feeding initially on the hatred of one or a few peers, escalation becomes a game in which members of the group incite one another toward ever increasing levels of violence. To do his part and "prove himself," therefore, each offender feels that he must surpass the previous atrocity.

Few would dispute that the murder of James Byrd in Jasper, Texas, was a hate crime. In contrast, for over a decade the case of the Central Park jogger has been an important object lesson for those who investigate hate crimes. It epitomizes the difficulty of determining whether or not an attack is in fact a hate offense. At one end of the continuum, there are numerous crimes that are unequivocally crimes of hate directed against individuals strictly because of their belonging to a group or category. At the other end of the continuum, however, there are some offenses for which it is difficult, if not impossible, to determine the extent to which hate was a motivating factor.

The attack on the Central Park jogger has many of the elements that we designate hate crimes. It was a crime committed by multiple offenders who employed excessive brutality against a total stranger. The ambiguity concerns the basis for the attack, whether it was really motivated by gender, race, both, or neither.

In many hate offenses, there is a "spillover" effect that can easily give the appearance of indiscriminate violence, at least at a superficial level. The offenders' anger may be so intense that it generalizes onto in-group members as well. It is conceivable, for example, that the wilding youths who assaulted the Central Park jogger set out exclusively to molest and harass Whites or women but were so caught up in the frenzy of the group experience that almost anyone present would have been selected.

It is also possible that the youngsters involved in that attack actually set out to get even, in some abstract sense, with "society at large" or "humanity"—and especially with that segment of society that has "made it." Thus they lashed out against privileged Whites who have the leisure to jog at whim. In their minds, race becomes an indicator of class; White means wealthy.

An offense against property in two upscale Massachusetts communities, where a spillover effect apparently occurred, clearly qualifies as a hate crime. At twenty-seven different locations in the affluent towns of Wellesley and Dover, two young men left ethnic and racial slurs—swastikas, "Adolph Lives," "White Only," "Final Solution," and the like—on homes, cars, roadways, and retail stores. At the home of a Greek-American family in Dover, they painted a row of swastikas and the words "Fuck Greeks" on the driveway. The pair also vandalized the car of a racist skinhead they had known who probably would have agreed with their views on Jews, Blacks, and Greeks.

Was this a mistake? Were the perpetrators simply attempting to be offensive? Or was their hatred so extreme and out of control that any target was better than none?

Many who commit hate crimes are at the margin of their community. They may have dropped out of school either spiritually or physically and see little likelihood of ever making it in terms of the American success ethic. But if they can't succeed in a middle-class sense, they can at least garner the respect and approval of their friends. Peer influence therefore becomes crucial to their sense of belonging and self-esteem.

The 1999 massacre at Columbine High School in Littleton, Colorado, would probably never have occurred in the absence of social influence. Many teenagers are notoriously other-directed, relying on their peers for their self-esteem and a sense of belonging. Being ignored or even bullied by the popular students at school has at least two important consequences for vulnerable youngsters. First, the victims of bullying come to see themselves as outsiders who resent their rejecting schoolmates and may decide to seek revenge against them. Second, the rejection by mainstream members of the student population serves to enhance the value of bullied students bonding with other bullied students who share the same sense of being marginalized and alienated. The Trenchcoat Mafia represented for the Columbine shooters an alternative source of status and belonging. For youngsters who were regarded by the popular students as geeks, nerds, or outcasts, the image of evil forces—Nazism, organized crime, gothic incivility—reinforced that they were actually important, even powerful, members of a secret fellowship.

In the following pages, we raise and answer many questions about the causes, conditions, and consequences of hate crimes. What are the origins of hate crimes in society and within the individual? Are all perpetrators "sick" deviant types, or do they actually reflect aspects of the dominant, mainstream culture in which they live? What can the criminal justice system do to combat these offenses? Can the police be convinced that the victimization of groups whose members have been historically antipolice deserves their serious attention? Can prosecutors and judges be persuaded to treat hate crimes as serious violations of law rather than childish pranks? Will administrators in prisons and jails be willing to deal with the racism and homophobia that presently run rampant in their institutions? And, finally, what can we do as individuals to ensure that hate crimes do not destroy us or our way of life?

In 1993, when we wrote *Hate Crimes: The Rising Tide of Bigotry and Bloodshed,* we felt a pressing need to address the issue of bigotry in America. Ten years later, we are no less concerned about the divisive and damaging impact of hate crimes on members of our society. The times have certainly changed and, to some extent, so have the victims of hate. Yet in the aftermath of September 11, it has become painfully evident that we are dealing with a problem that may change its form but refuses to go away.

two

NASTY PICTURES IN OUR HEADS: BELIEFS, STEREOTYPES, AND LEARNING TO HATE

Learning to hate is almost as inescapable as breathing. Like almost everyone else, the hate crime offender grows up in a culture that defines certain people as righteous, upstanding citizens, while designating others as sleazy, immoral characters who deserve to be mistreated. As a child, the perpetrator may never have had a firsthand experience with members of the groups he later comes to despise and then victimize. But, early on, merely by conversing with his family, friends, and teachers or by watching his favorite television programs, he learns the characteristics of disparaging stereotypes. He also learns that it is socially acceptable, perhaps even expected, to repeat racist jokes and use ethnic slurs and epithets.

Columnist Walter Lippmann long ago coined the term "stereotype" in reference to the "pictures in our heads"—the generalizations that we have concerning different groups of people. All the members of Group W are "terrorists who hate Americans." All the members of Group X are "dirty" and "lazy." All the members of Group Y are "money hungry,""powerful," and "shrewd." All the members of Group Z are "sexual predators."

Such stereotypes are so powerful, so widely accepted, and so enduring that many people, based solely on these unattributed characteristics, can easily identify Groups W, X, Y, and Z. Even if they do not agree that these images are correct, they probably recognize that the "pictures" are often associated with Arabs, African-Americans, Jews, and gays, respectively.

To some extent, the tendency to generalize about other people is probably universal. Almost everybody, based on personal experience that may or may not be limited, makes at least some generalizations about what other groups of people are like. The beliefs that we call stereotypes are, however, of a different order. First, almost every member of a stereotyped group is seen as a rubber stamp of everyone else in that group. Individual differences are totally obscured. Second, stereotypes usually cannot be modified by contradictory evidence. No argument or evidence is compelling enough to change the hatemonger's mind. He is emotionally invested in believing the worst about the members of a stigmatized group. Third, the person who accepts the validity of a nasty stereotype isn't simply trying to make sense of his world. More likely, he is looking for a convenient excuse to express hostility, to attack and victimize the people he despises.

Clearly, stereotypes tend to be all-encompassing: applied without regard for individual characteristics to each and every member of a group. From this viewpoint, there is no good reason to get to know "them" on a personal basis, since "to know one Latino is to know them all—to be familiar with one Asian is to be familiar with each and every one of them."

On the other hand, those who stereotype often recognize exceptions to the rule: cases they inevitably encounter in everyday life that simply don't fit their stereotyped preconceptions. For example, two freshmen—one Black, the other White—recently roomed together in the dormitory of a large northeastern university. Both grew up under rigid racial segregation in their neighborhoods, churches, and schools; both initially expressed negative beliefs about members of other races. Neither previously had a close relationship with a person of another race. Both were apprehensive about whether they would get along. Yet after two months, they developed a close friendship. When later questioned about their compatibility, both students expressed very positive regard for their roommate while continuing to hold stereotyped beliefs about each other's racial group. Each of them reasoned as follows: "My roommate is a great guy, but he's *different*: other members of his group simply can't be trusted." In a sense, then, by assuming that one case is unusual, the presumed exception allows a bigot to accept the "special case" while he continues to believe the stereotyped image.

The "exception to the rule" rule also minimizes the impact of a bigot's exposure to the successful members of a despised group. How does a White racist—someone firmly convinced of the intellectual superiority of Caucasians—explain Colin Powell, Condoleezza Rice, Bill Cosby, or Martin Luther King? He really doesn't have to explain anything: After all, a *few* exceptions can always be found. (If forced to explain, he can always talk about some Blacks having "White blood" or getting special treatment.) At the same time, the presence of a few exceptional cases in the mind of a hatemonger also helps him disregard the possibility of economic inequities between racial groups. He reasons, "Why can't they all be like Colin Powell and pull themselves up by their bootstraps? If Powell made it, so can the rest of them. But I guess they'd rather deal crack and loot stores."

Understanding a stereotype requires familiarity with its social and historical context. Even the most flattering image when applied to one group of people can become a damaging stereotype when applied to another. During warfare, the enemy is called "bloodthirsty" but our fighting force is "courageous," even if both sides violate the same rules of battle. In the business sector, male bosses are sometimes seen as "motivated" and "assertive" whereas female bosses under the same conditions are considered "pushy bitches." Having rhythm may be flattering when attributed to a White but is not always taken as a compliment by an American Black who is historically sensitive enough to recognize that the image of "the musical and ignorant Black" was employed to justify slavery. Acquiring power and wealth may sound like a laudable goal (indeed, the fulfillment of the American Dream), but not necessarily when ascribed to Jewish Americans whose ancestors were kicked out of several countries or even exterminated because they were charged with being too rich or having too much power.

Though declining over the decades, the stereotype of Jews as unscrupulous, aggressive, and too powerful continues to be accepted by millions of Americans. These stereotypes best express anxiety among Americans in general about *being able to compete for scarce resources* and moral outrage that a particular group might be getting *more than its share*—"*at my expense.*"

Even though verbalized in an apparently harmless joke or an innocuous television sitcom, stereotypes are often more pernicious than they first appear. Time and time again, they have been used to *justify* committing atrocities against the members of stigmatized groups. Thus the image serves an important purpose: Adult men can't be beaten, enslaved, or murdered with impunity. But those considered subhuman or childlike can be enslaved and treated as though they were animals.

Throughout history, many groups have been *infantilized*. So long as they were forced to "stay in their place" and play the inferior role to which they were assigned, they were stereotyped as children or infants. For example, women were traditionally regarded as "girls" who remained at home—in the kitchen and bedroom—where they "belonged," or so it was said. The particular image varied from generation to generation, but the intent was always the same—to keep women in a subservient position in their relations with men. To be in style, women of the 1920s were asked to look like children. Some wore their dresses cut to look like the shirts worn by little boys some ten years earlier. Others bobbed their hair like a baby's, hoping to give their face the appearance of "a small child: round and soft, with a turned-up nose, saucer eyes and a pouting "bee-stung" mouth."[1] During the 1960s, young women similarly dressed as if they were "little girls." They wore very short ruffled frocks and made up their eyes to create a "baby-faced look."[2] Miniskirts, baby-doll nightgowns, and lacy baby-doll dresses all made "grown women look like toddlers with a glandular affliction, or like severely retarded nubile teenagers."[3]

Much like children, women were viewed as diminutive or as the "weaker sex" and therefore in need of masculine protection, often whether they wanted it or not. Just to make sure that they remained weak enough, for example, stylish women of the nineteenth century were expected to wear tight corsets to achieve the stylish hourglass figure. Women who complied may have been in high fashion, but they also suffered weakness, shortness of breath, and back pain, sometimes severe enough to cause disability (and therefore greater dependency on men).

Race has also served as a basis for infantilization. During slavery, the "little Black Sambo" image depicted Black American men as "boys" who lacked either the sophistication or the intelligence to fend for themselves. Hence, the justification for what was popularly believed to be a

"White man's burden": Because some Whites regarded Blacks as inherently inferior, slavery was widely considered as absolutely essential for the survival of the Black race.[4]

The members of a group are typically infantilized only as long as they conform to playing a docile and obliging role vis-à-vis those in positions of power. If the members of a stigmatized group get "too uppity"—perhaps even rebellious—they are no longer stereotyped as having the characteristics of children but are regarded as animals or demons. In a word, they are *dehumanized*. After all, you cannot kill children and infants—regardless of how much they misbehave; but it is perfectly acceptable—perhaps even obligatory—to slaughter an animal or kill "the devil."

During the European witch hunts (from the late fifteenth to the mid-eighteenth centuries), women who dared challenge the prerogatives traditionally assigned to men or competed against men in the workforce were summarily labeled as witches and then burned at the stake or crushed to death under heavy rocks. According to some estimates, millions of women may have been destroyed as witches. At the turn of the twentieth century, Irish immigrants who competed with native-born Americans for jobs were depicted in editorial cartoons as nothing more than fully clothed apes, while Jewish newcomers were portrayed in caricature as giant octopuses whose tentacles enveloped the world. Members of organized hate groups have long contended that Jews are the descendants of Satan and that Blacks are a different and inferior species they call "mud people."[5] During the 1960s and early 1970s, leaders of the women's movement were sometimes stereotyped in cartoon fashion sporting horns, a tail, and the look of evil in their eyes—ugly and vicious "she-devils."[6]

Stereotypes turn particularly nasty whenever a vulnerable segment of society is regarded as threatening the power, prestige, or privileges of the dominant group. After a lengthy period of rising tolerance for racial and ethnic equality throughout society, Americans are increasingly concerned with "cutting their economic losses" vis-à-vis other groups. Most Americans, in principle, continue to support equal treatment of Blacks and Whites in jobs, housing, schools, and public accommodations. But when it comes to supporting these efforts through action, enthusiasm begins to wane. In other words, at an abstract level, most Americans believe in equality, yet in practice we really don't want it—not if it means personal sacrifice!

What is more, as economic conditions have worsened, opposition to measures that promise racial equality in some areas has either remained very strong or actually increased. Few Whites object to integrating schools or neighborhoods when a small number of Blacks is involved. But when substantial numbers of Blacks move into a classroom or a neighborhood, Whites feel *threatened* and so reject integration.

Although Black Americans tend to view themselves as victims of White society, White Americans typically no longer acknowledge the persistence of prejudice and discrimination in the lives of Blacks. Instead, they claim that many Black Americans are unmotivated or lazy. In this way, Whites are able to downplay their own responsibility for why Blacks tend to have worse jobs, lower incomes, and poorer housing than Whites and, at the same time, justify their own opposition to programs—for example, affirmative action—designed to achieve racial parity.[7]

When a perceived threat is economic, so are the stereotypes applied to a particular group in order to explain its inferior status. Thus, according to a recent Harris survey commissioned by the National Conference for Community and Justice, 21 percent of White Americans, 31 percent of Asian-Americans, and 26 percent of Latino Americans say that Black Americans "want to live on welfare." Similarly, 20 percent of White Americans, 35 percent of Asian-Americans, and 24 percent of Black Americans agreed that Latino Americans "lack ambition and the drive to succeed." Asian-Americans too were characterized in a negative light by a sizable proportion of Americans. In fact, 27 percent of White Americans, but 46 percent of Latino Americans and 42 percent of Black Americans, were in agreement that Asian-Americans are "unscrupulous, crafty, and devious in business."[8]

Even more threatening to Whites, as well as to subjugated groups, is the complementary image of Asians as the "model minority"—newcomers who have been spectacularly successful in American society. This stereotype serves to obscure important pockets of poverty within the Asian-American community and exacerbates the resentment felt by Americans who simply aren't "making it" themselves. Even if Asians are successful, they are believed to be inordinately successful. Why?

How is it possible for a group of Americans to excel economically despite their presumed defects of motivation and character? *Perhaps Asians are the undeserving recipients of extraordinary treatment.* This is precisely the unsubstantiated charge that many Americans make in an effort to explain what they believe to be an "unfair advantage" for Asian-Americans. For example, a rumor that circulated among blue-collar workers throughout the United States recently was the claim, totally without basis in reality, that all Asian newcomers received the gift of a new automobile from the U.S. government.

In some cases, the inordinate success of a few Asians has been used to justify withholding aid from all Asians. For example, most colleges and universities no longer grant Asian-Americans special consideration in the admissions process and in financial assistance awards. Indeed, certain institutions of higher learning have actually "rigged their admissions standards to handicap Asian students."[9]

The threat posed by the September 11 terrorist attack ensured that Americans would adopt more negative images of Arabs. According to the Gallup News Service, more than half of all Americans were willing to support increased security measures directed specifically at Arabs in the United States. About the only measure that continued to be disapproved by the majority was expressing violence against Americans of Arab descent.

Negative stereotyping of Arabs existed long before the attack on America. In 1998, a *New York Times* survey discovered that 68 percent of Americans agreed that "Arab-Americans are more loyal to Arab countries than to the United States." Shortly after the bombing of the World Trade Center in 1993, George Gallup found that 32 percent of Americans held an unfavorable opinion of Arabs. Also during 1993, a Gallup poll reported that almost 67 percent of all Americans believed there were too many Arab immigrants entering the country. An earlier survey of public opinion taken in 1991 during the Persian Gulf war similarly determined that 41 percent held Arabs in low esteem. The majority of Americans agreed that Arabs were "terrorists," "violent," and "religious fanatics."

The importance of the personal threat in the stereotyping process can be seen in the acceptance of vicious beliefs concerning a range of groups apart from Arabs and Muslims whose members, having challenged the status quo by their new visibility, are currently the targets of hatred. As more and more Americans have grown fearful of contracting AIDS, for example, they have also stereotyped lesbians and gay men as "a pervasive, sinister, conspiratorial, and corruptive threat." The traditional view of gays as essentially laughable—"as queens, fairies, limp-wrists, and nellies"—could hardly have put them at so much risk. But to stereotype gays as the destroyers of civilization is to make life easier for potential gay-bashers everywhere who seek justification and support for their criminal behavior.[10]

Many people have a distorted view of social reality because they usually don't bother to validate or test their beliefs about others in any systematic way. Thus they can go through a lifetime clinging to old stereotypes that are patently false, never considering that they are essentially inaccurate and unfair.

If an Italian-American makes headlines as a member of organized crime, everybody remembers that he is of Italian descent. If someone who is French does the same thing, his ethnic identity seems irrelevant. If a rapist is Black, some Whites attribute his sexual deviance to his race. If a Black police officer risks his life to arrest the rapist, the same Whites forget about the color of the officer's skin or treat him as an exception to the rule.

The distorted perception of the reality of life in America can be easily demonstrated by questioning even the most sophisticated individuals about elementary social facts. For example, what percentage of the population of the United States is Black? Latino? Jewish? According to a recent Gallup national survey, the average American estimates that 30 percent of the population of the United States is Black (actually, the figure for those who regard themselves as Black or African-American is about 12 percent); that 25 percent of all Americans are Latino (actually, the figure is close to 13 percent); and that 15 percent of our population is Jewish (actually the figure is only 2 percent maximum).

What difference does it make that so many Americans have a distorted view of social reality? That they operate on the basis of false stereotypes? That they are misinformed about other people and maybe about themselves? The answers lie in the relationship between the way we define the world and the decisions we make about it.

Jews are commonly stereotyped as "unscrupulous, aggressive, and too powerful." If they are mistakenly believed to make up 15 percent of our population, then the myth of a dominant Jewish presence in banking or the press sounds more plausible. *Maybe we should restrict Jews so they can no longer work for banks and newspapers.* If Blacks, who are often regarded as "violence-prone," are also thought to constitute 30 percent of all Americans, then we might support making our inner cities into armed camps. *Let's spend less for social programs and more for police intervention.* Not only do stereotypes sometimes confirm our worst suspicions—in this case, that minorities are taking over—but they also suggest that hatemongers take action to limit the influence of those minorities.

Whatever the causal factors responsible for hate offenses, those who attack other human beings because they are different want *validation* in doing so. To an increasing extent, hatemongers find solace, if not inspiration, in the humor, entertainment, music, and politics that we share as a people—in a growing culture of hate, overflowing with nasty stereotypes, that is being directed en masse toward members of our society.[11]

three

HATRED IS HOT: THE MIXED MESSAGES OF POP CULTURE

W e laugh and the world laughs with us; at least some people in the world laugh with us . . . *Others weep*—those who are the butt of the joke. We clap along with the beat of a popular tune on FM radio. It makes us feel happy, excited, uplifted . . . *but at whose expense?* Perhaps at the expense of groups maligned in the lyrics. We feel a surge of solidarity and self-esteem in response to the ravings of a bigoted, charismatic politician . . . *but somebody suffers*—usually the innocent people on whom all our personal problems are blamed. Hatred has long been an integral part of American mass culture, finding expression in its art, music, politics, religion, and humor.

Our popular culture both reflects and affects the attitudes and concerns of Americans. We may therefore look to recent changes in music, humor, and art in order to identify larger trends in public attitudes that might not otherwise be so obvious, at least to a casual observer.

Bigotry has not taken a backseat to tolerance. Various forms of popular culture continue to be saturated with negative stereotypes that characterize various minority groups in the United States. Hatred continues to be hot; intolerance is still in. Whether or not it is intended, we are in the midst of a *culture of hate:* from humor and music to religion and politics, a person's group affiliation—the fact that he or she *differs from people in the mainstream*—continues to provide a basis for dehumanizing and insulting treatment.

Sociologists and psychologists have long recognized the role of humor in subtly communicating malice under conditions of competition and conflict. Put-down jokes are designed to make one's adversary appear ludicrous or absurd. At the group level, racial humor is primarily created to attain some sense of self-esteem and solidarity at the expense of another racial group.[1] Under the guise of *merely joking*, individuals can give voice to racist ideas and emotions while maintaining that they are only having a little fun.[2]

These racist jokes remain with the listener and may be retold time and time again to much wider audiences. Moreover, even if they are not retold, the racist ideas on which such humor is based tend to remain with the audience as a subtle reinforcement of society's stereotypes.

Among standup comics who capitalize on our sense of collective intolerance, Andrew Dice Clay in the 1990s made the art of slurring women, gays, and minorities a highlight of his raunchy routines. His audience laughed at the expense of newcomers, for example, when he referred to Asians as "urine-colored people with towels on their heads."[3] Clay's slurs directed against women sparked some outrage. When the comic hosted *Saturday Night Live*, Nora Dunn, a former cast member, and singer Sinead O'Connor both refused to perform on the same stage, claiming that Clay's appearance would provide a legitimate arena for the sexist ravings of "a hatemonger."

But Andrew Dice Clay is hardly the Lone Ranger among contemporary comics who have made people of color, women, gays, Jews, and vulnerable people the butt of their humor. A new form of "attack comedy" has emerged, in which the most downtrodden, least fortunate members of our society are verbally assaulted. During the 1960s, comics Lenny Bruce, Dick Gregory, Richard Pryor, and George Carlin were notorious for denigrating others in a humorous format. But they typically directed their anger against the "establishment" elements in society whose members could easily protect themselves—the wealthy, the powerful, and the prestigious—or against the prejudices, hypocrisies, and mindless slogans that these comics ascribed to mainstream society. Bruce regarded his comedy as a vehicle for achieving social change.[4] Like Dick Gregory, he used humor to attack popular establishment targets—the military or the president—and to provoke his audiences to question their commonly held beliefs. His humor provided an alternative perspective.

In sharp contrast, modern "attack" comics like Andrew Dice Clay, the late Sam Kinnison, Eddie Murphy, Bobcat Goldthwait, and Jay Charboneau have made no pretext of having some higher purpose. They aim their savage barbs simply to achieve an effect—to make their audiences cringe, squirm, and, of course, laugh—especially at the expense of those who cannot defend themselves from exploitation and cruelty.

Sometimes the victim is a defenseless individual; other times, it is an entire group of vulnerable people. In his standup routine, Kinnison used to joke about a famine in Africa: "Of course those silly motherfuckers in Ethiopia are dying," he moaned. "Whoever told them to live in a desert? Human beings are not supposed to live in the fucking desert!" During a television performance, Don Rickles points to an elderly woman in the audience: "Hi there, Ma'am. I spoke to the home . . . you go in Friday." [56789] During *Late Night with Conan O'Brien,* comedienne Sarah Silverman repeatedly uses the racial slur "chink" and jokes about avoiding jury duty by scribbling "I HATE CHINKS" on the jury information questionnaire. [10] In a stage routine, Chris Rock suggests giving midgets to blind people. "Midgets find it hard to get work," Rock says. "Just get a midget to walk around in front of a blind man saying, 'Yo, man, you gotta make a left.'" [11]

The culture of hate has permeated popular music as well, especially in the lyrics of recordings directed specifically to younger audiences. [12] In the language of the streets, Black rap artists of the 1990s like Ice-T, 2 Live Crew, and N.W.A. (Niggas with Attitude) expressed a violent sexual theme supported by the view that women are "whores" and "bitches" who are "only asking for it anyway." Extreme rap lyrics fuse sex and violence, so that one becomes a metaphor for the other. For example, N.W.A.'s Eazy-E described in sexual terms how he went to his girlfriend's house, knocked down the door, and blasted her with an assault rifle.

Some rap violence has also been directed against gays. In the song, "Watcha' Looking At?" by Audio Two, for example, a man who appears to be gay is warned that his sexual orientation is enough to get him punched in the face.

Popular musicians have also cast aspersions on groups that are different in terms of race or ethnicity. Calling himself "Supreme Allied

Chief of Community Relations," a member of the rap group Public Enemy (Professor Griff), once told the press that "Jews are wicked. They create wickedness around the globe." Public Enemy subsequently released a single, "Welcome to the Terrordome," that again espoused the Christ-killer anti-Semitic theme.[13]

Over the last decade, however, rap as the principal musical expression of hip-hop culture has become increasingly mainstream and diverse. Although created by Black teenagers on the streets of inner-city neighborhoods as rhythmic stories of violence, drugs, and crime, hip-hop has actually replaced rock 'n' roll as the most popular genre of youth music in the United States. Millions of American teenagers—White, Black, Latino, and Asian residing in big cities and suburban towns alike—adopt the uniform of hip-hop, including the caps worn backward, baggy pants, and expensive sneakers, use inner-city street slang, and collect CDs recorded by rap artists.[14]

Notwithstanding its bad reputation, much of contemporary hip-hop is neither violent nor bigoted; indeed, some is decidedly multicultural and antiracist. The late rapper Tupac Shakur, for example, in his song, "I Wonder If Heaven's Got a Ghetto," raps about the scourge of racism and about the need to bring Blacks and Whites together.[15]

Yet there is a continuing theme in the "gangsta" strain of hip-hop culture in which racism, misogyny, and homophobia are frequently expressed. White rapper Marshall Mathers (a.k.a. Eminem), who raps about despising gays and killing women, has become an icon among those American teenagers who eagerly embrace his message of violence and hate.[16] He lyrically confesses believing that his purpose on earth is to "put fear in faggots" and informs his male fans that drinking allows them "to officially slap bitches." Listening to rebellious and antisocial rap music may not inspire most youngsters to go out and commit murder, but it does seem to increase their level of anger.[17]

Also during the early 1990s, the lyrics of some heavy metal records—loud and guitar-driven rock music—emphasized violence, sexism, power, and hatred. In Motley Crue's song "Live Wire," for example, all of these themes came together in a scene of brutal assault and murder.[18] Moreover, the heavy metal rock band Guns N' Roses sold more than 4 million copies of "G N' R Lies," whose lyrics were blatantly antiBlack, antiimmigrant, and antigay. In "Used to Love her," the same group attempted to justify violence against women by depicting a young man being incessantly nagged by his girlfriend until he could take no more and killed her. Guns N' Roses leader Axl Rose defended his beliefs to members of the press as follows: "He's mad at immigrants because he had a run-in with a Middle Eastern clerk at a 7-Eleven. He hates homosexuals because one once made advances to him while he was sleeping. He uses words like "niggers" because you're not allowed to use words like "nigger." [19]

The message of much of heavy metal is quite benign. Unfortunately, however, the fans of metal, especially its most youthful followers, tend to understand the lyrics of their favorite songs in an unsophisticated way. Their interpretation tends to be literal, failing to take into account the complex metaphors frequently depicted by metal artists. Considering that heavy metal advocates tend to come to the music with an antisocial predisposition, there is reason to be concerned about the impact of the most bigoted and violent metal on the attitudes and behavior of its audience members. [20]

Into the new millennium, as the popularity of heavy metal has gradually waned, a new and even more sinister form of specialized metal music has recently emerged. Known widely as Black metal or the Satanic Metal Underground, this latest genre represents the hardest strain of heavy metal, emphasizing cold-blooded murder, hate and prejudice, nihilism, and the unbridled expression of masculine lust. Moreover, running as a general theme through the lyrics of Black metal is a preoccupation with eliminating Christianity and its basic tenets from the face of the earth. Support for the virulently anti-Christian (and, in many cases, anti-Jewish) position comes from at least two sources. Many of the fans of National Socialist Black metal are followers of Satan (considered to be the archenemy of Christ), whom they praise and honor in their music and their behavior. Others cling to ancient pagan rituals and beliefs that were supplanted by an onslaught of Christian conversions throughout Europe a thousand years ago. They dress in Viking clothing, wear "corpse paint" makeup, and carry skulls to their concerts. [21]

A closely related genre of music has recently given inspiration to the extremist thinking of the members of racist skinhead groups and White supremacist organizations. Known as "White power" or "hate core" rock, the lyrics preach hate, support acts of violence directed against Blacks, gays, and Jews, and encourage RaHoWa—a racial holy war. The nation's largest hate music record label, Resistance Records, is led by White supremacist William Pierce, whose novel *The Turner Diaries* reportedly gave Timothy McVeigh his blueprint for blowing up the federal building in Oklahoma City and killing 168 innocent victims. In one hate rock song entitled "Third Reich" produced by Resistance Records, the lyrics suggest that killing all Blacks, Jews, and gypsies would feel "darn right."[22] In the album *Hail AIDS* by the band Ethnic Cleansing, songs include "Alien Gook," "Fertilizer Bomb," and "Piles of Dead Jews."[23]

Religious leaders have also given expression to anti-Semitism. In the 1980s, the president of the Southern Baptist Convention, later insisting that he was only teasing, remarked in a radio sermon that "Jews got funny-looking noses." Louis Farrakhan, leader of the Black Muslim sect known as the Nation of Islam, once referred to Judaism as a "dirty religion." Speaking at Madison Square Garden in 1985, Farrakhan remarked, "The Jews talk about 'Never again'. . . listen, Jews, this little Black boy is your last chance because the Scriptures charge you with killing the prophets of God. . . . You cannot say 'Never again' to God, because when he puts you in the oven, 'Never again' don't mean a thing."[24]

More recently, Farrakhan has made some conciliatory remarks about Jewish-Americans. Yet, in the election campaign of 2000, when Senator Joseph Lieberman was chosen as Gore's running mate, Farrakhan warned that Lieberman's Jewish identity gave him "dual loyalty" to the United States and Israel.

Farrakhan's denigration of Jews is reminiscent of the inflammatory speeches of Iran's Ayatollah Khomeini in which he once attributed all of his nation's problems to America and called all Americans "the world's Satans." Ironically, the Nation of Islam leader's rantings and ravings also mirror—but as a reverse religious image—the dehumanized impressions of Americans portrayed by Islamic extremist Osama bin Laden in his speeches after the September 11 terrorist attacks. In the aftermath of the assault on New York City and Washington, D.C., relations between Christians and Muslims were further soured by Franklin Graham, son of evangelist Billy Graham, who remarked that Islam was violent and that Muslims did not worship the same God as

Christians. At about the same time, Reverend Jerry Falwell blamed the September 11 attacks on "abortionists, feminists, gays, and lesbians."

Certain politicians have sought to elicit a favorable response from their constituents by couching their racist messages in legitimate issues. Louisiana's David Duke raised this strategy to an art form when he spoke eloquently about the need to get the federal government off the backs of the people (meaning: end federal programs that benefit Blacks and Latinos) or about our right to expect a quality education for all our children (meaning: White children should not have to go to school with Black children). Concerned about such matters, many Americans might support a candidate who addresses the important issues of the day—even if he also happens to espouse racism.

Duke's successes in Louisiana politics as a state representative and, to a lesser extent, at the national level underscore his former role as a Ku Klux Klan Imperial Wizard and the founder of the National Association for the Advancement of White People (NAAWP). In a 1986 fund-raising letter distributed by the NAAWP, Duke stated:

> Unless we act soon, Whites will become outnumbered in the nation that we created—*within a generation*! No issue is more important than our people preserving its identity, culture, and rights. An America ruled by a majority of Blacks, Mexicans, and other Third World types will not be the America of our forefathers, or the kind of nation for which they struggled and sacrificed.[25]

In the last few years, Duke has headed the European-American Unity and Rights Organization. On the organization's Web site, Duke has argued that the attack on the World Trade Center was actually a plot concocted by Israeli intelligence to discredit Muslims and gain support for Israel in its conflict with the Palestinians. He suggests not only that Israelis had prior knowledge of the terrorist attack but that they were behind it. His evidence? Simply that there should have been "many hundreds, if not thousands of Israelis in the World Trade Center at the time of the attacks." Why? Because, Duke asserts, "the International Jewish involvement in banking and finance is legendary. For instance, two of the richest firms in New York are Goldman-Sachs and the Solomon Brothers; and both firms have offices in the Twin Towers." Yet, according to Duke's best estimate, no more than 130 (and possibly only one) Israelis lost their lives in the September 11 catastrophe.[26]

Even the most respectable commentators have been willing to publicly voice their personal biases, without regard for the consequences that their statements might have on intergroup tensions. Syndicated columnist, cable-TV celebrity, and former presidential candidate Patrick Buchanan—aide to the Nixon/Agnew team—has suggested that the Anti-Defamation League was out to smear him. Referring to the Congress of the United States as "Israeli-occupied," he claimed that the Israeli defense minister and "its amen corner in the United States" tried to drag the United States into its war against Iraq because it would serve Israeli interests (He failed to foresee Baghdad's Scud missiles aimed at Tel Aviv.) In pleading his case against the Persian Gulf war, he argued that if we went to war, those who fought would have names like "McAllister, Murphy, Gonzales, and Leroy Brown." Even his ally on the right, William F. Buckley Jr., could see the anti-Semitism in this assertion: "There is no way to read that sentence without concluding that Pat Buchanan was suggesting that American Jews manage to avoid personal military exposure even while advancing military policies they (uniquely?) engender."[27]

Buchanan's remarks regarding the war against Iraq are part of a series of anti-Jewish, anti-Israeli statements. He previously proclaimed his skepticism about whether hundreds of thousands of Jews actually had been executed at Treblinka. (Like David Duke, he says the estimate of concentration camp deaths has been severely inflated.) He defended former President Reagan's visit to a cemetery in Germany where SS troopers were buried. (Reagan later claimed that he had been misled into believing that German soldiers who had risked their lives to save Jews were buried there.)[28] In questioning the necessity of America's involvement in World War II, Buchanan wrote in his best-selling 1999 book, *A Republic, Not an Empire,* "that Adolf Hitler had actually posed no threat to the United States."

Also in the political arena, a growing number of "shock jocks" have emerged as the controversial hosts for popular radio talk shows around the country. To the delight of a national audience of millions, right-wing talk master Rush Limbaugh regularly castigates feminists, animal rights advocates, and gay rights activists. In New York City, long-time talk host Bob Grant once characterized Mayor David Dinkins, a Black American, as "a washroom attendant." Similarly, syndicated shock jock Don Imus described network correspondent Gwen Ifill, who is an African-American, as "the cleaning lady."[29] Howard Stern's popular talk show has made a fetish of targeting any vulnerable group—Blacks, gays, women, and the disabled. Stern's "shuck-and-jive" imitation of Black political leaders has helped propel the contentious talk show host into the national limelight.[30]

A particularly appalling version of the culture of hate is the om-nipresent portrayal of women being victimized by grotesque forms of sexual violence in motion pictures. Though these films are supposedly made for adults, they actually appeal to teenage audiences. These R-rated "slasher" films—widely available to members of all age-groups in theaters as well as video cassettes—depict the assault, torture, and murder of women, but in erotic and romantic contexts. In *Tool Box Murders*, for example, a "glassy-eyed lunatic" type is shown literally nailing a nude young woman to a wall as romantic music plays softly in the background. In *I Spit on Your Grave*, several men are shown track-ing, taunting, and then "playfully" gang-raping a terrified young woman whom they have trapped on a desolate island. Using the cine-matic innovations introduced in the semicartoon feature *Roger Rabbit*, the film *Evil Toons* portrays an animated demon who stalks and then sexually assaults female college students played by live actors. Such films contain even more sexual violence against women than do their less available X-rated counterparts. The R-rated versions may send a message that sex and violence are inseparable; that you cannot or *should not* have one without the other. Moreover, research indicates that a heavy diet of slasher movies can make some men more aggres-sive toward women and more accepting of sexual violence .[31]

We do not suggest that everyone who promotes the culture of hate *means* to defame or injure others. Still, just because some-thing is *intended* to be entertaining doesn't necessarily mean that it's also benign. Because a musician's "heart is in the right place" doesn't always guarantee that his message is without harm. Even when an artist's motive is honorable, his effect on a youthful and unsophisticated audience can be deceptively dangerous. A comic's sexist and racist jokes may be hilarious, but, at the same time, perpetuate the nasty stereotypes that many people hold of those who are different. A rap or heavy metal artist may engage in hyperbole only to make a point with his audience or espouse a philosophical position that only he *really* understands and still bring a sexist or racist fan to the precipice of violence. Similarly, a particular R-rated film may keep you on the edge of your seat yet act as a catalyst for violent behavior toward women.[32]

We would like to presume that hatred reflects a sick, pathological fringe element that has little, if anything, to do with the dominant American culture. We comfort ourselves believing that vicious acts of bigotry originate outside of mainstream society; that they reside only in the darkest recesses of the marginal or abnormal mind. To the extent that this view is accepted, we see ourselves as innocent, blameless, and clean, whereas *they* are as guilty as sin. We are free of prejudice, while *they* are rednecks, racists, and bigots. *We* can continue to go about our business as usual, whereas *they* must change their evil ways.

Yet the large numbers of people who continue to rent hate- and violence-filled movies and buy tickets to see racist musical groups in concert indicate that the threads of a culture of hate are woven into the fabric of American society. Clearly, we are not talking merely about the acts of a few entertainers or politicians who operate outside of the mainstream of American culture. If TV audiences were actually repulsed by the humor of Howard Stern, he would never have been asked to host a weekly late-night television show opposite *Saturday Night Live*. If Patrick Buchanan's guest appearances on national talk shows (e.g., *Today)* caused their ratings to drop, he would hardly be asked back. Yet he is.

The culture of hate is part of a vicious cycle of hate and crime; it both reflects and affects the growth of hate crimes in the United States. It supports and encourages those who seek to express their personal version of bigotry in some form of criminal behavior. As suggested earlier, stereotypes serve an important but dangerous function: They *justify* hate crimes in the mind of the perpetrator by providing him with the essential dehumanized images of vulnerable individuals. It would be difficult, if not impossible, for most people to assault another human being, but it becomes a good deal easier to attack or kill "a urine-colored person with a towel on his head," "a Christ killer," "a whore," "a bitch," "a nigger," "a gook," "a cracker," or "a rapist."

Young Americans are frequently targeted as the primary audience for the culture of hate, especially its films, music, and humor. Partially because they lack diverse personal experiences, young people are generally unprepared to reject prejudiced claims coming from sources they regard as credible. Moreover, because they are less likely to handle their frustrations with tolerance and self-control, young Americans are more likely to resort to violence to resolve conflicts. In fact, most hate crimes are committed by offenders under the age of twenty-five.

The continuing presence of a culture of hate reminds us that hate crimes are only the extreme tip of the iceberg of bigotry and prejudice. Popular culture often represents a more pervasive, if less extreme, version of the very same underlying hostilities that trigger criminal behavior. There are many members of society who are very angry—if not quite angry enough to vandalize a cemetery or assault someone whose skin color is different. Instead, they might only parrot the racist lyrics of a White power song, shout their agreement with a racist talk show host, laugh at a racist standup comic, or vicariously relish the murder spree of a deranged killer depicted in an R-rated slasher film. For a few misguided souls, however, the culture of hate is simply not enough to satisfy their need for malice, their quest is one for personal justice.

In the culture of hate, we find the posture that is politically correct (PC) for the social and economic climate of the new millennium—divisiveness and group conflict rather than intergroup harmony and cooperation. Those who believe that tolerance for diversity is PC must be sleepwalking through the decade. Certainly, there was a period in history when nonviolence, egalitarianism, and multiculturalism were actually in style. On college campuses around the nation, baby boomer college students— wearing bell bottoms and love beads—once protested en masse against racism, war, and sexual harassment. During the 1960s and early 1970s, many boomers were intent on changing the world, or at least the world on their campuses. The culture of that time—its music, films, humor, and politics—often reflected the desire of young people for social change.

Of course, that was almost thirty years ago, and the old egalitarian version of political correctness has long since been dead and buried. It went out of fashion just as the Carter administration left office, and Americans began blaming the so-called welfare parasites for everything that had gone wrong with our country.

Even in the aftermath of the 9/11 terrorist attack, the solidarity felt by many Americans was never extended to millions of fellow residents—those of Arab or Muslim descent whose loyalty and patriotism were essentially unblemished, yet who were collectively regarded with suspicion at every turn. Actually, the animosity toward terrorists generalized not only to Middle Easterners but to anyone having a Middle Eastern look, whether their homeland was Egypt, India, Italy, or Peru, whether they were Muslim, Hindu, Jewish, or Christian.

In the culture of hate, liberalism has become about as popular as leprosy. In its place, we find a new brand of political correctness—one that fits better with the prevailing conservative proclivities of the American people and our harder economic times, with the recent influx of newcomers from eastern Europe, Asia, and Latin America being blamed for challenging job opportunities. If anything, the rising tide of multiculturalism is being met by growing resentment among native-born White males who believe that their masculine advantage has eroded. Far from being PC, anyone who in the opening decade of the new millennium dares take a position in favor of diversity and egalitarianism is committing PS: political suicide.

four

RESENTMENT: MOTIVATIONS BEHIND THE HATE

Nathan Thrill joined a local neo-Nazi organization in Colorado because he resented what "racial minorities" were doing to his country. He believed that his success in life was being somehow blocked by "those people being here." In November 1997, Thrill observed Oumar Dia, a thirty-eight-year-old bellhop from Senegal, waiting at a downtown bus stop. Thrill watched Dia for a time and, according to law enforcement officials, decided he would be easy to kill. He approached the Senegalese immigrant and began to threaten and bully him. After subjecting Dia to verbal abuse, Thrill shot and killed his victim. At his trial Thrill argued that he was the real victim of injustice—that because of the way he had been treated by society, "can you really blame me for being out of control with my anger?"

Thrill is hardly alone in feeling victimized from childhood on. At the tender age of four, David Lewis Rice lunged headfirst through a sliding glass door, leaving him with a badly scarred face and blindness in one eye. During his teenage years, he burned the left side of his face in a freak welding accident, which only worsened his already grotesque appearance. Some of Rice's schoolmates routinely targeted the disfigured and pitifully skinny youngster with harassment and ridicule; the "nicer" kids simply avoided him.

Depressed by his failure both in and out of the classroom, Rice dropped out after his second year of high school and went to work. But his ill fortune continued in full force. He had a brief and miserable marriage and an extended period of moving in and out of menial jobs. By his twenty-seventh birthday, Rice was destitute and living in a shelter in Seattle, Washington. He held part-time jobs whenever he could get them, which wasn't very often.

Totally down on his luck and unable to function in everyday life, Rice sought aid and comfort. He found them by joining the ranks of the Seattle Duck Club, an organization notorious for its violently antigovernment, anticommunist, and anti-Semitic philosophy. He gradually developed the belief that his personal problems were a result of some vaguely defined global conspiracy involving Jewish lawyers, communists, the Federal Reserve system, and international bankers.

In line with his friends in the ultraconservative fringe, Rice was particularly enraged by a prominent attorney in Seattle, Charles Goldmark. Years earlier, Goldmark's father had waged an unsuccessful election campaign for state representative. He was widely regarded as a communist sympathizer, based only on his membership in the American Civil Liberties Union and his wife's previous association with the Communist Party as a young girl in New York City. Following his defeat, Goldmark's father filed and won a libel suit against his detractors that received months of national attention. Because of the publicity, however, he continued to be unfairly linked to communism. And, in later years, so was his wealthy son, Charles.

On Christmas Eve, in the middle of the night, Rice decided single-handedly to eliminate the "top communist" and "head Jew" in Washington State. The bearded, anemic-looking vagrant walked into an affluent Seattle neighborhood and, posing as a delivery man, gained entry into the home of the "enemy"—Charles Goldmark. At the point of a realistic-looking toy handgun, he handcuffed Goldmark, his wife, and their two sons and then used chloroform to drug them all into unconsciousness.

Rice slaughtered his victims as they slept. He viciously bludgeoned Goldmark and then, taking a carving knife from the kitchen drawer, he fatally stabbed Goldmark's wife and children.

While Rice was slashing and bludgeoning the members of the Goldmark family one by one, their Christmas tree sat conspicuously by the fireplace in the living room and their Christmas ham baked slowly in the oven. It didn't seem to occur to Rice that Charles Goldmark was neither Jewish nor a communist, but a wealthy Protestant capitalist at-

torney who had attended Quaker schools as a child and later graduated from Harvard Law School. But then such"details"are unimportant
to someone on a mission.[1]

Whether or not David Lewis Rice was psychotic, there are many
other individuals who are just as bitter, indignant, hostile, or irate, even
if they are not severely mentally ill. Like Rice, they may feel left out and
abused, may be fearful of being left out or abused, or convinced beyond
a shadow of a doubt that their way of life is being destroyed and their
rights are being ignored. *They* are the victims, from their distorted perspective, of a society that is out of control, and *they* are looking for
someone to blame.

Resentment can be found, at least to some extent, in the personality
of most hate crime perpetrators. The interchangeability of victims gives
us a clue that this resentment may be immense and that it likely serves
a deep-rooted psychological need. Extremely prejudiced individuals
are frequently *ethnocentric*; they harbor a generalized hostility toward
groups that they perceive to be different. Thus one Black victim can
easily substitute for another; one Jew is as good (or, more precisely, as
bad) as the next. But the choice of victim also can cross group lines: If
Blacks aren't available to victimize, then Latinos will do. If Latinos can't
be found, then gays will be targeted, and so on. After all,"none of them
really have a right to be here in my country, anyway!"

The generalized resentment that often forms the basis for hate
crimes is frequently aimed at either society as a whole or a broad definition of"the government" rather than at any particular individual or
group. It is the wider society from which a perpetrator is estranged and
it is the wider society that he perceives as having rejected him. He is
convinced that the country has changed for the worse, that political
leaders are taking us down the road to total ruination, and that people
like himself—the"little guys"—have lost all control of their destiny.

At the same time, however, hate crimes have a basis in what the
members of a society are *normally* taught when they are growing up.
Thus the perpetrator of hate crimes is socialized in the values and rules
of conventional society. He learns to hate in the same way that he
learns to love country, motherhood, and church. He may be raised by a
set of parents who repeat bigoted jokes at the dinner table, may watch
stereotyped portrayals of minorities on television, may listen to racist

lyrics from popular artists, and may listen to friends recount their negative experiences with the members of different groups. Every time he
passes through the inner city on the way to work, his stereotyped attitudes are reinforced. Every time a news report highlights violence committed by Blacks, academic awards achieved by Asians, or acts of terrorism are committed by Middle Easterners, he feels validated in his
fears and concerns. He learns his culture and, as a result, knows precisely those groups against whom he is supposed to vent his anger.
These are the groups that his culture has stereotyped as inferior in an
intellectual or a moral sense; these are the people who deserve to be
disparaged and belittled in the culture of hate. By defining the enemy
in unmistakable terms, the offender's culture has given him permission
to attack.

Decades ago, the authors of *The Authoritarian Personality* recognized
that prejudice serves a deep-rooted psychological need to protect or
enhance self-esteem. An authoritarian child as described by Theodore
Adorno and his associates is raised with harsh and threatening forms
of discipline. He is expected to be weak and to submit to the desires of
his parents. In the extreme case, he may be physically assaulted. The
parents, in turn, assume a dominant posture in relation to their child.
As a result, an authoritarian child makes only a superficial identification with his parents, actually harboring much latent hostility and resentment toward them.

The outcome of such childhood experiences has relevance for an understanding of the psychological roots of hate crimes: Authoritarians
may finally become hatemongers, and they come to treat others in the
manner that their parents treated them. As adults, they identify with
power and the powerful; they *identify with the aggressor*, maintaining a
general contempt for the allegedly inferior and weak members of society. Thus they despise such diverse groups as Blacks, immigrants,
Latinos, Jews, Arabs, and gays. In the process, they bolster and protect
their own self-esteem whenever it is threatened.

Threat to self-esteem may have a basis in objective reality, not only
for a few authoritarian types but for Americans in general. Resentment
is a state of mind, but it is also a state of our society. Some observers
have applied the term "downward mobility" to characterize the economic plight of an entire generation of middle-class Americans who

are slipping and sliding their way down the socioeconomic ladder. According to William Clark in a study conducted for the Center for Immigration Studies, the culprit can be located in a long-standing economic trend that began in the 1980s and will probably continue into the indefinite future. Clark's research found a decline in real numbers in families identified as middle class in American society, fueled in large part by significant increases in the cost of purchasing a home and providing a college education.

This trend has involved a dramatic shift away from manufacturing and toward services, a shift that has transformed us into a postindustrial society. In 1959 production of goods represented some 60 percent of all employment; by 1985 this figure had dropped to 26 percent, and the overwhelming majority of Americans were employed in the service sector of the economy. During this transitional period, new jobs were created—mainly "bad" jobs that paid poorly and provided few opportunities for upward mobility. Thus large numbers of Americans were forced to take a substantial drop in pay and, therefore, in their way of life. The trend toward service employment continued during the 1990s, when, according to a report from the Bureau of Labor Statistics, 90 percent of the job growth during the 1990s was in private service industries.[2]

The rich really have been getting richer, doing so at the expense of poor and middle-income Americans who have seen their achievements evaporate over time. Through at least the past two decades, the biggest losers have been Blacks, Latinos, young men, female heads of households, farmers, and steelworkers; but almost everyone has suffered to some extent. Most troubling, the group continuing to fall behind most dramatically is our nation's children. According to a study by the Center for Budget and Policy Priorities, "The average poor child fell farther below the poverty line in 1998 and 1999 than any year since 1979."[3]

According to political analyst Kevin Phillips, the widening gap between rich and poor may have been encouraged by national economic policies of the 1980s—a period that represented a strong reversal of almost four decades of downward income redistribution. At the upper end of our class system, the after-tax proportion of income controlled by the wealthiest 1 percent of Americans climbed from 7 percent in 1977 to 11 percent in 1990. Even when adjusted for inflation, the number of millionaires doubled between the late 1970s and the late 1980s, resulting in a record 1.25 million households with a net worth exceeding $1 million. Through the 1990s this trend continued."IRS data show that between 1995 and 1997 the average after tax income of the 1% of the tax-filers with the highest incomes jumped 31% . . . by contrast . . . the bottom 90% of tax filers . . . rose just 3.4 percent."

For families positioned on the lower rungs of the socioeconomic ladder, however, the economic quality of life has deteriorated. Since 1977, the average after-tax family income of the bottom 10 percent of Americans declined 10.5 percent in current dollars. According to a recent study conducted by the National Center for Children in Poverty, despite some improvement during the 1990s, more children live in poverty today than in 1979. Compared with seven other industrial countries (Sweden, West Germany, Australia, Canada, Britain, France, and the Netherlands), the United States has the dubious distinction of being the most unequal, having more poverty and fewer people who are middle class. In his most recent work Kevin Phillips concludes,"By 2000, . . . the United States was not only the world's wealthiest nation and leading economic power but the western industrial nation with the greatest percentage of the world's rich and the greatest gap between rich and poor."[4]

In order to maintain their standard of living, larger numbers of middle-class households have become dual-career families. When family earnings have grown at all, they have increasingly resulted from "greater work effort—from a rise in the number of earners per family and in the average weeks and weekly hours worked per earner. The primary source of the increased work effort has been women, including many with children."[5]

This option for keeping up economically—by increasing the number of people working in a family—is less available to poor Americans than ever before. More and more poor families are headed by a single parent. A study by the Center for Social Policy Studies at George Washington University determined that almost 70 percent of all poor families are headed by a single parent. In 1960 just the opposite was true: 70 percent of poor families included two parents.[6]

Polling data collected in conjunction with the 1990 presidential election reveal a watershed in public attitudes. For the first time in that century, most Americans believed that their children would *not* have a better standard of living than they did and that there is very little they can do to ameliorate this situation. This important shift in attitude contradicts a long-held American belief: Parents work hard to be able to provide a better quality of life for their children. If people now believe that their personal effort is ineffectual, they may look for an alternative means for improving their economic position. One way is to challenge those who are perceived to be causing their economic difficulties—Blacks, Jews, Hispanics, Asians, women, immigrants, and perhaps anyone else who is "different."

Many Americans now feel that their long-term economic condition is controlled by persons, groups, or forces that they can no longer influence. Again, hard work is not enough. The causal factors are seen as outside of personal control. The traditional American middle-class lifestyle is slipping away, and *somebody somewhere must be responsible.*

According to *American Demographics*, young people have been particularly hard hit by downward mobility. As a result, they are taking longer to finish college, living for a longer period of time with parents or other relatives, and delaying plans to marry. Young married couples are today less likely to own their own homes. As part of a William T. Grant study entitled "The Forgotten Half Revisited: American Youth and Young Families 1988–2008," Samuel Halperin found that the percentage of young families owning their own home actually fell from 49 to 38 between 1980 and the mid-1990s.[7]

Comparing their worsening economic circumstances with those of their parents, millions of teenagers and young adults have begun to experience what sociologists call *relative deprivation*—they question the essential validity of the American Dream and are less optimistic about prospects for their own future. In fact, many of them feel deprived and disillusioned in comparison with their parents' generation.

Called "selfish," "passive," and "ultraconservative" by those who remember the liberal activism of the prosperous 1960s, many young Americans are trying merely to maintain their current standard of living. In the face of income erosion, they regard tax increases as a burden they cannot afford. Instead of having an altruistic orientation toward those in need, young Americans feel *personally threatened* by the growing presence of newcomers and minorities who compete for diminishing amounts of wealth, status, and power. And in fact they are being *challenged*, to an increasing extent, for jobs, power, and prestige by a broad range of "outsiders." The growing presence of women, people of color, and international students threatens the dominance of White males on college campuses across the country. More and more lesbians and gay men "come out" to friends and relatives and then express their demands in assertive public demonstrations for inclusion in politics, work, education, and the military. Unprecedented numbers of newcomers from Asia, eastern Europe, and Latin America are competing for jobs with native-born Americans. Affirmative action guidelines and quotas are widely regarded as "reverse discrimination" policies which, at the expense of White males, grant special treatment to undeserving minorities and women. More than just cultural baggage left over from a previous era, bigotry may to some extent also be a reaction to a continuing and objective threat to group position. Thus racial tolerance drops as the size of the minority population grows enough to challenge the status quo.[8]

Criminologists have long recognized that absolute levels of economic deprivation do not necessarily correlate with measures of either violence or prejudice. At the national level, for example, there is no relationship between the unemployment rate and the homicide rate. Research suggests, however, that a strong relationship exists between income inequality and murder. That is, the greater a country's income disparity, the higher its homicide rate.

Income inequality represents a form of relative deprivation whereby individuals may appear to be doing well financially but actually feel economically threatened. In an early study, Bettelheim and Janowitz uncovered no relationship between income level or objective socioeconomic status and intensity of anti-Semitism, but found that downwardly mobile men—individuals who had moved lower in terms of socioeconomic status by comparison with their previous civilian employment—expressed greater hostility against Jews than did men who were stable with respect to their socioeconomic status. For these men, loss of occupational status apparently constituted a frustration sufficiently intense to generate considerable ethnic hatred.

The attack on September 11, 2001, made a difficult situation even worse. While the economy had already begun a decline that was a recession in all but the formal definition, the attack on the World Trade

Center and the Pentagon drove our economy deeper into decline. This time, however, there was someone to blame. The attack planned by Osama bin Laden and carried out by members of his Al Quaeda terrorist network deepened the economic fears of the nation and created widespread anxiety about the possibility of further acts of terrorism being committed on our shores.

It did not take very long for the purveyors of hate across the country to quickly blame the attack on Arabs and call for the deportation of all Arab-Americans. The Southern Poverty Law Center reported that Ann Coulter, a contributing editor for the *National Review On-Line* argued, "We should invade their countries, kill their leaders, and convert them to Christianity." What followed was an unprecedented increase in attacks on Arab-Americans and a broad-based scapegoating of Arabs for all economic and military problems.

Although hatemongers may grow up learning the conventional culture, they are *abnormal* with respect to their lack of power and prestige in mainstream society. According to police officials who specialize in responding to hate offenses, many of the young people who commit hate crimes have been particularly hard hit by economic bad times and, as a result, feel on the margins of society. Bill Johnston, formerly the director of the Boston police department's Community Disorders Unit, which investigates hate crimes, suggests that these kids may be in school, but they are not successful in school. They believe that "the system" has failed them . . . not just the schools or their job, but the entire American way of life. Thirty years ago, they would have worked in a factory and made a decent living. Now there are few well-paying jobs available for those with only a high school education. In the past these young people used their hands to build things. Now they are using their hands to destroy things. For them, the American Dream is dead. Whether a result of the dramatic change from a manufacturing to a service economy or simply the consequence of inept government policies, it really makes no difference to them. They believe they have no future but won't blame themselves for their situation. And to some extent they shouldn't. Still, they fail to place the responsibility on large-scale abstract social and economic forces or on the government. They are looking for *someone* to blame . . . someone who is concrete, visible, and vulnerable. Someone who is different.

One example of the worst kind of result of this type of thinking happened in Boston, where two gay men were shot and wounded in an apparent civil rights violation (the assailant was reported to have called both of his victims "faggots" and "queers"). Robert Weinerman, victim advocate for the Fenway Community Health Center, tried to explain to members of the press why hate-motivated violence against gays and lesbians in Massachusetts had increased 29 percent in only one year. "It is happening more now than in the past because more and more gay and lesbian people are openly visible and holding positions of power in state and city government," he said. "That increased visibility brings a backlash."[9]

To an increasing extent, then, Americans engage in *zero-sum thinking*. They view two or more individuals or groups as striving for the same scarce goals, with the success of one automatically implying a reduced probability that others will also attain their goal, be it a job, raise, or promotion. If you believe that the "pie" is shrinking, you might not be so willing to give up a slice for someone who doesn't have his own piece. After the economic boom of the 1990s the new millennium has brought an economic decline, at least temporarily, and with it a fear that the economic pie no longer appears to grow—if anything, it seems to be getting smaller.

Zero-sum thinking is not limited to economics. It can also be applied to relative judgments of moral worth, even to evaluating the basic value of others as human beings. In the same way that an individual feels in competition with others for money or prestige, so he may feel in competition for moral righteousness. That is, he can only feel righteous when he compares himself with someone who is evil; he can only gain in moral worth to the extent that someone else loses in moral worth.

Zero-sum thinking engages the individual in a competitive struggle to upgrade himself and downgrade others. Respectability demands deviance; good requires bad. Thus a strong position against Jews, Muslims, or gays can make an individual feel that he is a good Christian; a radical stand in opposition to Christians, Jews, or gays can make an individual feel that he is a good Muslim; and so on. At the extreme, an individual who engages in zero-sum moralistic thinking gives himself a shot of moral adrenaline each time he assaults or harasses those he deems deserving of it.[10]

Resentment takes many forms. Some groups are actually blamed for the misery of the perpetrator. Throughout history, Jews have been held responsible for just about everything that has gone wrong—the crucifixion of Jesus, the Black Plague, inflation and depression, rampant capitalism, rampant communism, mortgage foreclosures, and the AIDS epidemic, to mention only a few. The recent attack on the World Trade Center has been blamed on Jews by many leaders of organized hate groups. Just days after September 11, William Pierce, leader of the notoriously racist and anti-Semitic National Alliance, argued, "What happened this week is a direct consequence of the American people allowing the Jews to control their Government and to use American Strength to advance Jews' interests."[11]

In eastern Europe, we are currently witnessing a revival of the same kind of anti-Semitic thinking, in that Jews are being blamed for a host of economic and social problems over which they could not possibly have control. In the United States, the members of organized hate groups have similarly blamed Jews for causing bad economic times and for creating racial antagonism between Black and White Americans.

Decisions made in far-off places like Washington, D.C., Moscow, Tel Aviv, or Baghdad can determine whether we place the responsibility for our problems on people who are different from us. Under conditions of war, cold war, or the threat of war, anxious citizens may direct their wrath at members of the local community who are perceived to be in league with the "enemy." Japanese-Americans were cast in this unfortunate role during World War II. Iranians were victimized during the hostage crisis in 1978. More recently, many Arab-Americans have been detained for questioning by federal law enforcement authorities about possible involvement in the September 11 attack. Many who were detained were eventually released; while in custody they were denied access to their attorneys and were not permitted to notify their immediate families.

In response to the Iraqi invasion of Kuwait and the American involvement in the Persian Gulf war in 1991, local resentment turned toward Arab-Americans. Dozens received death threats or harassing phone calls. In Detroit, the publisher of the largest Arabic-language newspaper in the United States got an anonymous call warning that he would be killed if Americans in Kuwait were harmed. In Boston, a forty-one-year-old Palestinian-American was forced to move from his apartment after several neighbors called his landlady to demand his eviction. At midnight, he heard a voice outside the front window of his apartment telling him, "You move out or you'll die."

In the months following the attack on America, the FBI initiated 318 hate crime probes involving Arab, Muslim, and Sikh Americans. These probes resulted in charges against some eighty people. According to the Council on American-Islamic Relations, there were seventeen hundred acts of hostility toward American Muslims and Arabs and those perceived to be American Muslims or Arabs, over the same period of time.

On September 15, for example, only four days after the attack on America, a forty-nine-year-old Sikh Indian wearing a turban was shot down in front of his gas station in Mesa, Arizona. The next day in Buffalo, New York, an Arab-American was knocked unconscious by an eighteen-year-old male in the bathroom of a local food market. The victim reported that he was called an "Arab terrorist" before having his head smashed against the bathroom door. The attack was exacerbated when the victim struggled from the bathroom and asked for help. A number of store employees laughed at him and refused his request. There were murders and assaults around the country. In Dallas, a Pakistani Muslim was found shot to death in his convenience store. In Huntington, New York, a Pakistani pedestrian was nearly run down by a motorist who had threatened to kill her. In San Gabriel, California, an Egyptian Christian was killed in his grocery store. In Brockton, Massachusetts, an Arab-American man returned to work to find his pizza shop engulfed in flames.

Asian-Americans have also served as convenient targets for the anger of many Americans—and not only because they are mistaken for Middle Eastern terrorists. During World War II, hundreds of thousands of Japanese-Americans were rounded up and thrown into camps, their possessions confiscated, and their lives profoundly disrupted. Because they were at war with Japan, Americans could easily rationalize their treatment of Japanese-Americans as a defensive strategy necessary to minimize anti-American activities among a population susceptible to divided loyalties. (It is interesting that neither Italian-Americans nor German-Americans were interned, though the United States was also at war with Italy and Germany. Italian and German immigrants were, however, rounded up and detained.) The treatment of Chinese-Americans could not be so easily justified because China was an ally. Yet the harassment of Chinese-Americans—pelted with rocks and racial slurs—became so pervasive that *Life* magazine, in 1941, felt compelled to run a two-page story instructing its readers how to distinguish "friendly Chinese" (higher cheekbones, flatter nose, ruddier complexion, etc.) from "enemy alien JAPS." After all, we wouldn't want to throw rocks at the *wrong* U.S. citizens or visiting dignitaries!

During the 1982 recession, anti-Asian sentiment once again gained momentum, as many Americans blamed Japanese car manufacturers for massive layoffs in the automobile industry. Detroit was particularly hard- hit, not only by unemployment but also by hate and violence. Capitalizing on anti-Japanese attitudes, automobile dealers sought publicity by giving angry Americans a chance to get even, if only symbolically, with Japan. They placed a Japanese car in a conspicuous section of their lot and encouraged residents to smash it with a sledge hammer. Incorporating both American capitalism and resentment, the sign on one car lot in Detroit read, "Pay a Dollar—Bash a Toyota."

The bashing occasionally turned from cars to human beings. In June 1982, a twenty-seven-year-old Chinese-American, Vincent Chin, was spending his Saturday night drinking in a topless bar located in one of Detroit's many working-class neighborhoods. The young man was enjoying his "final fling" at his bachelor party. Before he could extricate himself, two strangers—a Chrysler autoworker and his stepson—had engaged Chin in a shouting match and then an all-out brawl. Shouting "it's because of you we're out of work," one of the attackers took a baseball bat to the Chinese-American's skull and bludgeoned him to death. Apparently these enraged hatemongers didn't worry about making fine distinctions between Japanese- and Chinese-Americans. From their point of view, any Asian was the enemy.

In March 1983, Vincent Chin's killers—Ronald Ebens and Michael Nitz—were sentenced after confessing to the murder. Wayne County circuit judge Charles Kaufman gave the two men three years of probation and fines of $3,780 each. Explaining his lenient ruling, the judge said that the defendants were "not the kind of people you send to prison. . . . These men are not going to go out and harm somebody else." Needless to say, the Asian-American community was furious.[12]

Resentment is a thread that runs through the fabric of society today. In all quarters, Americans take exception to demands made by those who seek to preserve or increase their own share of economic resources at "our" expense. When a group has suffered some degree of oppression, it becomes easier for its members to blame the advantaged group and justify criminal behavior. In extreme cases, resentment may be translated into brutal acts of violence.

From 1981 to 1987, for example, members of the Temple of Love in Miami, a Black separatist cult, plotted fourteen killings and two attempted murders in the name of Old Testament vengeance. Their charismatic leader Yahweh Ben Yahweh (God, Son of God in Hebrew) preached that all Whites were "serpents" and "demons." He taught that Blacks were the only true Jews and that Whites who identified themselves with Judaism were actually "false imposter Jews" who worshiped in "the synagogue of Satan."

Under Yahweh's direction, at least six Black separatists conspired to kill "White devils" in retribution for the oppression of Blacks by Whites. As part of the initiation ritual for joining their temple, recruits had to murder a "White devil" and then bring back the victim's severed ear as proof of the killing. Eight of the victims were White vagrants who were in the wrong place at the wrong time. But several victims were Black people who had somehow challenged Yahweh's directives. One disobedient "blasphemer" was decapitated; two others were shot to death for failing to vacate an apartment owned by the temple. A female ex-member had her throat slit. And one Black man was killed because he had chased from his home temple members who were seeking donations.

In his sermons, Yahweh told his followers, "All hypocrites must die." Before his plan could be completely carried out, however, the fifty-five-year-old son of a Pentecostal minister was convicted and sent to prison for conspiracy to commit murder.[13]

Following the acquittal of Los Angeles police officers charged in the videotaped beating of Rodney King, another episode of Black-on-White violence captured the attention of the country. During the riots in Los Angeles, a White truck driver, Reginald Denny, was literally dragged from the cab of his truck and, as the TV cameras rolled, was beaten without mercy by five Blacks. The victim, whose only crime was being White, had stopped his truck at a red light during the early hours of the rioting. The five Black men beat Denny with the fire extinguisher from his truck and then robbed him of his wallet. One offender shot him with a shotgun while others hit him with beer bottles and savagely kicked him in the head. The long-haired truck driver survived because four bystanders, also Black, risked their own lives to stop the beating and rushed the victim to a local hospital.[14]

Blame is only one expression of resentment. Other groups are deeply resented but are not necessarily viewed as responsible for the problems suffered by the offender. Instead, they are seen as the *undeserving recipients* of some advantage. At the close of the American Civil War, during a period known as "reconstruction," ex-slaves were given a series of legally guaranteed opportunities for equal treatment. Unfortunately, the reaction to this promise of equality took the form of increased lynching of Blacks throughout the South. White Americans simply could not accept efforts that they thought might reduce their own advantaged position in society.

At present, Blacks and Latinos may similarly be regarded as receiving preferential (and undeserved) treatment under affirmative action–type programs in schools and companies. Asians may be commonly (and incorrectly) perceived as getting a special government "handout" in the form of financial assistance when they come to this country, which helps them get ahead. As women continue to earn places in previously all-male occupations, they too are confronted with accusations that they only got their jobs because of their gender.

In the final analysis, many individuals suffer low self-esteem, dislike entire groups of people, and feel profoundly resentful; yet they would never actually commit a crime motivated by bigotry. Perpetrators of hate crimes feel in addition some *personal threat* originating in the groups they despise. Jews have too much power; they are responsible for our recession and therefore *my* unemployment. Blacks benefit from reverse discrimination; because of affirmative action, *I* can't get into law school. Feminists are taking more than their share of jobs; their presence makes it more and more difficult for *me* to feed *my* family. Asians are grabbing all the college scholarship money; because of them, *my* son might not be able to attend college.

What are disgruntled and resentful Americans—fed up with "unfair competition" and sick and tired of feeling disadvantaged—to do? Ten or fifteen years ago, they might have grabbed a beer from the refrigerator and turned on the reruns of *NYPD Blue* or snoozed on the couch. They were variously labeled, sometimes unfairly, as the "silent majority" or the "me generation," by reporters and political pundits eager to characterize what they saw as a trend toward indifference and apathy.

But Americans are now taking their cues from a new breed of hero: idols of activism who are admired and respected not for their ability to keep us entertained nor for their success in business, but for their courage to take active charge of their own lives and the lives of others. In the face of overwhelming and impersonal social, political, and economic forces, Americans feel increasing admiration for those who come forward from their place among the spectators. In the aftermath of the September 11 terrorist attack, we have also found idols of activism in firefighters, police officers, and passengers on doomed airliners who refused to let terrorists fly into the White House.

Thus our choice of idols reflects our growing determination not to stand idly by but to respond to perceived injustice and to act on our important beliefs. At the same time, some idols of activism also express a growing impatience with legitimate avenues of making it in mainstream society. *You can no longer depend on government or corporate America; it is now entirely up to you—Let's roll!*

In the spirit of renewed activism, Americans are generally more willing to express their resentment, even if it means committing acts of discrimination and violence. In his abortive campaign for the governorship of Louisiana and later the presidency, David Duke became an activist voice for White blue-collar workers who felt that "welfare parasites," corrupt government officials, and civil rights advocates were at the root of America's economic woes. To many of his supporters, Duke was courageous for *daring* to act on beliefs that other politicians shared but presumably were afraid to acknowledge in public, let alone act on.

At the extreme, members of organized hate groups—Aryan Nations, the National Alliance, the White Aryan Resistance, and the Ku Klux Klan—have become increasingly willing to translate their bigoted attitudes into bigoted behavior. Militant revolutionaries have taken on new prominence within the White supremacist movement, giving it a broad political and economic activism that incorporates racism among such issues as taxes, foreign aid, immigration, crime, and AIDS. During the 1980s, members of organized hate groups were responsible for committing armed robberies, assaults, and murders across the country. During one eighteen-month period in 1984–1985, for example, members of the White supremacist group known as the Order killed two FBI agents, a sheriff, and a state trooper. By late 1985, twenty-three Order members had been convicted of racketeering offenses and sentenced to long terms in prison.[15]

Resentment often gets played out in themes that are apparent only at the level of motivation. As in the case of Nathan Thrill, from the viewpoint of the hatemonger, a criminal act may seem perfectly justified, even necessary. He may believe sincerely that his violence is defensive or that he is only getting even with those who have ruined his life or even the country. In some cases, the perpetrator may even see his hate crime as a recreational sport, in which he gets together with "the boys" for an evening of drinking beer and bashing gays.

five

FOR THE THRILL OF IT: THE STRONG PREYING ON THE WEAK

ike young men getting together on a Saturday night to play a game of cards, certain hatemongers get together and decide to go out and destroy property or bash minorities. They want to have some fun and stir up a little excitement—at someone else's expense. In a *thrill-seeking hate crime*, there need not be a precipitating incident. The victim does not necessarily "invade" the territory of the assailant by walking through his neighborhood, moving onto his block, or attending his school. On the contrary, the assailant (or group of assailants), looking to harass those who are different, searches out locations where the members of a particular group regularly congregate. The payoff for the perpetrators is psychological as well as social: They enjoy the exhilaration and the thrill of making someone suffer. For those with a sadistic streak, inflicting pain and suffering is its own reward. In addition, the youthful perpetrators receive a stamp of approval from their friends who regard hatred and violence as "hot" or "cool."

The leader of a thrill hate crime episode may be the only member of the group to be motivated by intense hatred of the victim. He manipulates the others by playing on their need to prove their loyalty, by daring them not to back out. Most members merely follow along; they conform, they accept the challenge in order to avoid being rejected by the people in their lives who mean the most—their good friends. Each one believes that he alone is hesitant to go along and that, if he resists, the others would consider him a coward or a "wimp."

Indeed, many youths who participate in a hate-motivated rampage against gays, Blacks, Arabs, or Asians would probably not engage in such behavior on their own. Groups provide both inspiration and security. For a teenager who is on the verge of flunking out of school and doesn't get along with his parents, group membership is especially influential. Being accepted by his pals makes him feel special. Indeed, being rejected by them may be tantamount to being given a death sentence, at least in his eyes.

Moreover, an individual in the presence of his friends may take risks that he would otherwise find unacceptable. Under such circumstances, he feels free from accountability—responsibility is shared with his buddies, and so is the blame. Members of the group act within a division of labor and are typically asked to play only specialized roles in the commission of a violent act. One of them selects the victim, another knocks her to the ground, still another tears off her clothing, and so on. According to Robert Panarella, a professor of police science at the John Jay College of Criminal Justice, the result is that "while the action of each individual can seem relatively minor, the action of the whole may be horrific."[1]

On November 4, 2000, in the small town of Angelica, Wisconsin, Robert and Cindy Lee pulled their truck over to the side of the road to switch drivers. Meanwhile, a Black pickup truck skidded to a stop and pulled behind the Asian couple. The two nineteen-year-old men in the pickup, Grant Heim and Jeremy Martin, asked if they needed any help. The Lees said they were fine, thanked the two strangers, and then drove off. But moments later, Heim and Martin got back onto the highway and decided to have a little fun by scaring their Asian victims. The two men ran their pickup across the path of the Lees, causing them to swerve off the road and onto the gravel shoulder.[2]

During the early morning hours of October 5, 2001, on the campus of the University of Kentucky, two local high school students roamed the campus in their Black pickup truck, looking for a little fun at the expense of international students who might be walking back to their dormitory after a night of hitting the books. In two separate incidents, the teenagers approached a student of color who was leaving the campus library—in one case, a Japanese student; in the second, an Indian student—and asked for directions. Each student walked over to the truck and was punched in the face.[3]

Many of the hate crimes directed against property—acts of desecration and vandalism—can be included in the thrill-seeking category. In an incident in Wellesley, Massachusetts, two alienated White youths looking for excitement went on a spree of destruction and defacement that resulted in attacks on twenty-three properties in three different communities. The two went out at night when "there was nothing else to do" and defaced walls, driveways, and automobiles with slurs against Jews, Blacks, Greeks, and even skinheads. After their arrest, the two young men claimed that they hadn't intended to hurt anyone and were drunk at the time.

The selection of victims in the incidents at Angelica, Wisconsin, the University of Kentucky, and Wellesley, Massachusetts, are typical of thrill hate crimes in general—victims are chosen more or less on a random basis. Thus interchangeability occurs not only within a target group—for example, among Blacks, Jews, or Asians—but across groups as well. Almost any vulnerable and easily identified victim will do.

The culture of hate is important for singling out the victims of thrill hate attacks and justifying the violence perpetrated against them. Offenders target the members of certain groups because they regard them as inferior—perhaps even subhuman—and because they are convinced that their criminal behavior will simply not engender the negative sanctions that crimes against more respectable groups might. These youths see gays, Blacks, Asians, Arabs, Jews, and women being used as the butt of jokes by certain comedians (not to mention members of their audience who repeat the jokes), belittled in the lyrics of popular music, and discredited by thinly disguised political messages. In some cases, young people looking for a thrill learn a dangerously misguided message: Nobody will care if we attack the members of this group, and we might be applauded!

The utter randomness of these thrill-seeking hate crimes—especially those aimed at property—makes it particularly difficult to apprehend the perpetrators. Their motives tend to be obscure and their patterns of committing the crimes are haphazard at best. Because they usually do not have an economic motivation—they gain no money, property, or jobs—such hate crimes may be relatively easy to deter with the threat of appropriate sanctions. According to some experts, the offenders get little more than "bragging rights," the ability to tell their friends about how they "trashed that temple" or "beat up that gook."[4]

Thus the hatred behind thrill-seeking violence is for most perpetrators superficial; they hold on to their disparaging images to justify victimizing strangers. Consequently, offenders are usually not profoundly convinced of the legitimacy of their criminal acts and can be dissuaded from repeating them. In many crimes the threat of sanctions may not deter future criminal behavior (e.g., serious drug use), but in thrill hate crimes the threat of criminal sanctions may be just enough to convince a group of bored young men to stay home rather than go out looking for someone to beat. It is important, therefore, to apprehend hate crime perpetrators at this point, especially in light of the possibility that at least some property offenders who go undetected later graduate to hate crimes directed against people. Because what the perpetrators derive from committing such crimes is minimal, they may be strongly influenced by a strong statement from society at large which demonstrates that this type of behavior won't be tolerated.

Assaultive hate crimes can also occur as a deadly game in which the perpetrators express a need to feel powerful and dominant in destructive behavior. In 1990, for example, unidentified vandals in Madison, Wisconsin, first smashed the windows and then cut the brake lines of a bus that was supposed to take Jewish children to a day camp. Fortunately, the act of sabotage was discovered and no one was injured. But the climate of anti-Semitism became so dangerous in Madison that armed police had to be stationed outside local synagogues while worshipers celebrated the Jewish New Year, Rosh Hashanah.[5] In September 1998 in Queens, New York, a twenty-year-old man from Trinidad was beaten into a coma and hospitalized as a result of a confrontation with three White men wielding baseball bats who were out looking for some fun.

Thrill hate crimes are occasionally committed by couples—two friends or relatives who share a deep disappointment with life and have time on their hands, so they team up to go bashing. In a racially mixed area of Wheaton, Maryland, for example, two young White men—both unable to find work—were charged in a particularly bizarre hate crime. The incident occurred in the early morning hours of March 3, 1992, as two Black women—ages twenty-nine and thirty-nine—were walking from their apartment to a pay phone in a nearby shopping center. According to police reports, the two White men—one nineteen, the other twenty-one—stopped their car and then chased their victims on foot. One woman ran toward a house in the neighborhood and was rescued by the occupant, a thirty-year-old man who heard one of the assailants warn, "If you knock on that door again, I'll kill you."

The other woman tried to escape into the woods, where she fell to the ground. The attacker, catching up, beat her around the head and face, ripped off her clothes, and doused her with lighter fluid. While he was attempting to light the fluid, however, police cars arrived on the scene. Before they had a chance to burn their victim, both men escaped. They were later apprehended and charged with attempted murder, assault with intent to murder, assault with intent to maim, kidnapping, and attempting to injure a person for racial reasons under a 1988 hate crimes statute. One woman was left hysterical but otherwise unhurt. The other victim was left naked from the waist up and bleeding from cuts to the head.[6]

When large numbers of young people go on a rampage, they are said to be "wilding." Smaller groups of hatemongers can also go wild, even if not in a state of frenzy. Most thrill attacks take the form of vandalism, intimidation, and assault. Occasionally, however, a group of young people looking for some excitement attack their victim with lethal force. This is what happened in the case of twenty-year-old James Burmeister and his two buddies, all of whom were soldiers stationed at the Fort Bragg army base outside of Fayetteville, North Carolina. The three young men were also racist skinheads who hated Blacks, Latinos, and Jews. By day, they completely immersed themselves in the disciplined military training required of all recruits on base. At night, they shed their military uniforms in favor of the steel-toed boots and green leather jackets associated with the Nazi skinhead movement.

During the early morning hours of December 7, 1995, the three skinhead soldiers drove their Chevrolet Cavalier into a Black neighborhood located in the middle of town. They spent the night drinking, playing pool, and watching topless dancers at a local sports bar.

All the while, Burmeister had made his intentions clear enough—he talked to his friends about finding the enemy and having a little fun, about wanting to earn the racist badge of honor in the form of a spider web tattoo worn only by members of the movement who had killed in order to further the Nazi cause. He liked the excitement, the thrill, and the bragging rights.

Shortly after midnight, while driving along a dirt road, the three racists spotted their victims, Michael James, thirty-six, and Jackie Burden, twenty-seven, who were walking together along the road. Burmeister jumped out of the car and immediately opened fire on the Black couple with his 9-millimeter Ruger handgun, killing them both.

Although members of any "inferior" group will usually do, gays are most frequently targeted as the victims of thrill-motivated attacks. They usually receive serious injuries when bashed. Comparisons of national and several state reports on the percentage of assaulted hate crime victims from each group (as opposed to being victims of harassment or vandalism) indicates that gay, lesbian, and bisexual victims were the most likely to be assaulted when compared with other hate crime victim groups.

Gays make particularly "good" victims for groups of bored young men looking for a thrill. First, gays are known to congregate in certain areas of major cities and are thus relatively easy to find. Second, gays may represent a particularly difficult psychosexual threat to teenage males who are in the process of establishing their sexual identity. The members of skinhead gangs frequently dress to emphasize their toughness and masculinity—for example, steel-toed boots and motorcycle jackets. Their exaggerated "macho" appearance may indicate underlying confusion and doubt as well as a sense of powerlessness associated with the developmental stage of adolescence. Finally, gays may be particularly reluctant to report attacks against them. Those who have not "come out of the closet" may fear people discovering their sexual orientation and then using it as a basis for discrimination. Some gays may be concerned about the practical problems of possibly losing their apartment or their job. Others may worry that they will be rejected by disappointed family members or ignored by unsympathetic police. Criminologists Kevin Berrill and Gregory Herek have described this process as *secondary victimization*, the negative response of others to a crime victim because of his or her sexual orientation.

Unlike offenders who bash the members of ethnic and racial groups, those who target gays are more typically "average young men" without criminal records who come from any of a number of different lifestyles, backgrounds, and social classes. Even when they are from economically secure families, however, most gay bashers still suffer from a form of *marginality* stemming from a sense of powerlessness that often accompanies the teenage years. Based only on their status as adolescents, even those who appear from an adult perspective to be successful and well-adjusted may search for ways to overcome their feelings of alienation and inferiority. They bash gays for the same reason that other teenagers steal hubcaps, shoplift, or hold wild parties when their parents are out of town. But young men who have been socialized to be aggressive and find violent solutions to their problems may end their search for power by physically attacking others who themselves lack the power to retaliate.

According to Matt Foreman, executive director of the New York City Gay and Lesbian Anti-Violence Project (AVP), gay bashing ("Let's go beat up some queers") has actually become a fad or a sport among certain high school students. In the typical case, two or more young men arm themselves with knives, bottles, hammers, or baseball bats and then target a part of the city in which they suspect that large numbers of gays congregate or reside. The intruders rush in, assault their unsuspecting victim, and rush out again.

This is precisely the sequence of events that transpired during the early morning hours of July 2, 1990, in a New York City schoolyard widely known as a homosexual hangout after dark. At 2:00 A.M., Julio Rivera, a twenty-nine-year-old Puerto Rican who worked as a bartender in gay bars and as a prostitute, was passing through the schoolyard on his way home. He was suddenly surrounded by three young men who, without warning or provocation, literally hammered him with repeated blows in the face and head, viciously kicked him, and then stabbed him in the back. Rivera was still conscious when his assailants left the scene. He managed to stagger from the schoolyard to get help and was taken by ambulance to a nearby hospital, where he died a few hours later.

In a videotaped confession, Daniel Doyle, a Union College freshman, later implicated two of his friends in the assault on Rivera. Prior to the attack, they had spent four hours guzzling beer, said Doyle. Then he and his friends had decided to take a little walk. Sure, it was almost two o'clock in the morning, but none of them could sleep. So they walked without purpose or destination. Before leaving the house, according to Doyle, one of them had slipped a claw hammer into the waistband of his pants. Another had taken along a wrench and a knife that he had snatched from Doyle's kitchen. But they had had no particular place in mind to go. They just couldn't sleep.

The Bias Review Panel of the New York City police saw the assault somewhat differently. Alleging that the perpetrators despised homosexuals and that they were connected with a gang of skinheads in the neighborhood, the review panel concluded that the incident was a vicious hate crime—an attack perpetrated against Rivera because of his sexual orientation.[7]

In November 1991, Daniel Doyle took the stand in a packed Queens, New York, courtroom. He was present not as a defendant but as the prosecution's star witness against the two defendants, Eric Brown, twenty-one, and Esat Bici, nineteen. Doyle had previously confessed making the fatal wound by plunging his knife into Rivera's back. But in a plea bargain with the prosecuting attorneys, the charges against him had been reduced from second-degree murder to manslaughter. In exchange, Doyle agreed to testify against his two friends.

According to Doyle, he had held a "skinhead" party at his Jackson Heights apartment on the evening that Rivera was slain. As the party was winding down, Doyle suggested to Brown and Bici that they go out and "beat some people up."

Later that night, the trio walked along the Long Island Railroad tracks, hoping to run into "a drug addict, a homo, or homeless" person to assault. Along the way, they knocked over a temporary shack left vacant by a homeless person and then—for the hell of it—set it on fire. When an appropriate victim failed to appear, the three friends left the tracks and walked toward the Jackson Heights schoolyard known as an area in which gays congregate. Rivera was just coming around the corner as the trio approached. The attack was swift and deadly. "We stabbed him and killed him," Doyle told the court in a calm tone of voice. "I killed him because he was gay."[8]

❖   ❖   ❖

It would probably not be an exaggeration to suggest that many teenagers are "temporary sociopaths," generally lacking in either a strong sense of conscience or profound empathy for the problems of others. In psychiatric terms, a sociopath often engages in irresponsible and antisocial behavior such as lying, stealing, vandalism, and fighting. He is typically manipulative, cruel, and reckless. By the time a sociopath reaches middle age, it is highly unlikely that he can be rehabilitated. You don't suddenly develop a conscience at the age of thirty-four or forty.

But teenagers are a different story. Even the brightest and most popular fourteen-year-old may be searching for guidance and a sense of belonging that he cannot find at home or in school. During the indefinite period between childhood and adulthood, many young people are profoundly confused and easily persuaded. As a society, we expect them to begin their journey toward independence and responsibility, but we also keep them in a dependent and subservient relationship with adults. They come to depend on one another—their peers—for emotional support and direction. Many young people will therefore do things when they are fifteen that they wouldn't dream of doing at the age of twenty-five or thirty-two. Even an act of extreme violence may not be out of the question.

Of course, young males are not the only ones who commit hate offenses. Adults too attack others based on their race, religion, national origin, sexual orientation, or gender. Hate crimes committed by middle-aged adults, however, differ in at least one important respect. They usually don't regard their hate offense as a game or sport committed for the fun of it. Instead, they sense that a personal threat is being directed against them and are deadly serious in what they consider to be an appropriate reaction.

six

DEFENDING AGAINST A PERSONAL THREAT: TO HATE IS TO PROTECT

It was little more than a week after the horrendous assaults on the Pentagon and the World Trade Center. Forty-five-year-old Ali Almansoop, a Yemeni immigrant, had fallen asleep at his girlfriend's Lincoln Park, Michigan, apartment. At 6:30 A.M., he was suddenly awakened by her former boyfriend, thirty-eight-year-old Brent Seever, who had broken into the house. According to police, he was incensed by the devastation of the terrorist attacks and stormed into her apartment in a fit of rage. Shouting anti-Arab slogans, Seever threatened Almansoop with a handgun. In a futile attempt to save his life, the forty-five-year-old Yemeni immigrant begged for mercy and then tried to escape into the yard but was shot twice in the back. When arrested, Seever confessed to the police that he had been driving around the neighborhood, thinking about the September 11 attacks and getting angrier and angrier. He had to do something to defend his country, even if it meant shooting to death an innocent man.[1]

Not all hate offenses are motivated by thrill or excitement. In *defensive hate crimes*, the hatemongers seize on what they consider a precipitating or triggering incident to serve as a catalyst for the expression of their anger. They rationalize that by attacking an outsider they are in fact taking a protective posture, a defensive stance against intruders. Indeed, they often cast outsiders in the role of those actively threatening them, while they regard themselves as pillars of the community.

Whereas in thrill-motivated hate crimes a group of teenagers travels to another area to find victims, the perpetrators in defensive hate crimes typically do not leave their own neighborhood, school, or workplace. Although the members of almost any group of "outsiders" can be targeted, the primary victims of defensive hate crimes are people of color. In the Howard Beach case, for example, three Black men drove through an all-White neighborhood and were assaulted because their very presence in the community was seen as an invasion by outsiders. Similarly, when Asian Indians moved into Jersey City, New Jersey, an East Indian chemist was severely beaten with an iron bar in his own apartment by a racist who resented the presence of "Hindus" in *his* neighborhood. And when a Black woman and her young son moved to a previously all-White block located in the North End of Boston, they were greeted with the words "No niggers" spray-painted on the front of their brownstone. When asked about the incident, a long-time resident of the neighborhood told a reporter, "We don't want them niggers. We never had them, and we never want to see them. That's true. They're terrible, strange people. I've been here for thirty-seven years, and I've never seen colored people here."[2]

From the perpetrators' point of view, their community, means of livelihood, or way of life has been threatened by the mere presence of members of some other group. The hatemongers therefore feel justified, even obligated, to go on the "defensive." Characteristically, they feel few, if any, pangs of guilt in savagely attacking an outsider.

In thrill hate crimes, almost any member of a vulnerable group will usually do as a target. In contrast, the perpetrators of defensive hate crimes tend to target a particular individual or set of individuals who are perceived to constitute a personal threat—the Black family that just moved into an all-White neighborhood, the White college student who has begun to date her Asian classmate, or the Latino who was recently promoted at work.

Just as in thrill hate crimes, the offenders in defensive attacks are not necessarily associated with any organized hate group (although, as we shall see, they may call on the members of an organized group to help "repel the intruders"). Typically, the perpetrators have no prior history of crime or overt bigotry. Their reaction may have an economic basis—they fear losing property value or opportunities for advancement at work. Sometimes they react to a symbolic loss of "turf" or "privilege"—for example, when "our women" begin to date "them" or when "they" come into our neighborhood and begin to "take over." Though particular victims are selected, there is still an element of interchangeability—any member of the victim group who dares to pose a threat will be targeted for abuse.

Thus defensive hate crimes are intended to send a message—for example, that Blacks are not welcome on this block or Latinos should not apply for that promotion. As such, these crimes are in their intended effect very much like acts of terrorism, meant to send a signal by means of fear and horror. If the original criminal response fails to elicit the desired retreat on the part of the victim, then the offender frequently escalates the level of property damage or violence. A Black family moving into an all-White neighborhood is first warned; if they don't heed the warning, then their windows are broken; and if they still refuse to move out, their house may be firebombed, or worse.

The escalation of violence was certainly a factor in a hate crime that occurred in August 2001 in Pemberton Township, Pennsylvania. Donald Butler, a twenty-nine-year-old Black resident, was targeted by two White supremacists who shouted racial slurs at him from their car as Butler stood on the front lawn of his home. Perhaps seeing the verbal abuse against their neighbor as an isolated and trivial event, Butler's White neighbors did nothing to assure him of their support or indignation. Three weeks later, the same two hatemongers returned with baseball bats, this time invading Butler's home in the dead of night and brutally beating him and his wife. The Butlers escaped with stitches and broken bones, but they felt hurt and alone, as if no one really cared. They have since relocated to another community.

The victims of defensive hate crimes are typically apprehensive and frustrated. Unlike thrill hate crimes in which many members of a group feel vulnerable to random attack, defensive hate crime victims are aware that their particular situation precipitated the attack and that they could be attacked again. The frustration that these victims feel comes from knowing why they were being attacked: simply for attempting to do something—moving into a new home, dating someone, accepting a promotion—that everyone else takes for granted as appropriate. In a sense, the victims of defensive hate offenses are being attacked for exercising their constitutional rights; for example, their right to live in a home free from intimidation and harassment or their right to equal opportunity for career advancement.

According to a survey conducted by the Klanwatch Project, a unit of the Southern Poverty Law Center in Birmingham, Alabama, about half of all racially inspired acts of vandalism and violence are directed at Blacks moving into previously White neighborhoods.

In 1997, Donald Green and his colleagues similarly determined that hate crimes occur most often in what they call "defended" White neighborhoods—predominantly White areas of a community that have experienced an in-migration of residents of color. Typical of such hate crimes is the case of Purnell Daniels, a forty-one-year-old Black engineer whose house was located in a mostly White section of Newark, Delaware. While retrieving the morning paper, he discovered a cardboard containing the raised letters KKK glued to the front door of his home.[3]

Recent court decisions requiring the desegregation of previously all-White housing developments have been a catalyst of hate attacks. During the 1990s in cities like Boston and Dallas, courts ruled that local efforts to keep public housing projects segregated by race could not continue. In Boston, the federal court ruled that previously all-White housing developments in South Boston and Charlestown had to be integrated. The first Black families to move into these projects met an unending series of insults and petty acts of vandalism. The Boston police responded forcefully, maintaining a visible presence in the developments where racial tensions ran high. Although police support helped reduce the level of violence between groups, a review of hate crime reports throughout the 1990s and into the new millennium revealed that these desegregated housing developments remain the single largest location of hate crimes in the city.

Building on Green's notion of defended neighborhood shows that bigots might decide to defend any aspect of their lives they feel especially entitled to hold. Given the competitive nature of the workplace, for example, it comes as no surprise that many defensive hate crimes also occur on the job. In their study of "ethnoviolence at work," sociologists Joan Weiss, Howard Ehrlich, and Barbara Larcom interviewed a national sample of 2,078 Americans. These researchers found that 27 percent of all respondents who reported "prejudice-based" episodes experienced them at work. These incidents included break-ins, property damage, robbery, harassing language, physical assaults, sexual harassment, or rape.

Hatred over job competition has occasionally involved organized hate groups. During the recession of 1981, White fishermen in the Galveston, Texas, area became troubled about the growing presence (and prosperity) of Vietnamese refugees who had settled along the Gulf Coast and were fishing in Galveston Bay. Complaining that the Vietnamese newcomers engaged in unfair competition, the White fishermen asked the Ku Klux Klan for help in driving their Asian competitors out of the area.[4]

The Klan gladly complied. Only a few weeks passed before thirty-year-old Louis Beam, a long-time KKK leader and Grand Titan of the Texas chapter, supervised a Klan rally in support of the Galveston Bay White fishermen. Carrying rifles and shotguns, the Klansmen raised their hands in a Nazi salute and shouted, "White power! We will fight." They then set fire to a cross. Several weeks later, a radio station in Houston reported that the Klansmen, under the direction of Louis Beam, had invited fifty White fishermen to participate with them in military training exercises.

The KKK then waged a vicious campaign of intimidation and violence against the refugees. Several Vietnamese-owned fishing boats were set on fire; crosses were burned in the front yard of a Vietnamese fisherman and near a marina in which the newcomers stored their boats. To the few White residents who had befriended their Asian neighbors, the Klan sent business cards warning: "You have been paid a social visit by the Knights of the Ku Klux Klan—Don't make the next visit a business call." As a final warning, fifteen Klansmen sailed their fishing boat within sight of the marina and the homes of many Vietnamese. Displaying semiautomatic rifles and shotguns, the Klaners wore robes or battle fatigues. They had hanged a human effigy from the craft's rear rigging. The Klansman paused for a moment, fired a blank round from a cannon they had brought on board, and then, only when they felt sure of having made the point, returned to shore.

The Klan's threatening gestures toward the Vietnamese refugees continued for months. It took a legal maneuver orchestrated by the Southern Poverty Law Center's Klanwatch Project and its civil rights attorney Morris Dees to finally end the KKK threat. In the spring, the Vietnamese Fishermen's Association filed suit in federal court to prohibit the Klan from operating paramilitary training camps in Texas.

After three days of testimony by the Vietnamese and a handful of their White friends and business partners, Judge Gabrielle McDonald issued an injunction that barred the Klan's menacing campaign.[5]

During the 1980s and early 1990s, New York City was the site of several major defensive hate crimes apparently precipitated by the presence of "outsiders" in a predominantly White neighborhood. Sociologists have noted that many of these areas in which Blacks have been assaulted are blue-collar communities consisting largely of second- and third-generation families of European immigrants. Thirty years earlier, many of the White residents had moved out of their former neighborhoods precisely to distance themselves from Black and Latino newcomers arriving from the South, the Caribbean, and Latin America. From the viewpoint of White residents, Blacks and Latinos had invaded their old neighborhoods—now they were doing it again.[6]

According to sociologist Robin M. Williams Jr. of Cornell University, young men in these lower middle-class communities must struggle to make a place for themselves where they feel a sense of power and control. They commit murderous hate crimes when they begin to believe that outsiders are contesting their right to neighborhood, community, or privilege.

On the evening of August 1989, a defensive hate crime in the Bensonhurst section of Brooklyn left the entire city of New York shaken to its core. Sixteen-year-old Yusuf Hawkins and three other Black teenagers had walked into the mostly White, working-class Bensonhurst neighborhood because they were interested in inspecting a used car they had seen advertised in the newspaper. But they never got to check out the automobile. Instead, they were immediately surrounded and then chased down the street by a gang of local White youths carrying baseball bats and shouting "Let's club the niggers." Provoked by a rumor that one of their former girlfriends had been dating Blacks and Latinos, the White youths had already been agitated. The sight of Blacks in *their* neighborhood who may have been visiting that local girl was simply too much to take. The thinking was all too clear: "Here come niggers. They don't belong here. They are probably here to take *our* women. We must protect our neighborhood, our women, ourselves." One of them yelled, "The hell with beating them up." He pulled out a gun and fired four times. Hit directly in the chest by two shots, Yusuf Hawkins collapsed to the pavement and died a short time later.

In June 1990, two of the defendants were convicted for their part in the Hawkins slaying. Identified as the trigger man, nineteen-year-old Joseph Fama was convicted of second-degree murder and sentenced to a term of thirty-two years to life. His codefendent, Keith Mondello, also nineteen, was named as the organizer of the gang of White youths who had attacked Yusuf Hawkings and was sentenced to five to sixteen years for rioting and discrimination. In a separate trial concluded in December 1990, a third defendant, twenty-two-year-old John Vento, was acquitted of murder and manslaughter but convicted of rioting. His conviction carries a maximum penalty of four years in prison.[7]

Canarsie, New York, has long been the focal point for crimes designed to protect the neighborhood from an "invasion" by outsiders. Situated in the southeast corner of Brooklyn, Canarsie looks like any other comfortable working-class community. Its streets are lined with two- and three-story brick houses, churches, and small businesses. On a tranquil summer day, residents can be seen sitting on their porches with friends and neighbors, walking to the park with their children, or fishing off Canarsie Pier. But there is another, more disturbing, side to Canarsie. The community has erupted in racial turmoil as Blacks from surrounding communities are seen as "invading" the neighborhood.

Racial antagonism is nothing new to the people of Canarsie. The community has a history of racial tensions dating back three decades. In the fall of 1972, the local school board demanded that Canarsie accept into its schools a few dozen Black children from neighboring Brownsville. But Canarsie's residents, the majority of whom were lower-middle-class Whites, refused to comply. The forces of reaction became swiftly mobilized in an effort to protect the community from what some residents regarded as an invasion by outsiders. A number of Canarsie residents marched through the streets, boycotted the schools, fire-bombed the home of a Black family, and hurled rocks at buses carrying Black children into the neighborhood. The rallying cry spread with incredible speed through the community of seventy thousand outraged people: "Canarsie schools for Canarsie children." What these residents actually meant, of course, was "Canarsie schools for *White* children. No *Blacks* allowed."

To be fair, it should be emphasized that the majority of Canarsie residents never participated in the racial incidents protesting busing (this is true in almost every community where racial conflict has occurred). Yet the effect of violent demonstrations by the antibusing forces was probably far greater than their small numbers might suggest. First, such episodes send a clear warning to Blacks in surrounding communities who might otherwise consider breaking the racial barrier: "Stay in your own neighborhood, or the same thing will happen to you." Second, the publicity given to violent acts ensures that most of the residents of Canarsie, whether or not they participated in demonstrations or illegal behavior, will be labeled as "racists" and "bigots."[8]

The efficacy of violent demonstrations notwithstanding, the "invasion" of Canarsie continued in full force to change the character of the community. The focus of this change was directly on the neighborhoods; an influx of Black homeowners between 1980 and 1991 reduced the proportion of Canarsie Whites from 90 percent to 75 percent. Many blocks that had been predominantly Irish, Jewish, or Italian became increasingly populated by newcomers from the Caribbean, East Asia, and Central and South America, but not without struggle and conflict.[9]

By 1991 the real estate market softened, and homeowners in Canarsie—as in countless other communities around the country—saw their property values plummet. As unemployment rates climbed, so did anxiety about the future. Then the trouble started again.

During a twelve-month period, there were more than fifteen racial incidents in Canarsie. Unknown arsonists burned a Pakistani grocery store and firebombed a Black-owned insurance office. A local real estate office was firebombed after it showed homes to Black families. Then three Black men beat a twenty-year-old White man after shouting racial slurs at him from their car.

Defensive hate crimes often occur during a well-intentioned outreach to increase the diversity of a community. An outbreak of racial hostility in the predominantly White city of Dubuque, Iowa, coincided with debate concerning a plan to encourage Blacks to move to this very city. Recognizing that only 331 of Dubuque's 58,000 residents were Black, an official task force decided to design and implement a program for increasing the city's racial diversity. During the spring of 1991, Dubuque city officials approved a plan whereby twenty minority families a year for five years would be recruited to move into the city. The official nine-page report entitled *We Want to Change* acknowledged the existence of racism in Dubuque and called on local businesses to bring in Black families for professional as well as lower-level jobs. To attract Blacks to the area, the city offered recruits subsidies to rent or own a home as well as guaranteed job security. According to Mayor James Brady, implementation of the plan over a five-year period would increase Dubuque's Black representation from 1.2 to 1.8 percent of the population.

Many Dubuque residents endorsed the idea, at least initially.[10] By August 1991, however, the residents of Dubuque found themselves in the grip of a major national recession. The town's factories laid off workers, and jobs became increasingly scarce. Dubuque's unemployment rate soared to 10 percent, and many city residents were questioning the legitimacy of bringing in "outsiders" to compete for jobs at a time when so many longtime residents were out of work. Talking to the Associated Press, for example, a twenty-four-year-old unemployed construction worker explained: "They want to bring 100 minorities in, and we just don't have the jobs for those people. If they want to move here, they should move here on their own."[11] Another unemployed resident argued that Blacks were getting special treatment, a form of reverse discrimination. Calling David Duke a "saint, a White Martin Luther King," he asserted, "Seems like they're getting everything and we're getting trounced on."[12]

The reaction was angry and swift. Burning crosses were found at homes, in parks, and on schoolyard playgrounds. The letters KKK were scrawled on a garage door. Racist slurs like "No niggers" and "We don't want them" were painted on school buildings, and fights between Black and White students broke out at Dubuque Senior High School. Some of the town's teenagers attempted to form a chapter of the National Association for the Advancement of White People. Thomas Robb, national director of the Knights of the Ku Klux Klan, traveled from his home in Zinc, Arkansas, to rally the residents of Dubuque in defense of "our heritage."[13] In November 1991, Alice Scott moved her family from Milwaukee to Dubuque to "protect her three children from the hazards of growing up in the inner city." Within a matter of days, the Black woman was welcomed by a brick thrown through her living room window and a cross burned on her front lawn.[14] The young granddaughters of another Black resident, Hazel O'Neal, walked three blocks to get some ice cream. Along the way, a truckload of White men screaming"niggers get out"tried to spit on them. O'Neal later told a reporter,"You're afraid to walk in the streets because you're harassed."[15] By December 1991, city leaders were promising that they would not spend tax dollars to implement the diversity plan, and recruitment dropped off.

It should be noted that many members of the Dubuque community now agree that Dubuque is a significantly more enlightened place than it was in the early 1990s. In responding to accusations of racism, a memorandum of understanding was reached in March 1993 between the Dubuque police department and the National Association for the Advancement of Colored People. Based on this agreement, the Dubuque Community Advisory Panel, which hears complaints about police misconduct regarding civil rights or discrimination, was created. Both the memorandum and advisory panel remain in effect today.[16]

During the early 1990s, Asian Indians experienced their share of abuse and harassment coming from those who resented the"invasion of outsiders"into their communities and acted to preserve the dominance of the majority group. Growing numbers of East Indians moved into the northern section of Edison, New Jersey, and the Iselin section of neighboring Woodbridge, towns located in Middlesex County. In these formerly White-dominated communities, some thirty miles south of New York City, there are now dozens of sari shops, Indian restaurants, and Asian jewelry stores as well as tens of thousands of Indian newcomers. For some period of time, there was also growing hatred.

According to police reports, such vicious anti-Indian gangs as the Dotbusters and the Lost Boys in central New Jersey targeted their campaign of terror at the Indian outsiders. On many occasions, groups of young White men drove through local areas populated by Indians, smashing automobile windshields or shouting anti-Indian slurs and threats (e.g.,"Dotheads come out. We're going to kick your asses."). On New Year's Day 1991, several Indians were accosted by a large group of young White men at a diner in Iselin. More than insults flew through the air as they hurled bottles and threw their fists, leaving several Indians injured. On May 23, 1991, in a particularly brutal crime, eight members of the Lost Boys allegedly assaulted a young Indian man behind a local convenience store. Carrying sticks, rocks, and bats, they encircled their victim and repeatedly struck him in the head. He required a two-day stay in the hospital and needed thirty stitches to close the ugly wound on his forehead and four stitches for an injury below his left eyebrow.[17]

In its narrow sense, the term "defensive" refers to behavior designed to protect against an attack. Hate crimes perpetrated in Howard Beach, Bensonhurst, central New Jersey, and Dubuque clearly fit this definition in the perpetrators' minds. In each case, the victims were regarded as making some illegitimate move into a community that was previously dominated by Whites. The perpetrators felt that their homes, schools, or neighborhoods were under attack by outsiders. This is typical of the thinking in defensive hate crimes.

Anyone with a cursory knowledge of international conflict realizes that the concept of defense can easily be expanded to include preemptive strikes, terrorist attacks, and even the wholesale slaughter of innocent civilians. The claims by Osama bin Laden that the attack on the World Trade Center represented an aspect of jihad—a holy war to protect the Middle East from the West—is only the most recent example. The massive displacement of Native American tribes by White settlers provides another case in point that is uncomfortably close to home. In some defensive hate attacks, it is similarly the perpetrators who were originally outsiders. Now they move in and attempt to displace their victims. The hatemongers typically possess an inordinate belief in their own *entitlement*. Once they occupy a neighborhood, it belongs to them. Even if Blacks or Latinos have lived on the block for decades, they are the "outsiders" who must now move. From the hatemonger's point of view, this is a White country, a White state, and a White community. "White is right; White rules." So, anyone who isn't White is expected to defer to the "ruling elite". . . or pay the consequences.

Benefiting from cheap real estate and highway construction, the town of Alton, Illinois, has—since the 1970s—attracted a growing White population from nearby St. Louis. The small number of Blacks in Alton can trace its presence in the community for at least 125 years, beginning when the New Bethel African Methodist Episcopal Church was founded by former slaves. For most of their history in the town,

Alton's Blacks lived in peace. But during the last three decades, as more and more Whites have moved in, Black members of the community have repeatedly come under attack.

Unlike the situation in Howard Beach, Bensonhurst, or Dubuque, in Alton it was Whites rather than Blacks who were the outsiders. Still, according to Linda Lindsey, a visiting professor of sociology at Washington University in St. Louis, the focal point of the attacks was the Black church. Thus, in 1974, two bombs were detonated inside the church. Throughout the 1980s, vandals broke windows, scrawled racial epithets on the walls ("KKK" and "Die nigger"), and desecrated tombstones in the church cemetery. In 1988, arsonists twice burned the church to the ground. From the viewpoint of some Whites wanting to take over the town, says Lindsey, New Bethel was a symbol of the population that should be removed.[18]

Some defensive hate crimes are retaliatory in nature. The offenders see themselves as getting even for some previous crime against members of their own group. After a highly publicized hate incident, the community in question is often subjected to a series of crimes seeking revenge for the original attack. Until the September 11 assaults on America, the greatest number of hate crimes in the history of New York City occurred during the month following the Bensonhurst murder. Young New Yorkers, White and Black, seemed to be saying, "You got one of ours; now it's our turn to get one of yours."

Of course, if you consider the terrorist attack on the Twin Towers and the Pentagon a hate crime, then the largest number of retaliatory incidents in this nation's recent history took place in the months after September 11, 2001. Citizens around the nation who were horrified by the assault on America focused their anger on Arab- and Muslim-Americans, if not on any immigrant with dark skin and a foreign accent. According to the FBI, there were more acts of bigotry directed against Arabs and Muslims—ethnic slurs, harassment, threats, assaults, and vandalism—during the first thirty days following September 11 than in the last five years combined.

Defensive hate crimes are generally aimed against particular "outsiders"—those who are regarded as posing a personal challenge to a perpetrator's workplace, neighborhood, or physical well-being. The attack tends to be narrowly focused. Once the threat is perceived to subside, so does the criminal behavior.

On occasion, hate crimes go beyond what their perpetrators consider reaction, at least in the narrow sense. Rather than direct their attack at those individuals involved in a particular event or episode—moving into the neighborhood, taking a job at the next desk, attending the same party—the perpetrators are ready to wage "war" against any and all members of a particular group of people. No precipitating episode occurs; none is necessary. The perpetrator is on a moral mission: His assignment is to make the world a better place in which to live.

seven

RIDDING THE WORLD OF EVIL: HATE AS A DELUSIONAL MISSION

The rarest kind of hate crime is an attack carried out by individuals with a *mission*; they seek to rid the world of evil by disposing of the members of a despised group. In their view, all out-group members are subhumans, either animals or demons, who are bent on destroying *our* culture, *our* economy, or the purity of *our* racial heritage. The perpetrator therefore is concerned about much more than simply eliminating a few Blacks or Latinos from his workplace, his neighborhood, or his school. Instead, he believes that he has a higher-order purpose in carrying out his crime. He has been instructed by God or, in more secular versions, by *der Führer*, the Imperial Wizard, or the Grand Dragon to rid the world of evil by eliminating *all* Blacks, Latinos, Asians, women, gays, Muslims, or Jews; and he is compelled to act before it is too late.

The perpetrator of a mission hate crime is typically a conspiratorial thinker. He suffers from a severe mental illness that may cause hallucinations, impaired ability to reason, and withdrawal from contact with other people. Moreover, he believes that he must get even for the horrific problems that he has suffered. In his paranoid and delusional way of thinking, he sees a conspiracy of some kind for which he seeks revenge. His mission may be suicidal: it may not. But on either case, he must attempt to eliminate the *entire category* of people he is absolutely convinced is responsible for his personal frustrations.

A missionary allegiance to hate was an important ingredient in a number of offenses of catastrophic consequences, including those aimed at the government. Timothy McVeigh, whose 1995 bombing of

the federal building in Oklahoma City destroyed the lives of 168 innocent people, was motivated by a belief that the federal government had
become perverted beyond repair. Apparently taking his cue from White
supremacist William Pierce's image in *The Turner Diaries* of the federal
government as the enemy of White Christian Americans, McVeigh was
enraged about the botched (and, in his view, unconstitutional) inter-
ventions of federal agents at Ruby Ridge, Idaho, and Waco, Texas. In
1992, on a remote Idaho mountaintop known as Ruby Ridge, White
separatist Randy Weaver's unarmed wife and fourteen-year-old son
had been killed in a federal ambush. In 1993, as ATF agents stormed a
compound outside Waco, Texas, more than eighty Branch Davidian
cultists perished in flames.

Accepting the view that government is dominated by Jews and
Blacks, McVeigh became convinced that the FBI and ATF were out of
control and guilty of murdering innocent citizens. In bringing down a
federal building, McVeigh sought to instigate a violent revolution that
would ultimately topple the repressive and illegitimate oppressors. He
would teach them a lesson they would never forget.

An even more recent mission attack was perpetrated in March 2000
outside of the city of Pittsburgh by thirty-nine-year-old Ron Taylor. The
Black resident of Wilkinsburg, Pennsylvania, was sick and tired of the
ubiquitous racism he had so long tolerated in everyday life. But the latest episode in a long-running feud with his White maintenance man,
John DeWitt, was the final straw. Taylor's front door had been broken
for some time. He demanded that it be fixed and, as usual, DeWitt was
taking his good time to repair it.

On March 1, Taylor decided to get even with the "racist" but searched
in vain for the maintenance man. Not finding DeWitt, he turned his attention and his anger toward John Kroll, a carpenter who hadn't been
involved in Taylor's arguments but may have reminded him of his original target. Leaving his apartment, Taylor informed a Black neighbor he
encountered nearby, "I'm not going to hurt any Black people, I'm just
out to kill White people."

Taylor raised his handgun and fatally shot his unsuspecting victim.
He then walked to a fast-food restaurant in the Wilkinsburg business
area and opened fire again, killing two and wounding two more. All of
Taylor's victims were White. As he started shooting, Taylor angrily

shouted, "White trash. Racist pig. I think I'll terrorize you for a while."
In his apartment, the police later found letters written by Taylor in
which he expressed his anger toward Whites, Jews, Asians, Italians, and
the police.

A few weeks after Taylor went on his killing spree, an unemployed
White lawyer—also located in suburban Pittsburgh—went on a rampage of his own. Richard Baumhammers, a thirty-four-year-old out-of-
work immigration lawyer, first shot to death his next-door neighbor, a
sixty-three-year-old Jewish woman he had known since childhood.
Next he set her house on fire and drove off to two nearby synagogues,
firing bullets into their windows and walls. He then sped off in his car
and drove through local streets, choosing his victims by their skin color.
Before being arrested by the police some twenty miles from his original
attack, Baumhammers had managed to kill five people. In addition to
his Jewish victim, he shot to death a man of Indian descent who was
leaving a local grocery store, a Vietnamese employee and Chinese manager of a popular Chinese restaurant, and an African-American man
who was leaving a local karate school.

On searching the home he shared with his parents, police discovered a number of documents detailing the killer's anti-immigrant anxieties. Baumhammers feared that White Americans were destined to
become a statistical minority, that Americans of European descent were
losing their advantaged position, and that American citizens would
soon be forced to live in isolated suburbs surrounded by Third World
minorities. In response, he had developed a three-page manifesto for
his fledgling "Free Market Party," advocating the rights of European-
Americans and denouncing immigration from Third World nations.
Apparently Baumhammers had been totally ineffective in his efforts to
recruit new members to his cause. When arrested, he was still the one
and only member of his anti-immigrant organization.

In 1989 Canadians were made painfully aware of a growing resentment toward *all* women by an outbreak of sexist acts on college campuses across the country, culminating in the largest mission hate crime in
Canada's history. A female law school professor at the University of
Western Ontario claimed sex discrimination; the male students at Wilrid
Laurier University in Waterloo reportedly conducted panty raids in the
female dormitories; and the "No means no!" catch phrase of the student

council's antirape campaign at Queen's University in Kingston, Ontario, was perverted by some first-year male students who jokingly displayed their own version of posters reading "No means more beer!"

But all other acts of sexism were overshadowed by the murderous rampage of twenty-five-year-old Marc Lepine. On the rain-swept afternoon of December 6, 1989, Lepine entered the engineering school at the University of Montreal carrying a .223-caliber semiautomatic hunting rifle, a hundred rounds of bullets, and a single-minded purpose: to get even with the women—especially the feminist women—whom he held responsible for all of his troubles. Weapon in hand, Lepine walked slowly into a classroom crowded with students and, in a calm voice, ordered everyone to stop what they were doing. With a smile on his face, he told the women to move to one side of the room and the men to leave. Firing a shot into the ceiling to move the students along, Lepine shouted, "I want the women. You're all a bunch of feminists. I hate feminists." Then Lepine opened fire—in the classroom, in other classrooms, in the corridors, and in the cafeteria. He moved quickly from floor to floor, room to room looking only for women. Two hours later, the police tactical squad entered the building. They found the bodies of fourteen women—ages twenty-one to thirty-one—all gunned down by Lepine before he took his own life. Lepine's final words: "Ah, shit."

On searching the body of the killer, police found a handwritten three-page suicide note in Lepine's pocket, in which he explained his hideous outburst. "I have been unhappy for the past seven years," he lamented. "And, I will die on December 6, 1989. . . . Feminists have always ruined my life." On page 3 of his suicide note, Lepine had scribbled the names of fifteen prominent Canadian women, the very "feminists" he so thoroughly despised.

Those who are psychoanalytically inclined might speculate that Lepine's contempt for women was a generalized form of his hatred toward his mother. Perhaps she abandoned him at an early age. Or perhaps he *believed* he was a victim of abusive behavior when he was a young child. Perhaps Lepine's murderous rampage at the University of Montreal could be interpreted as a desperate attempt to get even with his mother; his victims were mere surrogates.

There is reason to believe that Marc Lepine's resentment toward women was not merely a generalization of anger toward his mother.

Lepine seems to have detested his father, a man who had brutally assaulted both his wife and his children and showed little interest in his family. At their divorce proceedings in 1970, Marc's mother testified that her husband was very brutal, that he showed little control of his emotions. He had beaten her in front of the children; he had hit her in the face; he had hit Marc so hard that the young boy bled from his nose and his ears. When Marc was only seven, his father threw him, his sister, and his mother out of their apartment. By the time he was fourteen, the boy's resentment was so intense that he decided to take his mother's name—it was at that time that Gamil Gharbi, son of Liass Gharbi, became the man known as Marc Lepine.

Life was not easy for Marc. He attempted to join the army but, for reasons that were never clear, was rejected. His lifelong ambition to become an engineer was thwarted, at least in his mind, when his bid for admission to the engineering school at the University of Montreal failed. In his own twisted logic, women were to blame. They were responsible for his repudiation by the military and for his inability to be educated as an engineer. Indeed, *female students* had taken his seat at the University of Montreal. Perhaps it would not be too far-fetched to speculate that Marc Lepine's final assault was an extreme version of his father's behavior toward women. Marc Lepine may have hated his father, but ultimately he identified with the aggressor.

Marc Lepine's rampage was clearly a hate crime. His suicide note and his remarks about women to his intended victims lead us to conclude that Lepine blamed the entire category of women for his personal failures. He looked for "feminists" behind every negative experience he had.

Not every mission hate crime is clearly marked as such. Even when the crime is perpetrated exclusively against the members of a particular group, we cannot always be sure that it was motivated by bigotry or bias. Like Marc Lepine, Patrick Purdy was a young man filled with hate who went on a deadly rampage. But unlike Lepine, Purdy never broadcast his intentions, nor did he leave a note explaining his behavior. Purdy was almost always by himself, had no girlfriends, and seemed to dislike everyone. He was conspiratorial and paranoid in his thinking. In the end, he singled out a particular group as being especially blameworthy.

For some five years, the twenty-four-year-old loner drifted from place to place. Working as a laborer, a security guard, or a welder, he traveled—to Connecticut, Nevada, Florida, Oregon, Tennessee, and Texas—to any state where his past might not come back to haunt him. But wherever he went, Purdy argued with his bosses and simply couldn't hold a job for more than a few weeks at a time.

Along the way, Purdy repeatedly got into trouble with the law. In 1980 he was arrested in Los Angeles for soliciting a sex act from a police officer. Two years later, he was arrested on charges of possession of hashish. In 1983 he was convicted of possessing a dangerous weapon. A few months later, he was arrested on a charge of receiving stolen property. In October 1984, he spent thirty days in a Woodland, California, jail for his part in a robbery.

Three years passed and Purdy's behavior became increasingly bizarre. In 1987 he was apprehended in El Dorado, California, for indiscriminately firing a 9-millimeter pistol in the El Dorado National Forest and for resisting arrest. He kicked deputies who tried to arrest him, shattered a window of their patrol car, and then told the police that it was his duty "to overthrow the suppressers." While being held in jail, Purdy tried to hang himself and cut his wrists with his fingernails; but, like everything else in his life, even his suicide attempt was a failure.

It was now January 1989; by this time, Purdy despised almost everyone, but especially people in positions of authority and especially his "enemies," the newcomers to America's shores. He had been living for a few weeks in Room 104 of El Rancho Motel on the edge of Stockton, California, a riverfront agricultural city located some sixty miles southeast of San Francisco, plotting his final assault on those who were to blame for his miserable existence. To develop an effective military strategy, he would spend hours in his room manipulating the hundreds of toy soldiers, tanks, jeeps, and weapons that he had collected in order to simulate an attack. He kept them on the shelves, on the heating grates, even in the refrigerator. The words "freedom," "victory," and "Hezballah" had been carved into the stock of his rifle. On the camouflage shirt that he wore over his military jacket, he had written "P.L.O.," "Libya," and "Death to the Great Satan." He perceived a conspiracy involving people in charge. The symbols on his weapon and jacket were the symbols of anti-Americanism ("the great Satan").

On Tuesday morning, January 17, Purdy put on his military flak jacket, picked up a handgun and an AK–47 semiautomatic assault rifle, and drove his 1977 Chevrolet station wagon a couple of miles to the Cleveland Elementary School in Stockton—the same elementary school he had attended from kindergarten to third grade. When he had lived there as a child, the neighborhood was White; now it was predominantly Asian.

Arriving at the Cleveland school just before noon, Purdy could see hundreds of young children—most of them refugees from Cambodia, Vietnam, China, and Mexico—playing at recess on the Blacktop in front of the brown stucco building that housed the school. As a diversion, he immediately parked his car and set it on fire with a Molotov cocktail in a Budweiser bottle. Then, through a gap in the fence surrounding the building, Purdy walked onto the crowded school grounds and opened fire.

For a period of two minutes, Purdy sprayed sixty rounds of bullets from his AK–47 at screaming children in a sweeping motion across the Blacktop. He then took the handgun from his belt and shot himself in the head. Written on the pistol's handle was the word "victory."

Purdy's "victory" toll was incredibly high. Five children, all from Southeast Asia, were dead and thirty more were wounded before the gunman killed himself.[1]

Purdy's attack was based on racial hatred. He had frequently made hostile racial comments to coworkers about the influx of Southeast Asian refugees into the United States and had protested bitterly about the large number of Southeast Asian classmates in industrial arts courses he was taking at the local community college. He complained that the newcomers were taking too many jobs and he resented having to compete with them. In less than eight years, the population of Southeast Asian refugees in Stockton went from fewer than a thousand to more than thirty thousand.

But why had Purdy chosen this particular set of targets—innocent children in a schoolyard—in order to carry out his mission? Purdy hated the newcomers from Vietnam and Cambodia who had taken over his old elementary school, if not the entire community. He was angered by the presence of these foreigners in the school that he had attended as a child. He believed that Asian-Americans had taken his place. But Purdy also hated the school and everything that it symbolized in his mind. He recalled his early years as a child, a particularly painful period when the shy and socially inept youngster was routinely tormented by his class-mates. In his warped and delusional way of thinking, Purdy may have viewed his victims as little more than the toy soldiers he had manipu-lated back in Room 104 of El Rancho Motel. As a result, five innocent children died at the hands of a deranged gunman who was full of hate.

❖ ❖ ❖

Hate crimes represent the end point on the continuum of prejudice and bigotry. For economic, social, and psychological reasons, countless individuals feel resentful. They have suffered a drop in self-esteem or status and are eager to place the blame elsewhere. The selection of their victim depends a good deal on groups and individuals whom the culture of hate portrays as weak, immoral, or uncivilized.

Yet millions of Americans have suffered a decline in their standard of living and/or their self-esteem but would never commit a criminal act against individuals who are different from them. Perhaps some poten-tial offenders simply do not buy into the culture of hate; others may possess enough self-control that they are able to stop themselves from behaving in a deviant or violent manner, no matter how great the ap-peal. For a few, however, the attraction of committing a hate crime is overpowering. In the thrill-seeking version, an individual is drawn into a group activity so that he is not rejected by the people who are most important to him—his friends. In defensive hate crimes, an individual believes that he must protect himself from the encroachment of out-siders. And in mission hate crimes, an individual becomes convinced that his personal problems are a result of some conspiracy involving entire categories of people with whom he feels compelled to get even. Like Patrick Purdy, he may suffer from an extreme form of mental ill-ness that leaves him paranoid and delusional. As we shall see, how-ever, you don't have to be sick in order to commit a mission hate crime. The desire to rid the world of evil also motivates the activities of organ-ized hate groups.

eight

BROTHERHOOD OF BIGOTRY: ORGANIZED HATE ACROSS THE COUNTRY

L ife hadn't been easy for twenty-seven-year-old Mulugeta Seraw, but his future once looked bright. The dark-skinned young man with a foreign accent and a ready smile lived and worked in the city of Portland, Oregon. Having immigrated from Ethiopia seven years earlier, Seraw was a part-time student and worked as an Avis shuttle-bus driver at the airport. He was far from wealthy but hoped eventually to save enough money to finish college and improve his standard of living. As an ambitious newcomer, Seraw was every bit the embodiment of striving for the American Dream.

It was early on a Sunday morning in November when Seraw and his two companions, also of Ethiopian descent, were returning home from a nearby party. Before turning in, they stopped their car to chat awhile, totally unaware that they were being watched by three local skinheads. The three members of a group known as East Side White Pride were returning from an evening of recruiting, drinking, and partying. Wearing uniforms consisting of military jackets, steel-toed boots, and shaven heads, the racist skinheads—Kenneth Mieske, Steven Strasser, and Kyle Brewster—stood on the corner about one hundred feet from Seraw and his friends. Brewster said, "Hey, I see a nigger. Let's go over there and mess with him."

The skinheads hopped in their car and drove down the block, where their path was obstructed by the car of the three Ethiopians. Mieske got out of the car first and exchanged angry words with Seraw and his companions. Strasser and Brewster joined in and there was a scuffle.

Mieske would wait no longer. Moving up behind Seraw, he repeatedly struck him in the back of the head with a baseball bat, while Strasser and Brewster kicked all three Black men with their steel-toed boots. When it was over, Seraw and his companions were taken to Emanuel Hospital and Health Center. Two of the Ethiopians were treated and released, but Seraw was pronounced dead on arrival, resulting from a fractured skull.

In May 1989, Mieske pleaded guilty to murdering Seraw and admitted that his motivation was racist. He was given a life sentence. The other two skinheads, Strasser and Brewster, were convicted of first-degree manslaughter and are presently serving prison sentences of up to twenty years.

Despite the convictions, the courtroom battle was far from over. In October 1990 Oregon's Multnomah County courthouse became the scene of a civil action—a wrongful death suit—brought on behalf of the Seraw family by Morris Dees, chief trial counsel of the Southern Poverty Law Center in Montgomery, the Anti-Defamation League of B'nai B'rith, and attorney Elden M. Rosenthal.

This was neither the first nor the last time that Morris Dees had sought, through civil action, to drain an organized hate group of its economic resources. In 1981 Dees and the Southern Poverty Law Center successfully sued the United Klans of America after its members dragged Michael Donald, a Black man, to downtown Mobile, Alabama, where they hanged him from a tree. An all-white jury of six ordered the United Klans to pay the victim's mother, sixty-four-year-old Beulah Mae Donald, an award in the amount of $7 million. In 1997 Dees won more than $37 million from the Christian Knights of the Ku Klux Klan for burning down the Macadonia Baptist Church near Columbia, South Carolina.

In 2000 Dees argued a civil case that resulted in a $6 million judgment against an Idaho-based white supremacist group known as the Aryan Nations and its founder Richard Butler. As a result, Butler declared bankruptcy and his compound was shut down.[1]

With the same objective in mind in the Portland case, Dees targeted the lawsuit at not only two of the skinheads who had attacked Seraw and his Ethiopian companions in 1988 but also Tom and John Metzger and their White Aryan Resistance organization (WAR) headquartered in

Fallbrook, California. Tom runs WAR—hosts its long-running cable access TV program, oversees its newspaper, and is heard on its Washington, D.C., hot line. For a living, he repairs TV sets. In the 1960s, Metzger was a member of the John Birch Society. During the 1970s, he served as California Grand Dragon of the Knights of the Ku Klux Klan. In 1980, he won the Democratic nomination to the House of Representatives and later ran unsuccessfully for the Senate. Tom Metzger's son John, leader of the Aryan Youth Movement (formerly the White Student Union), is responsible for recruiting young people to the cause.

The Metzgers, both Tom and John, were accused of being liable for Seraw's murder. The suit claimed that, in their role as head of WAR, the two men had encouraged and instigated the skinheads, who "conspired to inflict serious bodily harm" on Seraw.

Writing in *The Nation*, Elinor Langer suggests that the influence of the Metzgers and their organization, WAR, on racial violence in the streets of Portland actually began months earlier. An Asian-American man, the white woman to whom he was married, and their young daughter were leaving a local restaurant when they were accosted by three skinheads shouting racial slurs and insults. The publicity surrounding this incident was considerable—so considerable that it caught the attention of the Metzgers at their Fallbrook, California, headquarters. During the summer of 1988, John Metzger began writing to Portland skinheads, including Mieske, Brewster, and Strasser, urging them to join his cause. By the fall, WAR organizers had arrived.[2]

Not unlike international terrorists, the members of organized hate groups have broadened the meaning of the term "defense" to include aggressive behavior attacking innocent victims. In a recent issue of his WAR newspaper, for example, Tom Metzger asserts: "We have every right to use force in self defense, in retaliation, and *in preemptive strikes against those who openly threaten our freedom.*"[3]

Thus no pretext of a precipitating event is even required. Blacks need not move into an all-white neighborhood; Jews need not join a "Protestants-only" club. The very *presence* of members of a particular group—knowledge that they exist at all, no matter where and in what numbers—may be considered enough to call for a group response.[4]

In civil court, Ken Mieske argued self-defense: his lethal attack on Mulugeta Seraw had been part of a spontaneous street fight; he had merely reacted to the Ethiopian man's attempt to strangle one of his skinhead companions. Representing the Seraw family, however, Attorney Dees was able to show that Mieske's notion of defense was absurdly inclusive and out of touch with reality. The Metzgers, through agents they had sent to recruit Portland's skinheads, had aided and encouraged the violent behavior that led to Seraw's death; in their campaign of hate, the Metzgers had conspired to do violence to Blacks and had been reckless in sending representatives, including a former vice president of John Metzger's Aryan Youth Movement, Dave Mazzella, to Portland as their agent.

Mazzella's testimony left little to the imagination. Testifying for the plaintiffs, he candidly confessed that he had in fact been sent by WAR for the purpose of recruiting and training Portland skinheads. Tom Metzger had taught him how to assault Blacks by provoking them first, attacking them with baseball bats, and then claiming self-defense. According to Mazzella, he would send "report cards" to the Metzgers consisting of newspaper accounts of his beatings. In addition he had distributed copies of John Metzger's Aryan Youth Movement newspaper as a tool for recruiting skinheads in Portland. An article in one issue entitled "Clash and Bash" introduced the "sport" of bashing, whereby "hunting parties of white youth seek out non-Whites and break their bones."[5]

In court, Tom Metzger attempted to distance himself from the murder. He had never met Mazzella and, anyhow, his freedom of speech was being abridged. But Seraw's side produced damaging evidence to implicate the Metzgers in a more direct manner. First, they showed records of numerous telephone calls between Fallbrook and Mazzella in Portland. Then they produced a photograph that showed Tom Metzger holding an assault rifle as he gave paramilitary training to a group of skinheads.

On October 22, 1990, after deliberating for little more than five hours, the jury reached a decision on a vote of 11–1. Tom Metzger was ordered to pay $5 million; his son John was ordered to pay $1 million; their White Aryan Resistance organization was directed to pay $3 million—all in damages to the family of Mulugeta Seraw. In addition, skinheads Kenneth Mieske and Kyle Brewster were ordered to pay $500,000 each. Another $2.5 million in damages was also awarded.[6]

It took only hours for Tom Metzger to publicize his defiant response to the verdict against him. In a recorded telephone message on his hate-filled hot line, the head of WAR issued a warning to his "new" targets everywhere. In an emotional statement of purpose, he proclaimed that "we will put blood on the streets like you've never seen and advocate more violence than both World Wars put together. . . . We have a new set of targets to play with. So if you're white and work for the system, watch your step. Whether you be a system cop, a controlled judge or a crooked lawyer, your ass is grass."[7]

The vicious murder of twenty-seven-year-old Mulugeta Seraw could easily serve as a textbook illustration of the operations of organized hate groups today. We learn that *Metzger's White Aryan Resistance supported and encouraged the violence committed by skinhead groups.* Though only 5 percent of all hate crimes, maximum, are perpetrated by organized groups such as WAR, their impact is extremely pervasive. Thousands of racist skinheads rely on such organizations for slogans, mottoes, and guidance.

Osama bin Laden was no less a terrorist because he was thousands of miles from the World Trade Center towers when they collapsed. Similarly, Hitler may not have been present at the scene of the Nazi atrocities, but they were orchestrated by him. In the same way, there may be thousands of alienated youngsters who look for a role model for expressing their profound resentment. Such impressionable youths may not actually join some hate group—they may not even be willing to shave their heads and don the uniforms of skinheads. But they are nevertheless *inspired* by the presence of such groups and *intrigued* by the use of their symbols of power. In some cases, they receive their marching orders from the leaders of organized hate.

The marginal teenagers who spray-paint racist graffiti on buildings are usually not members of WAR, but they are attracted by its slogans. In the murder of Mulugeta Seraw, the White Aryan Resistance attracted youngsters looking for a thrill and used them as instruments to carry out its group mission of ridding the United States, if not the world, of its "subhuman" residents. In this scenario, we see the potential strength of an organized hate group. It is able to mobilize more than one source of motivation for action. Its leadership may be motivated by missionary zeal. Many of its members may even believe that their violence is defensive, aiming to protect the "American way of life" or their "Aryan heritage." At a personal level, the leaders of organized hate gain something that would have been inconceivable if they had remained conventional in their behavior—they become "big shots," powerful and respected generals in the army for the white race. Their followers also exact a privilege. They are the "field soldiers"—youthful skinheads or other disgruntled youths—who may have minimal political consciousness, but are looking for a thrill and, at the same time, see a way of feeling a sense of belonging. They are typically working-class youngsters who have not been successful at school or on the job. Having often grown up in dysfunctional families, they usually don't get along with their parents or other family members. At school, they are regarded by the popular students as "geeks," "nerds," or "outsiders." Among fellow skinheads, however, they feel both accepted and important. Their intolerance of people who are different is the common bond that gives them a sense of "family" that they never had.[8]

Some racist skinhead groups lack formal structure and ties to organized hate groups. Their alliance is maintained by little more than common haircuts, shared racism, political alienation, and more or less spontaneous outbursts of violence that they direct against Blacks or Latinos in their communities. At the other end of the continuum, however, there are thousands of racist skinheads who have organized for action. They give themselves a name (Romantic Violence, American Front Skinheads, Reich Skins, Confederate Hammer Skins, or the like), select a leader, hold regular meetings, distribute racist propaganda, and attend rallies sponsored by organized hate groups like the KKK. Although there is no single national organization of skinheads, networks of skinhead gangs have been known to exist, at least for a while. For example, the Confederate Hammer Skins, Western Hammer Skins, American Front, National White, and Old Glory Skins have linked together in a loose confederation. Even among skinheads associated with organized hate groups, however, members typically move in and out of different groups and switch their allegiance.[9]

Skinheads with connections to organized hate groups often employ rock music as a means of putting forth their racist message and as a tool for recruiting. A number of "white power" rock bands have gained in popularity. Their members perform songs containing blatantly racist lyrics and advocating violence against the despised groups. Recognizing the power of a tune to persuade, the White Aryan Resistance has encouraged its members to use racist music as a recruitment tool. In its newsletter, WAR advises, "Music is one of the greatest propaganda tools around. You can influence more people with a song than you can with a speech."[10] For similar reasons, in its bid to influence American youths, the National Alliance has recently purchased Resistance Records, a company that specializes in creating and distributing angry white power music to racist youngsters.

Ken Mieske was the lead singer in the rock band Machine. Prior to the Portland incident, he was convicted of petty theft and served a sentence of one year in the Oregon state penitentiary. Mieski must have been listening carefully to those who advocate mixing music with violence. In heavy metal style, he sang about being consumed with the urge to kill and about the pleasure that he derived from watching his victims suffer and die. Mieske's attempt to fuse music and violence apparently helped inspire the subsequent rapid growth of the hate music industry in the United States.

Another important lesson to be learned from the Seraw murder over ten years after the crime was committed is that *the leaders of organized hate groups have tended to become mainstream rather than fringe, at least in the image they attempt to project.* Tom and John Metzger wear ties, not sheets. Some of their most influential members are former KKK members who recognize the futility of looking deviant, perhaps even anti-American. The new groups talk in code words and phrases about the issues that concern middle America. They preach that the *heritage* (meaning: race) of white Christians is being eroded by *foreign* (meaning: Jewish/communist) influence; they lament the rise of *government interference* (meaning: Jews in high places who force racial integration down the throats of white Americans) in the lives of *average citizens* (meaning: white Christians); and they condemn *welfare cheating* (meaning: Blacks), which they see as of overwhelming proportions and on the rise. They wear suits and ties. Some get facelifts or don hairpieces. Several have run for public office. Even in their support of bizarre-looking skinhead youths, they themselves are more concerned with projecting a respectable public image. They realize that younger people often reject the robes and ritual in favor of paramilitary dress. Concerned with the reaction of both the public and the police, some skinhead groups have recently taken a cue from their mentors by wearing their hair long and getting rid of their Black leather jackets.[11]

Even some Klan leaders have changed their tune, at least in the way it is played for recruiting purposes. The leader of the Knights of the Ku Klux Klan in North Carolina barred the participation of violent neo-Nazis from its meetings. The head of the Klan in Florida urged its members to become a group "known for hating evil, instead of being a group known for hating Negroes." And the leader of the Knights of the Ku Klux Klan has repeatedly suggested that his group does not hate anyone but "loves the White race."

The strategy to campaign among those in the mainstream may be paying off. According to socialist and Klan expert Kathleen Blee, the image of organized hate groups recruiting from the ranks of the dysfunctional, the hate-filled, and the impoverished is, for the most part, a myth. In her interviews with thirty-four women in White supremacist groups, she found an unexpected diversity.

Most of them had graduated from high school or college, were not poor and had not grown up poor, and had not followed a boyfriend or husband into racism. Not unlike millions of other Americans, most of the women who joined hate groups had already harbored some resentment toward Blacks and Jews long before they signed up, but they didn't acquire "racist urgency" until they began associating with the members of racist groups.[12]

❖ ❖ ❖

The September 11 terrorist attack provoked an ambivalent response from White supremacists. The last thing they wanted was to be identified as "un-American" defenders of the "immigrant threat." Instead, William Pierce of the National Alliance, Matt Hale of the World Church of the Creator, and other movement leaders argued that the attack on America was a result of the U.S. government acting on behalf of the Jews.[13]

At the same time, those in the White supremacist movement who were less public relations conscious praised the Middle Eastern instigators of the terrorist attack, suggesting that their own colleagues should long ago have had the "courage" to assault "Jew York City." Shortly after the attack on America, Nazi Party chairman Rocky Suhayda lamented that "a bunch of towel heads and niggers put our great White Movement to SHAME."

Many observers of bioterrorism have argued that the source of anthrax sent through the mail just a few days after the attack on America was the work not of Middle Easterners, but of American White supremacists eager to contaminate leftist-leaning elements in government and the media.[14]

A third, and lasting, important message derived from the Portland murder is that *organized hate groups are technologically sophisticated.* Metzger's WAR uses computer networking, answering machines that leave hate messages, shortwave radio programs, and public access cable television. He and his colleagues have been seen as guests on nationally syndicated programs like *Oprah, Springer, Dateline NBC, Prime-Time Live,* and *20/20.*

For purposes of recruiting and spreading the racist word, the most important innovation by far has been the Internet. There are currently hundreds of hate Web sites operated by White supremacist and skinhead groups where anyone who is interested, no matter how young, can find hate propaganda, announcements of meetings and rallies, and racists with whom to chat. Youngsters who may feel quite alone in their racist beliefs while at home can log on, enter a chat room, and meet any number of like-minded buddies. Moreover, thanks to the widespread accessibility of the Internet, White power music, which is difficult if not impossible to buy in mainstream music stores, can easily be purchased on line.[15]

Metzger's WAR telephone message line offers White supremacist news and philosophy. It chastises government officials for their economic policy (e.g., "All you worthless bastards in the House and Senate, what are you up to now? What's your beloved Pentagon pork barrel going to do for you now that the phony cold war is being flushed down the toilet? What other ways are you planning to destroy White working people in the U.S.?"), for their policy toward immigrants (e.g., "Stop bringing in all these Asians and make room for national parks. Boxcar a few million Mexicans and Central Americans south of the border and watch the streets get cleaner overnight."), and for their treatment of Jews (e.g., "Why do you allow the Jew Mossad secret police full freedom to spy on Americans from the seventh floor of the Jew Anti-Defecation League right there in front of you? You chicken-shits worship the Jews so much you must have holes in the knees of all your pants.").[16]

As of 2002, according to the Anti-Defamation League, the number of cable television programs devoted to preaching hate has grown over the years. Featuring interviews with skinheads, hate group leaders, and other hate activists, there are fifty-seven such programs being broadcast on public access channels in twenty-four of the country's top television markets. Many have been found in California, but programs preaching racial and religious hatred have also turned up in other top markets such as Boston, New Haven, Phoenix, Denver, Tampa, Atlanta, Chicago, St. Paul, Cincinnati, Albuquerque, Pittsburgh, Houston, Richmond, and Seattle.[17]

Concerned citizens in these communities often wonder how the media activities of hate groups like the White Aryan Resistance are financed. Such groups typically operate on a small budget provided by membership dues and private contributions. Even effective lawsuits taking millions of dollars from such hate groups cannot possibly hope to put them entirely out of business. Because of public access laws and technological advances, a minimal budget is probably all that is needed in order to express bigotry on a widespread basis. Cable access television and the internet provide an effective "soapbox" at virtually no expense. For the cost of a personal computer, a VCR, and an answering machine, an organization can easily create regional, if not national, exposure for itself. Moreover, the exact amount and source of funding for White supremacist groups is a closely kept secret intended to protect the confidentiality of donors and to create a false impression of widespread support.

On occasion, a hate group's benefactor is unexpectedly revealed. At his death in 2001, a newspaper article about Richard J. Cotter reported that he had served as a legal adviser to various neo-Nazi groups. More shocking, the one-time Massachusetts assistant attorney general left $750,000 to White supremacist organizations.[18]

❖   ❖   ❖

According to the Southern Poverty Law Center's Klanwatch Project in Montgomery, the number of organized hate groups has grown significantly, perhaps as a result of hard economic times during the last couple of years. More specifically, Klanwatch estimates there has been a 27 percent increase over this period in the number of White supremacist groups, mainly in Georgia, Florida, Southern California, and the northeastern states, as well as around Chicago. The size of the antigovernment civilian militia movement has gone in the opposite direction, dwindling to fewer than 200 groups.[19]

Toward the midpoint of the 1990s, the militia or patriot movement reached its pinnacle of success in terms of recruitment. Through the 1980s and into the early 1990s, more and more Americans—having seen their fortunes dwindle under the impact of economic recession and having witnessed major blunders of federal law enforcement at Ruby Ridge and Waco—were attracted to the cause. Then, in 1995, Timothy McVeigh blew up 168 men, women, and children in Oklahoma City, and even the most ardent antigovernment extremists felt that McVeigh had gone too far, that enough was enough. Recruitment to the militia cause became all but impossible. Finally, as the turn of the millennium came and went without revolution, many more militia members found themselves completely disillusioned. The militia movement was beginning to look frail and tired. Many Americans lost interest in it.

But rather than operate on their own, many former members of the patriot movement transferred their allegiance to the White supremacist movement, causing the number of such groups to grow through the opening years of the new millennium. Over the same period, the structure of the White supremacist movement shifted away from large and highly organized groups to small "cells" of a few close friends or acquaintances—so-called lone wolves who were only loosely connected to any larger movement. In addition to causing organized hatemongers to lose power and influence, this transition also served to increase the difficulty federal investigators experienced in attempts to infiltrate and investigate groups of extremists.

But numbers alone do not tell the full story—there may be fewer than thirty-five thousand and almost certainly no more than fifty thousand members of White supremacist groups across the country. It is not only their revolutionary activism, however, but the growing sophistication of such organized hate groups in reaching the young people of America—their apparent finesse and respectability—that represents the real cause for alarm. It should also be noted that hundreds of thousands of Americans agree to some extent, if not wholeheartedly, with the principles of White supremacy, even if they would never join a hate group.[20]

Most Americans are somewhat acquainted with the objectives of White hate groups like the Ku Klux Klan and neo-Nazis. Those who are familiar with American history know that the Klan has risen and fallen time and time again in response to challenges to the advantaged position of the White majority. During a short period of post–Civil War reconstruction, for example, many Whites were challenged by newly freed slaves who sought some measure of political power and began to compete for jobs with White working-class Southerners. Thus the Klan, responding with a campaign of terror and violence, lynched many Blacks. Klan-initiated violence increased again during the 1920s, as native-born Americans sought "protection" from an unprecedented influx of immigration from Eastern and Southern Europe. Those old enough to remember the 1950s and 1960s might recall uniformed members of George Lincoln Rockwell's American Nazi Party giving the Nazi salute and shouting "Heil Hitler" or Klansmen in their sheets and hoods marching in opposition to racial desegregation in schools and public facilities.

By contrast, the newer organized hate groups don't always come so easily to mind for their bizarre uniforms or rituals. As noted earlier, followers of the Metzger's White Aryan Resistance shed their sheets and burning crosses in favor of more conventional attire. They often disavow the Klan and the Nazi movement in favor of a brand of "American patriotism" that plays better among the working people of Peoria (not to mention Rochester, Akron, Burbank, etc.). Matthew Hale, the twenty-nine-year-old lawyer who heads the Peoria-based World Church of the Creator went to law school. William Pierce who directs the National Alliance from its West Virginia headquarters has a Ph.D. and comes across as a well-educated and articulate spokesperson.

Moreover, White supremacist organizations now often cloak their hatred in the aura and dogma of Christianity. Followers of the religious arm of the hate movement, the Identity Church, are only "doing the work of God." At Sunday services, they preach that White Anglo-Saxons are the true Israelites depicted in the Old Testament, God's chosen people, while Jews are actually the children of Satan. They maintain that Jesus was not a Jew, but an ancestor of the White, northern European peoples. In their view, Blacks are "pre-adamic," a species lower than Whites. In fact, they claim that Blacks and other nonWhite groups are at the same spiritual level as animals and therefore have no souls.

Members of the movement also believe in the inevitability of a global war between the races that only White people will ultimately survive. The survivalists among Identity followers prepare for war by moving to communes where they stockpile weapons, provide paramilitary training, and pray. According to an Identity directory, there are Identity churches in thirty-three states, Canada, England, South Africa, and Australia.[21]

The Aryan Nations was developed around Reverend Richard Butler's version of the Identity Church, which he calls the "Church of Jesus Christ Christian." Like other organized hate groups, the Aryan Nations is militantly committed to anti-Semitism and racism. Rather than demand only that Blacks and Jews be expelled from the United States, however, Butler's group proposes establishing a separate White racist state in what is presently the northwest region of the United States and Canada.

Each year, Butler holds an "International Congress of Aryan Nations." Attracting as many as two hundred racists, the annual festival is meant to bring together White supremacist leaders from around the world who share information, give speeches, and offer courses in guerrilla warfare.[22]

As noted ealier, rather than arrange themselves in large hierarchical groups that can be easily infiltrated, many in the hate movement now take a "lone wolf" or "leaderless resistance" strategy, operating on their own or in small "cells" only loosely linked with some larger organization. On August 10, 1999, for example, thirty-seven-year-old Buford Furrow decided that it was time to give a dramatic "wake up call to America to kill Jews." Though essentially a loner, the stocky racist had a history of connections with anti-Semitic groups, including Aryan Nations. Semi-automatic in hand, Furrow stormed into the North Valley Jewish Community Center in Los Angeles, where he immediately took aim and fired more than 70 bullets at a roomful of children. Three boys, a teenage girl, and a woman were wounded, though none fatally. Then, while attempting to flee the area, Furrow approached a Filipino-American letter carrier and asked him to mail a letter. Before the postal worker could reply, Furrow shot him to death.[23]

The particularly depressed economic conditions in rural areas of the United States since the early 1980s have provided a fertile breeding ground for organized hate. Playing on a theme that has special appeal to downtrodden farmers and small town residents, members of Posse Comitatus (Latin for "power of the county") argue that all government power should be focused at the county, not the federal, level. From this perspective, IRS agents and federal judges are mortal enemies of the White race, and the county sheriff constitutes the one and only form of legitimate government. Many members of the Posse refuse to pay taxes. They charge that Jews create recessions and depressions and control the Federal Reserve.

Consistent with its emphasis on maintaining local control, Posse Comitatus has no nationally recognized leadership and consists of a number of decentralized and loosely affiliated groups of vigilantes and survivalists. From time to time, the Posse has attracted national attention.

In February 1983, for example, Posse member and farmer Gordon Kahl murdered two federal marshals in Medina, North Dakota, who had come to arrest him for a parole violation. The sixty-three-year-old Kahl evaded apprehension for almost four months. While a fugitive, he wrote a letter to James Wickstrom, leader of the Wisconsin chapter of the Posse Comitatus, describing the shoot-out with federal marshals as an early response to a prophecy from God to eliminate all Jews and communists from the United States. "We are a conquered and occupied nation," Kahl wrote, "conquered and occupied by the Jews who plan to rule the world by destroying Christianity and the White race."[24] In June, federal agents located the small farmhouse in the Ozark Mountains of Arkansas in which Kahl was hiding out. They fired a volley of gunfire and tear gas through the windows of the house, igniting the ammunition stored inside. Kahl was killed in the fiery explosion.

Like the Posse, the Populist Party also takes a conservative political position with an anti-Semitic twist. They claim that Jews are running the media as well as the federal government, and they oppose the U.S. alliance with the state of Israel. Before being elected to the Louisiana State House as a Democrat, David Duke was an unsuccessful Populist candidate for president.[25]

The agenda of the Populist Party seems, on the surface, to be responsible and patriotic. Its platform calls for "a respect for racial and cultural diversity." By means of code words understood by its members, however, the party actually expresses a covert anti-Semitic theme. For example, alleged respect for diversity is twisted: "The Populist Party will not permit any racial minority, through control of the media, cultural distortion or revolutionary political activity, to divide or factionalize the majority of the society-nation in which the minority lives." The term "racial minority" refers specifically to Jews while "cultural distortion" refers to the allegedly corrupting Jewish influence in American life.[26] White supremacist groups represent a fringe element among those who commit hate crimes. In statistical terms alone, the membership of all organized hate groups combined constitutes a tiny fraction of American citizens, most of whom wouldn't consider burning a cross or wearing a swastika. Even so, the influence of White supremacist groups like Posse Comitatus, White Aryan Resistance, Aryan Nations, and the Klan may be considerably greater than their numbers suggest. It takes only a small band of dedicated extremists to make trouble for a large number of apathetic middle-of-the-roaders. Even in this age of ac-tivism, there are many solid citizens who have neither the time nor the inclination for political action.

It is of even greater concern that the bigotry espoused by White su-premacists has moved into the mainstream of American society, even if it is expressed in more subtle terms. No longer can we limit our attention to hooded Klansmen or uniformed Nazis. On the contrary, we must now examine our young, our own schools, and perhaps even ourselves.

nine

HATE GOES TO SCHOOL: STILL ALIVE AND WELL ON CAMPUS

Students on the Amherst campus of the University of Massachusetts sat glued to the tube. This was the final game of the 1986 World Series—a championship contest between the New York Mets and the Boston Red Sox that had raised the collective level of excitement to a feverish pitch. Watching TV in residence halls around the campus, groups of undergraduates rooted their approval, booed the opposition, and drank in excess. Having sat through a lengthy rain delay and a frustrating loss for the Red Sox the night before, the majority of them were eager to see the "hometown boys finally make good." Surely, this would be the night when the Red Sox—widely regarded as the "White team"—would put to rest their reputation for choking in the clutch, for never being able to win the Big Game. (The Red Sox had not won a World Series since 1918.)

When the contest ended, however, it was the much despised Mets—commonly considered the "Black team"—and not the Red Sox who had come out on top. Thousands of disappointed Sox fans on campus—many of them drunk and angered by their team's defeat—poured out of the dorms to gather in the courtyard. They were immediately confronted by a few hundred euphoric Mets supporters, loudly celebrating their team's triumph and unsparingly taunting their losing rivals. In response, some of the Red Sox fans threw homemade firebombs and bottles; others came armed with sticks. Sporadic fighting broke out between the two sides. A few students were injured.[1]

At the beginning, confrontations involved only White Mets fans against White Red Sox fans. But the focus of the assault quickly turned racial when a particularly loud and unruly White student decided to attack one of the Black students in the courtyard. As though looking for a target to blame for the loss of the Red Sox, the crowd of Whites moved menacingly in the direction of the fifteen to twenty Blacks.

In an instance, the distinction between Mets and Red Sox supporters had evolved into a shoving and pushing match based on race alone. A White football player threw a punch. A Black student began swinging a stick after being jumped from behind and punched to the ground. Shouting racial insults, groups of White students chased the Black students as they attempted to escape. Some of the Whites broke windows and hurled rocks; others yelled racial slurs. Many attempted to force their way into a building where some of the Black students had gathered to hide. One Black attempted to defend himself with a golf club but was tackled to the ground, kicked, and then beaten into unconsciousness. The crowd finally dispersed, but only in reaction to prodding by the Amherst police and the University of Massachusetts security police.[2]

❖   ❖   ❖

In November 2001, the Review of Higher Education estimated that at least 1 million bias-motivated incidents occur on American college campuses each year, the vast majority of which are never reported to school or law enforcement authorities. Such hate attacks range from relatively minor acts of vandalism to serious episodes of violence.[3]

Evidence of widespread bias among our young people may be surprising, but it is nothing new. In 1990, pollster Louis Harris set out to determine the views of a nationwide sample of students regarding the state of racial and ethnic tensions in America. Working on behalf of the Reebok Foundation and Northeastern University's Center for the Study of Sport in Society, Harris's staff talked with a cross-section of 1,865 high school students who were attending the tenth, eleventh, and twelfth grades in public, parochial, and private schools around the country.

The pollster's findings painted a rather bleak picture of race relations among American youth. Apparently confrontations between individuals of different races and religions were "commonplace" in the nation's high schools. More than half of the students interviewed claimed that they had witnessed racial confrontations either "very often" or "once in a while." One in four reported having personally been a target of such an incident. Only 30 percent of all students said that they were prepared to intervene to stop or even to condemn a confrontation based on racial hatred. On the contrary, almost half admitted that they would join in the attack or, at the very least, agreed that the group being attacked was getting what it deserved.[4]

The findings of a survey of all 1,570 elementary, middle, and secondary public schools in Los Angeles County also support the view that youthful hatred has become all too common in our schools. Thirty-seven percent of these schools encountered incidents of hate-motivated violence over the period of a year. As expected, students in middle and high schools were particularly likely to have experienced hate violence and had a response rate of 47 percent and 42 percent respectively. Somewhat more surprising was the finding that 34 percent of the elementary schools also experienced violent episodes based on hate.

The Los Angeles County survey also determined that no one group had been singled out as a target for violence. Schools reported hate incidents against Black, Latino, White, Asian, Pacific Islander, and Arab students, as well as incidents directed against Jewish students, gay and lesbian students, and immigrant students. As found in hate crimes generally, most students who engaged in forms of hate-motivated violence were not involved in any organized hate groups. In fact, only 5 percent of the incidents reported in the Los Angeles survey were committed by students with links to White supremacist organizations.[5]

In the spring of 2000 researchers from Northeastern University with support from the Governor's Hate Crime Task Force surveyed thirty high schools in Massachusetts. Students were asked if they had been the victim of one (or more) of the following crimes: assault, assault and battery, sexual assault, harassment, theft, or vandalism. In addition to asking if these crimes had happened to each student, the study questioned the respondents as to why they thought they had been targeted. More than one-third of the students (38 percent) reported that they had been victims of one or more of these offenses. When asked if they thought that the crime was motivated by bias, a surprising 7.7 percent of the entire sample of forty-five hundred students reported that they believed so. The Northeastern University study also concluded that certain groups of students were especially likely to be targeted in hate crimes. For example, students perceived to be gay, lesbian, or bisexual were four times more likely to be attacked than other students. African-American and Asian-American students were were twice as likely to be targeted, and Latino, Jewish, and disabled students were also at a higher risk of attack in a bias-motivated crime.

Perhaps the most startling finding of the Northeastern University research was that many of these hate-motivated incidents went unreported to authorities. The study discovered that less than 5 percent of all hate crime victims told law enforcement authorities about the incident and only a third told any school officials. It was far more likely that they would confide in their friends (67 percent) or their parents (32 percent). More than one-quarter of the hate crime victims in this study did not tell anyone about their victimization.[6] In response to this report, the Massachusetts Governor's Task Force initiated a program of training in schools to increase the reporting of hate crimes.

After September 11, 2001, the bigots who had previously directed their violence toward gay or Black students now focused on a new set of targets: Arab or Middle Eastern students, who were harassed or assaulted in schools across the country. In Palmdale, California, for example, a group of Arab students stayed home after they were named in a list found by school officials as targets in a massacre being planned to avenge the September 11 attack. Such incidents became so widespread and troubling in the aftermath of the terrorist assault that the U.S. secretary of education, Rod Page, sent a letter to educators across the country urging them to make certain that classes and assemblies intended to honor the victims of those attacks not inadvertently "foster the targeting of Arab-American students for harassment or blame."

The hate incidents against those who are different continued to accumulate: An Arizona State University student from India was pushed to the ground and then punched and kicked by three people. A Missouri University medical student of Arabic descent received an e-mail threatening to kill him and "all the Arab pigs of the world." An Indian graduate student at the University of Kentucky was struck in the face as he walked on campus. A Saudi Arabian student at Boston University was stabbed as he left a local nightclub. A Muslim graduate student at Harvard University, wearing her traditional Islamic headscarf (hijab), was verbally and physically harassed at a Cambridge T-station. An Arab student at Syracuse University found that someone had placed a "trash" sign on his dormitory door.

According to the American-Arab Anti-Discrimination Committee, there were more than 250 violent incidences on college campuses in the months following the September 11 attack on America. The American Council on Education reports that more than one hundred students from the Middle East studying in the United States, out of fear for their personal safety, decided to return home. On some campuses, moreover, Arab and Jewish students traded accusations. On other campuses, student newspapers have been charged with printing insensitive materials that might easily justify attacks on students from the Middle East.

Perhaps some part of youthful bigotry is a reflection of the latest version of an age-old conflict between the generations: an adolescent counterculture designed to attract teenagers to one another and, at the same time, to "freak out" older individuals, especially parents. At the extreme, rebellious members of the baby boom generation of the 1960s expressed their independence by espousing "free love," tripping on LSD, smoking dope, and voicing political dissent through demonstrations. Their behavior was at times so outrageous that it left little to the next generation of youthful rebels to outdo. Members of the punk counterculture of the 1970s and early 1980s made their own statement by emphasizing violence rather than peace, as well as drinking to excess, slam dancing, dying their hair bright purple, and retreating from politics altogether.

What is left for contemporary youth who wish to make a statement to their parents as well as their peers? Never fear. In their own version of a collective quest for independence, some youngsters have gone one more step by embracing out-and-out evil. At the extreme, there is now a growing interest in the darker side of life, a concern with satanism, murder, and nihilism in the service of racism. Alienated teenagers around the country have increasingly experimented with bizarre cult rituals. In the name of Satan, some have met clandestinely to cut off the heads of pigs, dogs, and cats and then drink their blood. Others have held secret "hell parties," where they listen to heavy metal, ingest mescaline and LSD, and then sacrifice animals. At the extreme, a few have even committed ritualized murder. For example, a fifteen-year-old girl from Daytona, Florida, was sentenced to fifty years in prison after pleading no contest to the kidnapping and satanic slaying of a Vietnamese immigrant, Ngoc Van Dang. The young devil worshiper, a ninth-grade dropout, had allegedly gotten the idea to commit a human sacrifice from reading *The Satanic Bible* and participating in a satanic ritual with the use of a Ouija board. Along with three friends, she abducted Dang after hitching a ride with him in Orlando. At gun point, she forced him into the woods and shot him seven times, killing him. She then carved a large inverted cross across her victim's chest.

As in previous generations, these latest incarnations of the generation gap have succeeded in transforming themselves enough to become marketable to the middle-of-the road American teenagers. Just as the hippies of the 1960s formed the basis for the music, dress, hairstyles, and politics of the so-called hip generation, just as punk culture was later incorporated into "New Wave" music, art, and fashion, so a softened version of extremist cultural and political themes has been absorbed into conventional culture. Whereas they were earlier denied access to the commercial mainstream, for example, a few metal bands espousing nihilism, violence, and bigotry have been positioned at the top of the popular music charts, finding a responsive audience on "contemporary hit" radio stations. The most vicious version of metal's pounding rhythm and painful noise level may differ only subtly from the "hard rock" of previous generations, but its lyrics speak to a new genre of adolescent concerns, including oral sex at gun point, murder by ice pick, anal penetration, necrophilia, physical abuse of women, and satanic sacrifice.[7]

As a youth-oriented counterculture that appeals to alienated teenagers, the skinhead movement has grown in dramatic fashion as well. Across the country, disgruntled youths—especially those who aren't getting along with their families, teachers, and classmates—have shed their hair as well as their humanitarian values to revel in the limelight of the latest version of a racial superiority complex. In the year 2000, according to the Intelligence Project of the Southern Poverty Law Center, there were racist skinhead groups operating in more than thirty states across the country. According to the Anti-Defamation League of B'nai B'rith, this figure represents some leveling off in a longer-term trend that began decades earlier. In England, moreover, where the movement began in the late 1970s, skinheads now number as many as ten thousand. There are some thirty thousand in Germany, where they have spearheaded hundreds of violent attacks on foreigners during the last few years. Skinheads are also found in all European and Scandinavian countries, Canada, Australia, New Zealand, South Africa, and in several Latin American nations.[8]

Of course, only a tiny proportion—far fewer than 1 percent—of all American teenagers can be characterized as racist skinheads. The progress of these groups should, however, be measured not in terms of numbers alone but also by their increasing dangerousness. There is a growing pattern of recruitment and activity across the country. As already noted, skinheads have tried to enlist students in high schools from a number of states including Arizona, Texas, Pennsylvania, New York, Oregon, Michigan, California, Colorado, and Florida. Their efforts at the college level have been less effective, being largely confined to a few campuses in the state of Ohio. In high schools and junior high schools, however, the skinheads have found a more receptive audience. In fact, skinhead gangs seem to be drawing their recruits from younger and younger age-groups, some no older than thirteen years of age.[9]

To examine an all too typical example, consider the series of events that transpired in Glendale, California, a medium-sized blue-collar industrial city situated in the San Fernando Valley, about eight miles northeast of Los Angeles. Rosemont Junior High School in Glendale was the scene of repeated skinhead activity. In February 1989, a thirteen-year-old skinhead, after being refused permission to wear his White power T-shirt for his yearbook photo, threatened his teacher with a loaded .357 Magnum. The student pleaded guilty to three felony and two misdemeanor charges. That same year, a Rosemont administrator ejected a skinhead who was not a student at the school. The reprisal took only a few days to occur. At first, it was directed solely at the administrator; he became the target of threatening phone calls and obscenities written on the door of his office. Several days later, however, the counterattack was generalized: The words "Jew bitch," "No Jews," "Happy Birthday Hitler," and "We are back in town" were discovered etched, along with SS symbols and swastikas, into the classroom doors of Jewish teachers. The words "Fuck Jews" were found scrawled across student lockers throughout the school.[10]

Skinheads have participated in a variety of racially inspired acts in high schools across the country. At Groves High School in Bir-ming-ham, Michigan, skinheads reportedly defaced school property with swastikas and the words "nigger," "White power," and "Skins." At Sprayberry High School in Cobb County, Georgia, a group of skin-heads purportedly gave Nazi salutes and shouted "Heil Hitler" while reciting the pledge of allegiance. At Oak Ridge High School in Or-lando, Florida, skinheads apparently were responsible for raising a White power flag above the school and spray-painting swastikas on the walls of temporary classrooms, and so on.[11]

Hundreds of skinhead attacks have been directed against persons as well as property. At Shawnee High School in Medford, New Jersey, for example, a White female student was threatened with death at the hands of a local skinhead group because she talked to a Black class-mate. In school, she was told by another female student, "I'll have my skinhead friends kill you." Death threats were also repeatedly made to her over the phone by the members of a skinhead gang. The female high school student who made the original threat along with Joseph Cotton, eighteen, and Brian Riccobene, nineteen, were later arrested and charged with making terrorist threats.

In Tulsa, Oklahoma, a group of skinheads harassed and attacked the owner and customers of a multiracial nightclub. In an attempt to put the establishment out of business, the skinheads posted racist leaflets around the local community and then firebombed the club with a Molotov cocktail. When the club still refused to close, the skinheads began to assault its customers and attacked its owner by hitting him on the head with a brick. Then the skinheads kicked a patron in the head with steel-toed boots until he was unconscious. The club remained open, however. The four youths involved in this assault are presently under indictment by a federal grand jury in Tulsa.

Though often taking a more sophisticated approach than the "in your face" skinhead version, students on college campuses have not been immune to intergroup hostility. At colleges and universities, acts of hatred directed against individuals perceived to be different have oc-curred with alarming frequency.

Toward the more benign end of the continuum of hate incidents, college students make jokes about the ethnicity of their classmates. For example, sociologist Gary Spencer studied the growth of JAP (Jewish-American princess) baiting on his campus, Syracuse University, as well as other campuses around the country. He concluded that these jokes clearly contain a major element of both anti-Semitism and sexism.

The predominant theme of JAP jokes has recently become more overtly anti-Semitic, and the people who relate them are increasingly non-Jews. Even in their more benign form, these jokes are a new variation on an old theme—Jews have too much money for their own good and believe in their own entitlement, going far beyond what is reasonable or healthy or good for society. In this view, espoused to an increasing extent by non-Jewish students, Jews continue to enjoy illegitimate power and wealth. This idea has been found on campus after campus, in graffiti, anti-Semitic slurs, and sexual harassment of Jewish women.

More insidious versions of JAP jokes on campus have also surfaced during recent years. Rather than emphasize the alleged ostentatiousness of Jews, they suggest in no uncertain terms that the world would be better off if all Jewish women were eliminated. Joke: A solution to the JAP problem. When they go to get nose jobs, tie their tubes as well. Another joke: What to you call forty-nine JAPs facedown in deep water? A good beginning![12] Apparently some college students have taken their bigoted jokes to heart by translating their hatred into action. At the University of Arizona, the windows of the Jewish Student Center were shattered one evening in a burst of gunfire by unidentified assailants. At Dartmouth College, the *Dartmouth Review* published alongside its logo an anti-Semitic statement taken from Hitler's *Mein Kampf*. *Review* staffers claimed that the incident was a hoax perpetrated by an impostor in an effort to discredit the publication. At the University of Wisconsin, an unknown hatemonger spray-painted "Think Extinction" on the walls of the Jewish student center. Then two Phi Gamma Delta fraternity students at Wisconsin entered a predominantly Jewish fraternity without permission and pelted its members with punches and anti-Semitic slurs. The two Phi Gamma Delta brothers were arrested for battery. At Rutgers University, unidentified vandals defaced the Hillel Foundation building with anti-Semitic graffiti and swastikas.

Acts of intolerance on college campuses have frequently also involved racial or ethnic differences. At Yale University, unknown vandals spray-painted a red swastika and the words "White power" on the walls of the Afro-American cultural center. At the University of Michigan, a disc jockey on the campus radio station aired racist jokes and then played a song entitled "Run Nigger, Run." He was later suspended. At Brown University, racist graffiti ("Niggers go home") were found scribbled in elevators, on restroom doors, on posters, and on the doors of Black students' dormitory rooms. At Stanford University, unknown students drew thick lips on Beethoven's image on a poster and then hung it on a Black student's door in a large residence hall, and so on.[13]

Most perpetrators of hate crimes on campus are themselves college students. An especially hideous exception was an incident that occurred on the evening of August 18, 1992, when several young White men shouted racial insults at Luyen Phan Nguyen as he left a party at nearby Coral Springs. When the nineteen-year-old premed student from the University of Miami objected to the slurs and then tried to escape, the men chased him down "like an injured deer," according to Coral Springs police chief, Roy A. Arigo, throwing him to the ground and then repeatedly punching and kicking him in the head until he was dead. Eight men ranging in ages from eighteen to twenty-two were later arrested for the fatal beating and charged with murder. None of the defendants were students; most worked in the area and had no record of criminal violence.[14]

The most persecuted students on college campuses do not necessarily differ from their assailants with respect to race, religion, national origin, or even gender; they differ in terms of sexual orientation. According to many Student Life staffers, lesbian and gay students are most frequently targeted for victimization. The Governor's Task Force on Bias-Related Violence in New York reached the same conclusion: "While evidence shows serious problems for many groups (on New York State Campuses), the most severe hostilities are directed at lesbians and gay men."[15]

On campuses around the country, lesbians and gay men have been threatened with violence. At Harvard University recently a resident tutor quit after being tormented by a series of homophobic acts of vandalism.[16] During gay pride week at the University of Oregon, a number of men burst into a movie being watched by a gay group on campus and then blocked the exits to the room. When the intruders tired of holding the gay students hostage, they surrounded a shuttle van carrying female students and shouted antilesbian remarks at them. Although never identified, the threatening group was believed to consist of fraternity members on campus. At the University of Alaska, several students wearing sweatshirts bearing the logo "Anti-Fag Society" shouted insults at gays and defaced the books and clothing of gays on campus. After a dance marathon at Northwestern University, the gay couple sponsored by the Gay and Lesbian Alliance on campus received anonymous death threats on their answering machine. At the University of Delaware, forty anti-gay slurs such as "a warrior needs to kill homos badly" and "fags are going to die from AIDS" were scrawled on sidewalks on the central campus. A group calling itself the Anti-Homosexual Federation signed some of the graffiti, which were strategically placed where members of the gay students' organization had earlier written messages of support for National Coming Out Day.

But you don't have to be gay to be victimized—you only have to "look gay." Male students with effeminate body language or speech may be regularly harassed by their peers in college dormitories or campus centers. At the same time, such indicators of sexual orientation can be unreliable; there are effeminate men who aren't gay and gay men who aren't effeminate.

This is a major reason why attacks against gays and lesbians are so often targeted at their campus offices and organizational meetings. Based on appearance alone, haters cannot always identify students who are gay. As a result, they look for places where they are sure to find a number of "them" together. Frequently, the flyers announcing meetings are torn down or defaced. At one university recently, campus bigots scribbled their message, "All faggots must die," across the announcements. At the same university, an anonymous caller phoned the office of the campus Gay and Lesbian Coalition to say, "I'm a Nazi skinhead . . . I'm going to bomb your office and blow all you . . . up."

On many college campuses, student organizations tend to be divided along racial, religious, and gender lines and therefore emphasize the *differences* that separate students from one another. Such associations frequently organize around the problems or concerns experienced in common by the members of their group. Hence the proliferation of such minority student organizations as the Black Student Union and the Gay and Lesbian Alliance.

Organizations based on shared racial identity, religion, or sexual orientation probably provide much needed support for minority students who would otherwise feel totally out of place in a predominantly White or majority institution. In this sense, then, such organizations may be absolutely essential to the academic survival of minority students in what they perceive to be a hostile, or at best uncomfortable, environment.

Unfortunately, many White students apparently misunderstand the defensive objectives of segregated organizations on campus. Thus whatever the benefits they have for their members, such organizations are used by bigots to reinforce the notion already prevalent among majority students that minority students *think they are special, want nothing to do with majority students,* and *desire separation.* It is not surprising that White students on about twelve campuses have established White student unions to protest what they regard as oppression directed against them.[17]

On the West Coast, White student unions were initiated by Tom and John Metzger's White Aryan Resistance as an element of its outreach program aimed at young people. In its publication, *The White Student,* the Metzgers' White student unions disseminate a virulent form of anti-Semitism. Specifically, they spread the word that "Communism is Jewish! Boycott Jew stores. Drive the rats out of town!" In hundreds of thousands of flyers distributed to California college students, the organization also declared that the Nazi extermination of Jews a total hoax.[18]

Organizations whose membership is limited to specific groups are nothing new on college campuses, and they didn't begin with minority students. College fraternities have long deserved a reputation for encouraging racial separation and elitism. Donald E. Muir's study at the University of Alabama suggests that fraternities may continue, at least on some campuses, to serve as a sanctuary for traditional forms of racism. Based on the questionnaire responses of some 1,166 University of Alabama undergraduates, Muir found that the White fraternities and sororities on campus tend to recruit students who already dislike Blacks and tend to support racial discrimination on the part of their members.[19]

It is true, of course, that what happens at the University of Alabama does not necessarily apply to all of the thousands of campuses across the country. Indeed, there are more than a few universities at which fraternities promote diversity rather than divisiveness among students. At Northeastern University in Boston, for example, students organized a fraternity around the theme of diversity. Rather than emphasize exclusivity, founders of this fraternity actively recruited members representing the full range of racial, religious, and national backgrounds of students on the campus.

Too many fraternities on too many campuses continue blatantly to transmit their unambiguously bigoted theme. At the University of Wisconsin, for example, members of the Zeta Beta Tau fraternity conducted a mock slave auction for which they painted their faces Black, wore Afro wigs, and lip-synched Jackson Five songs. At Oklahoma State University, fraternity brothers were costumed as Black slaves who serenaded their sorority sisters as part of a campus "plantation party." At the University of Cincinnati, fraternity members held a Martin Luther King "trash" party where invited guests were asked to bring Ku Klux Klan hoods, welfare checks, large radios, and "your father if you know who he is." At Brown University, fraternity members printed party invitations announcing that only heterosexuals would be welcome. At Arizona State University, fraternity brothers forced Jewish pledges to say: "My number is 6 million. That's how many Jews were killed and I should have been one of them, sir."[20] At Syracuse University, fraternity members distributed T-shirts reading: "Homophobic and proud of it!" and "Club Faggots Not Seals!"[21] At the University of Mississippi, an all-White fraternity left two of its members stranded, bound, and nude at a predominantly Black school twenty-seven miles to the north. Racial slurs and KKK had been written across their chests with a Magic Marker.[22]

According to research conducted by Andrew Merton, professor of English at the University of New Hampshire, college fraternities also serve as a refuge for the worst sorts of sexism. The overwhelmingly macho milieu of the all-male typical fraternity—as expressed collectively in everything from sexist jokes and language to harassment and violence—only reinforces and amplifies stereotyped thinking about women. Rather than regard women as their equals, fraternity brothers typically engage in activities in which females are treated as merely "objects of conquest." Fraternity members build a snow sculpture bearing the image of a woman's breast pierced with a sword; pledges approach a woman and bite her on the breast; fraternity brothers position a woman so that one of them can bite her on the buttocks; members run through a sorority house wearing only jockstraps and Black greasepaint; fraternity members congregate in front of a sorority house to sing an obscene tune and browbeat a young woman who had accused a brother of rape; members of a fraternity share a record of how many beers it should take to seduce certain women on campus.[23] During the 1960s, college students seemed eager to share the American Dream with such nontraditional classmates as people of color, women, and students from other lands. Many young people regarded college not just as a means to a job but as a place to pursue lofty ideals such as beauty, truth, and love. They gladly embraced the "other," donning East Indian and Native American beads and dabbling in Buddhism and other Eastern religions as well as transcendental meditation. By the early 1970s, Yale University's Charles Reich had written his counterculture manual *The Greening of America*, in which he predicted that it was only a matter of time before America became a nation of hippies. The catchwords of the day included love, peace, and tolerance. Reflecting the culture on many college campuses, rock idol Neil Young sang "Southern Man," in which he took Southerners to task for discriminating against Blacks. College students from around the country marched on the capital to voice their support for civil rights, the women's movement, and the antiwar effort.

And then Americans experienced the energy crisis of 1973. Without warning, millions of motorists were forced to stand in long lines to get their gas tanks filled; for the first time, they worried whether they would be able to buy enough oil to heat their homes during the cold winter months. They were concerned also about spiraling double-digit inflation that threatened to destroy the American economy. Interest rates skyrocketed to the vicinity of 21 percent.

So long as prosperity prevailed and the economy was healthy, White male students gladly accepted the increasing enrollment of Blacks and women on their campuses. White men felt a certain unity with these other groups insofar as they were, like minorities and women, at risk. That is, they were draftable and therefore in fear of being sent to a war that many felt was inappropriate, if not immoral. As soon as the economic pie shrank, however, increasing numbers of students began to regard civil rights and feminism with doubt and suspicion.

It could be argued that the college campus is a microcosm of the larger society and, in many respects, it is precisely that. Yet the campus has changed dramatically since the hip era of the 1960s and 1970s. It now represents an exaggerated version of the zero-sum game that we normally expect to find elsewhere. On campus, the competition is fierce and getting fiercer all the time. As the cost of tuition goes up every year and job opportunities tighten, students increasingly see themselves as "soldiers" on the field of battle who must fight for their small share of the economic pie. As a result, students don't always view one another as allies or friends, but as opponents or enemies with whom they must vie for scarce amounts of success both in and out of the classroom. Increasingly, White students regard their minority classmates as the undeserving recipients of financial aid and compensatory programs— what they believe to be special attention and special treatment. Similarly, some Black and Latino students expect to find a racist behind every obstacle to their academic advancement. Moreover, male students resent the challenge posed by a growing presence of successful female students and of gay students who have come out of the closet. And students of many different backgrounds take exception to the increasing number of Asian-American students—all National Merit scholarship winners in high school, at least according to the stereotype. If there is one sociological law, it is that "competition breeds hostility between groups," especially when the economic pie begins to shrink.

On the college campus, this law can be observed to operate in its purest, most dangerous form. Some of the hate incidents at colleges and universities consist of relatively minor pranks—thrill offenses— perpetrated by students with time on their hands and insensitive minds. For example, several Kappa Kappa Gamma sorority members at Stanford University dressed in Indian costumes and parodied "Indian hollers" outside the Native American Center on campus. Seven White students at Brown shouted "Chink, Ching, Chong! Chink, Ching, Chong!" at two Asian-American students as they passed on a street near the campus. To an increasing extent, campus hate attacks have become more defensive; they are committed by students in response to a particular student or campus event that they feel threatened by—Gay

Pride Week, the first Black student in a dormitory, hostilities in the Middle East, and so on. For example, at the University of California at Davis, after an unsuccessful attempt by some members of the student government to reduce funding for a minority-oriented campus newspaper, *The Third World Forum*, two of its Chinese-American reporters received threatening phone calls. Identifying himself only as a member of the Ku Klux Klan, the caller suggested that "something drastic" would happen to them if they did not stop writing for the newspaper. Similarly, a first-year Latin American student at Bryn Mawr College found the following anonymous note slipped under her dormitory door after she had complained about her test grade: "Hey Spic. If you and your kind can't handle the work here at Bryn Mawr, don't blame it on this racial thing. You are just making our school look bad to everyone else. If you can't handle it, why don't you just get out. We'd all be a lot happier."

Ironically, intergroup conflict also reflects growing diversity among students. Over the past three decades, there have been increasing numbers of women, Blacks, Hispanics, Asians, and disabled students, as well as the avowedly gay on campuses around the country. In a situation where everyone has more or less the same background—where almost all students are White, straight, able-bodied, male, and Protestant—intergroup relations are not an issue. Under conditions of increasing cultural diversity, however, the differences between groups become salient on an everyday basis. For the first time, students must learn to deal with classmates and roommates who are *different*.

For most students, whatever their racial identity, college is the first occasion to have extensive contacts with individuals who differ from them in socially significant ways. Because of the pervasive racial segregation that characterizes our communities, most students grow up going to school among only "their own kind." Then they go off to college, where they might meet a broader range of humanity.

Of course, the first few months of college represent a particularly stressful and threatening period. It is often the first time away from home; and students are in an environment where they could fail and be forced to leave. It is difficult to make friends with someone who is different from you when you are terrified of being rejected yourself.

Many students therefore react to this extremely stressful situation by seeking companions who are very much like themselves.

The process whereby students, fearing rejection, befriend other students with similar attitudes and similar life experiences can have another, more negative consequence. A small number of such students make themselves feel more secure by attacking, either verbally or physically, classmates they see as inferior by virtue of that group's background, race, or creed. The very presence of minority students on a campus may provide such an opportunity. At the Citadel, a military college in Charleston, for example, five White cadets wearing sheets and hoods burned a five-foot paper cross in the dormitory room of a Black classmate. One of the first Black students to attend the Citadel, the victim of this prank withdrew from school partly because of the harassment he received from his peers. The five cadets were later indicted by a Charleston County grand jury under a "Klan Statute" for wearing hoods when they entered the Black student's room.

A recent report by the Community Relations Service (CRS) suggests to campus administrators that they must be prepared to respond to hate incidents before they take place. The CRS recommends the formation of a campuswide task force composed of representatives from campus law enforcement, student affairs, counseling and psychology, religious life, public relations, the faculty, and the student body. This task force would be trained and available to respond to incidents when they occur. An important aspect of this proposed approach is the recognition that there are many victims whenever a hate crime is committed. Initially the targeted victim must be helped, often physically and always emotionally. Then the task force must look to support other community members who will also suffer from the trauma of a hate-motivated attack.[24]

Bigotry on campus is more than an isolated event at a single university: minority student athletes across the country frequently face racial epitaphs shouted by opposing fans. This practice became so offensive at one basketball game located at a small New England college that the opposing coach pulled his team from the floor and forfeited the game rather than have his players subjected to further abuse.

Students who attend college to pursue lofty goals and embrace the finest ideals of the mind may regard going to school with different kinds of people as a benefit, even a privilege. In an environment fraught with fierce competition, however, the presence of diversity can represent a *personal threat*. The following flyer discovered hanging on the campus of Brown University epitomizes how some White students now perceive cultural diversity on their campus: "Once upon a time, Brown was a place where a White man could go to class without having to look at little Black faces, or little yellow faces or little brown faces, except when he went to take his meals. Things have been going downhill since the kitchen help moved into the classroom. Keep White supremacy alive!"

ten

MINORITY AGAINST MINORITY: PITCHED BATTLES OF HATE

On February 7, 1992, some four thousand grieving and incensed people attended the funeral of Phyliss LaPine, a thirty-eight-year-old Hasidic Jewish woman who had been brutally murdered after interrupting a burglar inside her Crown Heights, New York, apartment. She and her husband had recently moved with their four young children to this beleaguered Brooklyn neighborhood—home to thousands in the ultra-Orthodox Lubavitcher sect—in order to live in peace and to strengthen their religious ties.

According to the police, the killer followed LaPine into her home, where he stabbed her dozens of times in the chest and neck and then left her to die. When the police arrived at the scene of the crime, they found LaPine's blood-soaked body on the living room floor. Her clothing had been pushed up over her waist in an apparent act of sexual assault.

Although the only eyewitness told police he had seen a White man running from the scene of the crime, members of the Hasidic community were convinced that the culprit was Black, and they were enraged. Religious leaders pleaded with the Hasidic community for restraint, but to no avail. Three hundred Black-hatted and bearded men assembled in front of the local police station to express their outrage and demand an arrest. As a bottle was hurled in the direction of the demonstrators, they shouted "Go back to Africa" and "No more welfare." Three days later, after an intensive investigation, the police arrested Romane Lafond, a twenty-three-year-old Black unemployed handyman who lived a half mile away and charged him with the murder of Phyliss LaPine.[1]

The hostility between Blacks and Jews in the Crown Heights section of Brooklyn has a long history. The precipitating event for open warfare occurred in August 1991, after a seven-year-old Black child, Gavin Cato, was accidentally killed and his seven-year-old cousin injured by an Orthodox Jewish motorist whose car jumped a curb, pinning the children to the wall of an apartment building.

False rumors spread quickly through the Black community that a Hasidic-sponsored ambulance refused to attend to the injured Black children, instead speeding away with the three Hasidim involved in the accident. Unknown to witnesses at the scene, the police had given orders to the ambulance driver to remove the Jewish motorist from the scene in order to protect him from the anger of the crowd. Acting on rumors, a mob of Black youths rampaged through neighborhood streets, shouting racial slogans ("Kill the Jews"). Some of them later retaliated by stabbing to death a twenty-nine-year-old rabbinical student from Australia, who was chosen entirely at random and had no connection to the accident. During three days and nights of confrontations between Blacks and Jews, homes were damaged, cars were vandalized, and dozens of people were injured. For one week, Blacks and Jews exchanged racial epithets and hurled bottles and rocks.[2]

The presence of Black leader Reverend Al Sharpton on the following Tuesday added fuel to the fires of dissatisfaction. Sharpton claimed that Hasidim in the Crown Heights neighborhood had long enjoyed special treatment from the police—immunity from being targeted for investigation and arrest—and that the incident in which young Gavin Cato was killed was just another in a long series. At 6:00 P.M., Sharpton led a rally near the site of Gavin Cato's death. Within minutes, however, the angry crowd dispersed. There was widespread looting and the windows of nearby stores were shattered. People were hurling bottles and rocks, and youthful demonstrators pounded on the doors of frightened Jewish residents.

The history of relations between Blacks and Jews illustrates more generally factors in the development of minority against minority hate crimes. Because of their physical proximity in the neighborhood, Jews are often regarded by local Black residents not as another oppressed minority but as representatives of the White power structure. The visibility of Jewish wealth on the block—for example, Jewish-owned stores and shops—only supports the view that Jews get special breaks from local government not enjoyed by Black Americans in the same community.

Perhaps out of a growing impatience with racial inequality, some Black leaders have promoted hostility between Blacks and Jews. In a recent book, *The Secret Relationship Between Blacks and Jews* commissioned by Louis Farrakhan, leader of the Nation of Islam, Jews were singled out as responsible for exploiting Blacks during the centuries of the slave trade. Yet, according to Henry Louis Gates Jr., director of Harvard University's Afro-American Studies Program, American Jewish merchants were actually responsible for less than 2 percent of the slaves brought to the New World.[3] Gates contends instead that such "pseudo-scholarship" undermines the historical alliance between Blacks and Jews and, at the same time, weakens the moral credibility of Black Americans' struggle against racism.

Although possibly self-defeating, Black anti-Semitism may give us a clue as to the depth of discontent among Black Americans vis-à-vis other groups. One leader, a leader of the Nation of Islam, has called for a restructuring of Black-Jewish relations: "Our relationship to Jews has historically been one of tenant to landlord. We don't always want to be the tenant. We want to be the landlord."[4]

But Jews aren't the only minority in occasional confrontations with Black Americans. Since the 1970s, conflicts between Blacks and Asians have erupted in major cities across the United States. From Washington, D.C., to Philadelphia to Los Angeles, growing numbers of Koreans have taken over retail stores in areas populated by Blacks, who often charge that the Asian shopkeepers do not treat them with respect. Likening the Asian newcomers to Jewish merchants during the 1950s and 1960s, some Blacks similarly resent the fact that Korean immigrants have achieved success so rapidly after arriving on the scene.

In April 1992, the four White police officers involved in the beating of Black motorist Rodney King were acquitted by a predominantly White jury. Violent demonstrations broke out around the country. In Los Angeles, three days of rioting by Black and Latino residents resulted in 58 deaths, 2,400 injuries, $717 million in property damages, and almost 12,000 arrests. Rather than target Whites, however, most of the rioters directed their hostility against Korean stores and shops in the neighborhood. The majority of the more than three thousand Korean-American companies in Los Angeles were damaged, totaling $350 million.

Important differences between Blacks and Koreans account for much of the conflict that separates them. Koreans enjoy a considerable economic advantage because of their middle-class status in the "old country." Long before coming to America, they had already developed the managerial skills, through formal education and family guidance, that are necessary for effective entrepreneurship. To make matters worse, cultural differences make communication all but impossible.

Moreover, the very proximity of Asian-Americans to residences of Blacks and Latinos gives them a special vulnerability. Blacks and Latinos complain that ethnic Chinese landlords in the San Francisco area rent only to Asians. Moreover, not having the economic wherewithal to buy profitable businesses in middle-income or wealthy areas of the city, Asian-Americans instead operate marginally viable stores and shops in the inner city. Koreans are a middleman minority whose members are frequently victimized by members of the dominant group; in addition, they are scapegoats for the anger of Blacks with whom they are forced to compete for small shares of power, wealth, and status.[5]

Blacks have also been at odds with segments of the rapidly growing Latino community. Formerly staunch allies in the battle for equality, these two minorities now tend to see one another as opponents whose members must compete for jobs and political clout. One side charges that Latino immigrants are stealing jobs from low-income Black Americans. The other side contends that immigration laws discriminate against Latino workers. Blacks argue that Latinos are receiving benefits from civil rights victories that Blacks largely won without Latino help. Latinos respond that African-Americans refuse to treat them like equals in the fight for equality. To make matters worse, U.S. immigration policy has *in certain instances* favored Latinos. Whereas most of the would-be newcomers from Haiti have been regarded as economic refugees and repatriated, many Cubans have been treated as political refugees and allowed to stay in the United States.[6]

Ongoing tension between Blacks and Latinos has in cities like Miami, Houston, Los Angeles, Washington, D.C., and New York often provided the basis for political contests at the local level. On occasion, however, the intergroup rivalry has erupted into violent confrontations. Since 1981, at least six different riots have occurred because of tensions between Blacks and Latinos in the city of Miami. In January 1989, for example, two unarmed Black motorcyclists were killed by a Colombian-born police officer who had pursued the pair for a minor traffic violation. Shot in the head, one cyclist died at the scene. His passenger died the next day of injuries suffered when the motorcycle crashed. In response to this incident, Black neighborhoods throughout Miami turned violent. More than two hundred people were arrested as Blacks burned automobiles, looted stores, and threw bottles at the police. At least six people were shot and wounded, two by police officers, as the police returned sniper fire.[7]

In June 1991, Blacks rioted again on learning that the conviction of the Latino police officer responsible for the death of the Black motorcyclists had been overturned by the courts. But the antagonism between Miami's Blacks and Latinos is deeply rooted in economic competition.[8] Cuban immigrants have taken many of the menial jobs—particularly in the tourist hotel business—which had formerly gone to poor Blacks.

In Washington, D.C., the gulf between Blacks and Latinos has widened dangerously. In May 1991, a thirty-year-old Salvadoran immigrant, Daniel Enrique Gomez, was shot by a Black police officer. The policewoman claimed that Gomez had lunged at her with a knife while she was attempting to arrest him. But the word on the streets was that Gomez was handcuffed when he was shot. For two consecutive nights, the streets of Washington, D.C., were filled with angry Blacks and angry Latinos who set fire to buses and cars, hurled bricks, threw Molotov cocktails, and looted stores in the area. The rioting resulted in 225 arrests and $2 million in property damage. Twelve police were injured. Nothing that the rioters did, however, could possibly alleviate the fundamental cause of racial tension in D.C., namely, that growing numbers of poor Latinos are competing with inner-city Blacks for jobs and housing.[9]

The continuing competition between Latinos and Blacks ensured that time would not completely heal the wounds of the past. On the tenth anniversary of the shooting of Gomez, in May 2001, a Black police officer, Stacey Davis, fired his service revolver and hit two Latino men. The incident occurred on Friday evening, May 20, 2001, in Northwest Washington, D.C., when the out-of-uniform, off-duty policeman warned three men about drinking while driving. According to police, the three men got out of their car at a traffic light and pitched beer cans at Davis. When Davis identified himself as a police officer, they assaulted him with a metal pipe and a chair. At that point, Davis fought back, fatally shooting one man in the heart and wounding another in the neck.

Many Latino residents of the 2900 block of Sherman Avenue, where the confrontation occurred, considered Davis's use of force excessive. They also questioned whether his initial involvement was appropriate, given the fact that he was out of uniform and had not been provoked. Some regarded Davis's confrontation as the act of a "vigilante."[10]

On February 11, 2001, a limousine carrying a group of African American tourists through the streets of Washington, D.C., was forced to slam on its brakes to avoid hitting several Latino pedestrians as they crossed directly in front of the car. Stopping their White limousine, the tourists got out and argued heatedly with the Latino pedestrians, exchanging accusations and racial slurs. One of the Black passengers went beyond insulting talk. Taking a handgun from his coat pocket, he shot to death one of the Latino men and wounded three more.[11]

Racial tensions among prisoners have exploded into dangerous rioting. At the overcrowded ten thousand–inmate Los Angeles County jail known as Pitchess Detention Center, there have been more than 150 melees between Latinos and Blacks since 1991, typically set off by unwanted contact between the groups—a Black inmate who uses a telephone designated as a Latino phone, a Latino inmate who eats at a Black table, a false rumor that a Black inmate killed a Latino inmate, and the like. In April 2000, for example, hundreds of Black and Latino inmates rampaged through the facility, battling one another with their fists, knees, and homemade knives. Fighting between the groups continued several days, leaving several dozen men seriously injured.[12]

It is not shocking when a minority perpetrates defensive hate crimes on the members of another group. First, minorities are socialized within the framework of the dominant culture and, just like everybody else in a society, learn the dominant values, norms, and stereotypes. Second, underrepresented groups often develop negative attitudes toward one another as they battle for limited power, prestige, and wealth. In California, for example, the swelling population of Latinos and

Asians has gained political clout, but at the expense of African-Americans.[13] Third, though oppressed groups might be expected in general to express less ethnocentrism, compassion for others tends to remain within each individual's group. That is, whether majority or minority in status, individuals generally have a great deal of sympathy for the plight of *members of their own group*. The trick for those eager to reduce intergroup tensions is to get these individuals somehow to transfer their sympathy and understanding in the direction of the experiences of outsiders. A first step might be to help the representatives of competing groups recognize important areas of commonality between insiders and outsiders—to realize that problems that might be associated with their own group are actually *universal* or nearly so. Too frequently, however, the members of such groups are quick to see important differences and slow to recognize areas of commonality.

Even within the same racial, religious, or ethnic groups, animosity often arises on the basis of criteria that, to the outside observer, might appear inconsequential or even nonexistent. Among the members of that particular group, however, the differences may be regarded as essential. Thus West Indians versus American Blacks, Ashkenazic versus Sephardic Jews, Japanese versus Chinese versus Koreans, all represent *intra*group conflict that is not always obvious to the outsider yet is very real to insiders. Not unlike those that emerge between groups, stereotyped distinctions often develop within a group, sometimes purporting to explain the economic superiority of one segment over another. The more successful members might be stereotyped as arrogant and aloof, while the less successful members might be regarded as lazy and stupid.

Such stereotyped thinking occasionally becomes translated into heinous acts of discrimination. During World War II, for example, tens of thousands of Korean women were literally dragged from their homes and forced to act as prostitutes for the occupying Japanese soldiers. In addition, thousands of Korean men were kidnapped to serve in the Japanese army or work as slave laborers for the Japanese war machine.

In a local community, the animosity may deepen when members of different minority groups compete head-on with one another for the same jobs, live in the same neighborhoods, and send their children to the same schools. As they struggle to improve their social status, minorities may find themselves in fierce competition with the members of other groups who struggle with equal desire toward the same goals. Other minorities may be viewed as enemies rather than allies, as opponents in the contest for scarce resources. Thus the groundwork for intergroup hostility is laid.

Social scientists used to believe that intergroup contact almost inevitably promotes tolerance and harmony, that prejudice is literally a *prejudgment* used by the members of one group to characterize another in the absence of firsthand information. In this way of thinking, people from different backgrounds would like one another if they came to know one another as individuals rather than stereotypes.

Sadly, however, the conditions for enhancing intergroup relations are far more complex than was earlier believed. In some cases, groups whose members get to know one another better also get to despise one another more. For one thing, it doesn't always promote mutual admiration to connect the lower-class members of one group with the middle-class members of another. More often, they come to believe that they share little if anything in common with the members of the other group—that their differences are irreconcilable. It should come as no surprise then that middle-class Koreans or Jews in a squalid inner-city neighborhood may not be universally loved by their Black neighbors.

Even when the members of two groups possess equal status and income, whether they come to live in peace and harmony or go to war depends on the circumstances under which they interact. If one group is perceived as *challenging* the goals of the other, confrontation rather than peace may prevail. If the members of a group are seen as *threatening* the position of another group, then conflict may replace cooperation.

Psychologists Muzafer and Carolyn Sherif long ago demonstrated the link between competition and intergroup hostility in a series of experiments that took place in an isolated summer camp for eleven- and twelve-year-old boys. After a period of time together, the boys attending the camp were separated into two groups and placed in different cabins. When each group of boys had developed a strong sense of group spirit and identity, the Sherifs arranged for a number of intergroup encounters—a tournament of competitive games such as football, baseball, tug-of-war, and a treasure hunt—in which one group could fulfill its goals only at the expense of the other group. Though the tournament had begun in a spirit of good-natured rivalry, it soon became apparent that negative intergroup feelings were emerging on a large scale. The members of each group began to name-call their rivals, completely turning against members of the opposing group, even boys whom they had selected as "best friends" when they arrived at camp.

Muzafer and Carolyn Sherif's experiment didn't end after the competitive tournament that turned former friends into archenemies. Instead, the researchers staged a simple situation to make a point—a situation that required that the two groups of campers *cooperate* in order to achieve a common objective. The boys loved going into the nearby town on Saturday nights. But on this particular evening, the bus carrying all of them "got stuck" in the mud. In order to have a little fun in town, the boys from both groups were forced to put aside their differences—to pile out of the bus and push together to get it going again. Not only did the campers make it into town, but their intergroup hostility subsided as well. Their cooperation toward what the Sherifs call a *superordinate goal*—a common objective—helped reestablish friendships between former enemies. In the Sherifs' classic experiment, we find a ray of hope for the future: Human beings like one another more when they need one another to achieve a common goal.[14]

Competition between economically disadvantaged groups for status, power, and wealth is nothing new. Indeed, America's minorities have historically fought to climb the ladder of success while pushing their rivals off at every rung. At the turn of the century, the conflict grew between Irish and Italian immigrants; during the 1940s and 1950s, it was between Puerto Ricans and Blacks.

Unfortunately, Blacks have become the focal point of the largest number of minority against minority confrontations in cities across the country. In almost every violent encounter, it turns out to be Blacks who have unfortunate confrontations with other groups—Latinos, Asians, or Jews.

It has been accurately observed that the historical experience of Blacks in the United States is qualitatively different from the experiences of almost every other minority group. Only Blacks came to America in chains; only Blacks suffered the indignities of a legal system that forbade them to marry, own books, inherit money, or learn to read or write. Into the twenty-first century, Blacks have been stigmatized by a society that uses skin color and racial physiognomy as a basis for awarding educational and economic opportunities. Now Blacks watch in horror as newcomers from Asia, Europe, and Latin America go around them on their way up the ladder of success. In a radio interview, Nation of Islam leader Don Muhammad summarized the feelings of millions of Black Americans when he suggested that "Blacks have been in America 437 years, and people who have been here 437 days have walked past us."[15]

eleven

HATRED AROUND THE WORLD: KEEPING FOREIGNERS OUT

The voices of xenophobia and racism are once again reverberating throughout German society. The resentment associated with hate crimes can be clearly seen in a sweeping new wave of violence—the largest spree of racial violence in Germany since the early days of Nazism. Almost daily, there are skinhead attacks or public protests against immigrants, foreigners, or Jews.[1] Indeed, some racist skinheads have proudly proclaimed certain neighborhoods in German cities to be "national liberated zones," off-limits to Blacks, Jews, and immigrants who are beaten senseless or killed if they are caught there. Extremist Web sites have published the names and addresses of respectable and prominent liberals they claim are secretly Jewish.[2]

Changes in what used to be East Germany as it struggles to make the transition from a communist to a free market economy have set the stage for violent attacks on refugees and workers from eastern European and Third World countries. Unemployment has remained at 50 percent in some eastern cities, and the collapse of the once tightly controlled communist economic system has made living conditions deplorable. There is a housing shortfall in the major cities. Young Germans watch as their parents lose their jobs, their teachers are replaced, and their old political heroes are arrested. According to Heinrich Sosalla, director of social services in Magdeburg, "Young people are desperate for some sort of new authority." Some find it in a revised version of Nazi activism; they work out their frustrations on a new scapegoat—the hundreds of thousands of foreign refugees who struggle to gain a foothold in their host country.

Five million foreigners reside in Germany, including hundreds of thousands who seek political asylum and almost 3 million "guest workers"—émigrés who are permitted to reside in Germany because they are needed to fill a particular job—and their families, most of whom are permanently excluded from citizenship. In addition, about 400,000 ethnic Germans in the Soviet Union—persons of German ancestry—who return to the fatherland are automatically granted citizenship.[3]

The contributions of newcomers to a thriving German economy should not be underestimated. They provide a cheap source of labor that helps keep industry competitive, spur investments, and revitalize decaying communities. Many newcomers perform jobs that native-born Germans see as beneath them. Moreover, the population of Western Europe is waning and aging rapidly. The presence of large numbers of immigrants ensures that Germany will be able to maintain its current labor force.[4]

All of this is lost on the hordes of out-of-work neo-Nazi German youths who regard newcomers as little more than insects to be crushed underfoot. Since 1990, the targets of violence have remained relatively constant. The majority of victims (60 percent) have been foreigners; the perpetrators are young males ages sixteen to thirty, usually acting in groups.

Extremist assaults began to escalate in the early 1990s. During 1991 alone, there were almost fifteen hundred attacks against foreigners in Germany, but only a handful of convictions. In April 1991, a twenty-eight-year-old Mozambican was killed by a gang of neo-Nazi East German youths who pushed him from a moving trolley in the city of Dresden. In September 1991, six hundred right-wing German youths firebombed a home for foreigners and then physically assaulted two hundred Vietnamese and Mozambicans in the streets of Hoyerswerde.

More recently, normal tranquillity in the East German seaport town of Rostock was shattered by seven nights of organized violence in the streets. Armed with gasoline bombs and stones, a thousand Nazi youths attempted to force out foreigners seeking asylum in Germany. First, the mob firebombed a ten-story hostel in which Romanian Gypsies were housed. Then they stormed the building next door, a residence for Vietnamese "guest workers," and set it on fire. Some six hundred police officers in riot gear used water cannons and tear gas to subdue the crowd. At least 195 Nazi youths were arrested. Police evacuated 115 Vietnamese, and 200 Romanians were evacuated by police and re-located to a former East German army barracks under heavy guard.[5] Within days, the attacks in Rostock had touched off a massive wave of antiforeign violence in at least twenty cities around eastern Germany.

The transition into the new millennium did nothing to quell the numerous violent assaults on immigrants, Jews, and other vulnerable groups. In the year 2000, for example, neo-Nazi groups murdered four people and bombed a Düsseldorf commuter train station, injuring nine immigrants from the former Soviet Union. In a particularly vicious attack, Atiqur Rahman, a visiting scholar from India, was standing alone in a telephone booth in downtown Leipzig when he was confronted by a gang of racist skinheads looking for a foreigner to attack. First the young neo-Nazis took turns beating and kicking the Indian visitor. Then they set their dog on him until he was covered in blood. Rahman's life was spared only because he was able to find shelter in a nearby student hostel.[6] In the same year twelve youngsters in the town of Himbergen wearing brass knuckles and shouting "Sieg Heil" attempted to force their way into the home of a Turkish family. In the same week, four teenage skinheads who admitted they hated foreigners were tried in a juvenile court proceeding for their role in firebombing the apartment of asylum seekers in the Rhine River city of Ludwigshafen. The perpetrators threw a Molotov cocktail through a window that smashed the glass and exploded inside. An eleven-year-old girl was burned; two other children were cut by shards of broken glass.[7]

During fall celebrations marking the tenth anniversary of unification, Molotov cocktails were flung at a synagogue in the western city of Düsseldorf. In the eastern city of Weimar, a memorial bell tower at the former Buchenwald concentration camp was defiled with three Nazi swastikas. In addition, the windows of a Buchenwald museum were smashed. In April, a synagogue in the city of Erfurt, also located in eastern Germany, was bombed by neo-Nazis; in August, a bomb meant to blow up the residence of a former Jewish leader in the city of Bamberg was defused before it could do any harm.[8]

Violence against foreigners and Jews continued into 2001, especially in eastern cities where economic progress has been scant. In Cottbus, for example, a group of right-wing extremists threatened to kill a

Jewish couple. Just days later, also in the town of Cottbus, a gang of racist skinheads, aged seventeen to twenty-four, attacked and injured a twenty-four-year-old asylum seeker and a seventeen-year-old Ukrainian of German descent. The perpetrators were known to the police as troublemakers who had been previously prosecuted for inciting racial hatred.[9]

Also in December 2001, thirty-five hundred members of the far-right National Democratic Party held the largest neo-Nazi demonstration in Berlin since the Third Reich collapsed in 1945. To protest the reopening of an exhibition that documents war crimes perpetrated by the German army during World War II, they tried to march through the Jewish quarter of the city to the exhibition. Instead, the protesters clashed with more than a thousand anti-Nazi demonstrators who hurled stones and bottles and attempted to break through a security line near the city's main synagogue. Dozens of left-wing demonstrators and several police officers were injured, as water cannons and tear gas grenades were aimed at the surging crowds. Some twenty protesters were arrested.[10]

Much of the violence in Germany is perpetrated by a relatively small number of extremists—an estimated five thousand hard-core neo-Nazis and another thirty thousand racist skinheads out of a total German population of almost 78 million. In East Berlin, a chapter of neo-Nazis recruited a few hundred unemployed and alienated young men who give expression to bigotry and racism as a way of "fighting back." Several hundred neo-Nazis from former East German towns met in 1992 to commemorate the death of Hitler deputy Rudolf Hess.[11]

A recent survey reported that 40 percent of the fifteen-year-old residents of Rostock—an eastern German port city particularly hard hit by economic bad times—agree that foreigners are "totally" or "mainly" responsible for unemployment. Skinhead gangs victimize not only immigrants and Jews but also the members of any group—gays, disabled, liberals, and even single mothers—that they associate with the "enemy." The scapegoating motive is lost on those who resent their impoverished status and are looking for a convenient victim to blame. They strike out at the vulnerable, but they really want to attack the economically advantaged West Germany.[12]

Though the perpetrators of violence tend to represent a small proportion of the German people, the degree of resentment in Germany can be easily underestimated. There are actually millions of "silent sympathizers." In a recent national poll, up to 40 percent of all Germans expressed some sympathy for the issues—"Germany for Germans,""racial purity," and "foreigners out"—espoused by right-wing extremists. A survey of German youngsters recently found that more than a third believe that Hitler's regime had "a good side" and nearly 40 percent said that Nazism had its good points. Moreover, 15 percent of Germany's youths said they now consider Adolph Hitler a great man.[13]

Across Europe, xenophobic and anti-Semitic rhetoric has been inspired by a combination of increasingly diverse populations whose members believe they have been left out of a new prosperity. In Germany and surrounding European countries, violence is taught by means of underground Nazi computer games that circulate among high school students. In the game Aryan Test, players are asked to indicate the most effective method for exterminating Jews. The winning answer is to kill them in gas chambers. In the game Concentration Camp Manager, the objective is to kill as many Turks with as little gas as possible.[14]

Thanks to the Internet and the popularity of transatlantic travel, racist music has provided extremists around the world with a common language and a common "pan-Aryan" ideology. When neo-Nazi skinheads recently held a concert in the state of Georgia, it drew racists from England, Spain, Holland, Ireland, France, Canada, and Austria. Racist bands in Poland have sold tens of thousands of their CDs, and 12 percent of Swedish teenagers listen to White power music "sometimes" or "often." Before being banned, German neo-Nazi organizations organized about 180 concerts a year. In European countries White power music has become difficult to obtain because of government intervention; meanwhile, the racist music business in the United States has thrived and prospered from its ability to act as an international distributor of hate.[15]

In France, resentment against its 4 million Muslim Arab immigrants has provoked the government to tighten controls against illegal immigration. Public opinion pollsters report that 76 percent of all French citizens now believe that there are too many Arabs in their country; some 20 percent report feeling an aversion to Jews. Themes involving racist beliefs about North Africans and Black Africans and the threat of immigration—

formerly espoused only by marginal political parties—have entered the political discourse of the mainstream right.[16]

Speeches by the likes of Jean-Marie Le Pen are now filled with neo-Nazi ideology.[17] His right-wing National Front, a powerful if factionalized political force in some regions of France, has called for the eviction of all immigrants. Over the last decade, Le Pen has made his greatest inroads in areas of France having high unemployment and large immigrant communities. But he has also capitalized on widespread anti-immigrant sentiment at the national level, capturing 18 percent of the vote in France's 2002 presidential election.

Le Pen's antiimmigrant position is matched in fervor only by his anti-Semitism. He has openly disputed the authenticity of the Holocaust, dismissing stories of Nazi gas chambers as "historical detail" and has often raised the issue of national loyalty among French Jews. In a widely shown television debate, Le Pen repeatedly asked Lionel Stoleru, a Jewish government minister, whether he held both Israeli and French citizenship. "We have the right to know who you are," Le Pen told Stoleru.[18]

France has also been forced to deal with a rising tide of crimes against Jews. Through the 1980s and into the 1990s, numerous Jewish cemeteries were vandalized. In May 1990, a particularly grisly series of desecrations occurred. At the cemetery in Carpentras in southern France, vandals shattered thirty-four tombstones with sledgehammers and iron bars. They then dragged one woman's body halfway out of her grave and exhumed the body of an eighty-one-year-old man buried only two weeks earlier. As an expression of their disdain, the vandals impaled the man in the middle of his chest with an umbrella to hold in place a Star of David.[19]

Violence against French Jews rose sharply in September 2000, in response to heightened tensions between Israelis and Palestinians and then escalated again in 2001 after the September 11 attack on New York City. In 1998 France had only one serious anti-Semitic attack; in 1999 there were nine. The number of serious acts of violence against French Jews soared to 116 in the year 2000, almost all of them after the Palestinian uprising began in October, and to more than three hundred in 2001.

Some of the inspiration for anti-Jewish violence may have been located in France's right-wing politics and in the failure of left-wing parties to speak out for fear of alienating voters of Arab descent. Most of the recent attacks against French Jews have been perpetrated by Arab immigrants.[20]

In Italy, a traditional haven for newcomers, hospitality has similarly turned from hot to cold, depending on the health of the Italian economy. Whenever unemployment rises, Italians have a tendency to blame the influx of newcomers. Since the early 1990s, hardly a week passes without conflict between immigrants and Italians. In March 1990, for example, a large gang of Florentine youths battered their way into an immigrant dormitory and beat up immigrant workers. In May 1991, a crowd of Italians cheered as the police arrested a group of Albanians who were demonstrating in the city of Asti to protest the living conditions in their refugee camp. Also in May 1991, two Italian workers placed a high-powered air-compression hose into a Moroccan co-worker's anus, destroying his intestines and killing him.[21]

There are between two thousand and three thousand racist skinheads in Italy, who have recently shown renewed vitality. In September 2000, Luis Marsiglia, a teacher from the prosperous city of Verona, was attacked near her home on Monday evening by a gang of teenagers who sported motorcycle helmets. Discovering their Catholic victim's part-Jewish ancestry, the young neo-Nazis beat Marsiglia with metal batons as they shouted anti-Semitic epithets and laudatory comments about Austria's far-right leader, Joerg Haider. Earlier in the year, Marsiglia had received a number of anonymous threatening messages sent to his home by his former students at the Scipione Maffei school, where he taught.[22]

There are about 800,000 legal immigrants in Italy, many of whom hold jobs as domestics and physical laborers. Some Italians argue that, given their country's very low birth rate, immigrants are necessary to the vitality of the economy. But most Italians see the high unemployment rate and argue instead that immigrants are taking their jobs. In fact, 75 percent of all Italians now favor closing the borders to all new immigration.[23]

Even the most homogeneous White-skinned Scandinavian nations have been impacted by the recent arrival of unprecedented numbers of immigrants from developing countries. In Norway, for example, whose people have traditionally enjoyed more than their share of tranquillity and welfare, there are now 200,000 dark-skinned newcomers in a population of almost 4.5 million. The impact of this demographic change has not been lost on the Norwegian electorate. In elections in September 2001 Norwegians ejected the Labor Party, which held the upper hand for eighty years, and replaced it with a coalition supported by the antiimmigrant Progress Party. Moreover, the growing presence of dark-skinned foreigners in Norway's big cities has inspired the Scandinavian version of the neo-Nazi skinhead movement to respond with violence.[24]

On the evening of January 26, 2001, fifteen-year-old Benjamin Hermansen—the son of a White Norwegian mother and a Black Ghanaian father—was stabbed to death on the icy streets of Oslo's multiracial Holmlia suburb. It was almost midnight. Some five hundred yards from the apartment he shared with his mother, Hermansen and a friend, also a dark-skinned teenager, were walking together in a well-lighted area in front of a neighborhood grocery store.

Cruising the area, three neo-Nazi members of a skinhead gang known as the Bootboys spotted the two dark-skinned teenagers. Rushing from the car, they chased the two teenagers down the block and over a fence. Hermansen's friend was fast enough to escape, but Benjamin was not so lucky. Two of the neo-Nazis caught him, knocked him to the ground, and repeatedly stabbed him in the chest, back, and arm. Rising from the ground, Hermansen staggered along for a few yards and then collapsed. He was dead when he hit the ground.

As the economic woes in eastern Europe have worsened, so has the resurgence of racism and anti-Semitism. In Moscow, twenty-five-year-old Zimbabwean student Gideon Chimusoro was fatally shot in the neck by police after he kicked a dog belonging to the owner of a kiosk. When Chimusoro's classmates marched in protest, riot troops clubbed and kicked them to the ground. Some of the African students were pinned against walls and pounded viciously with clubs. Dozens of Russian onlookers, disgusted by the sight of protesting Africans, made obscene gestures at the demonstrators. All of them attended classes at Moscow's Patrice Lumumba People's Friendship University, once a showcase of communist propaganda but now a rundown institution beset with charges of neglect and racism.[25]

In the former Soviet Union, much of the overt hostility against the millions of Gypsy residents that was dormant under communism was given new impetus as eastern European populations struggled to deal with the reality of harsh economic times. Since 1990, many hundreds of Gypsies have been murdered and thousands of their homes destroyed in arsonist assaults committed by neo-Nazi, racist skinhead gangs.[26]

Gypsies living in the Czech Republic have been particularly hard hit by racist violence. In September 1993, for example, eight racist skinheads attacked a group of Gypsies in Pisek, south Bohemia. Out of desperation, the Gypsies jumped into the river Otava to avoid being assaulted but were trapped in the water by their assailants. A seventeen-year-old drowned. In May 1995, four teenagers carrying baseball bats broke into the home of a Gypsy family in Zdar nad Sazavou. In the process of ransacking the house, they beat to death a father of five young children. On the evening of November 22, 1999, a group of Gypsies was celebrating at Prague's Modra hvezda restaurant when more than twenty skinheads attacked. Shouting "Gypsies to the gas chambers, the White race, the Black bastards and nothing but nation," the youthful skinheads threw stones and beer bottles into the crowded pub, injuring six Gypsies and causing considerable property damage.[27]

Gypsies are not the only group to be targeted by citizens of eastern European nations searching for a scapegoat. In Russia, political factions have focused their assault on the small Jewish minority in an effort to force Jews to give up good jobs or to leave the country. Hundreds of thousands have already left; millions more are on their way out. Pro-communist groups have used Jews as scapegoats to explain the demise of Soviet Marxism; anticommunists have blamed Jews for the current state of economic misery. In February 1992, anti-Semites marched through the streets of Moscow, shouting "Beat the Yids and save Russia" and demanding the dismissal of Jews from important public positions.[28]

Given the minuscule number of its Jewish citizens, Poland has a continuing anti-Semitic impulse that seems particularly absurd. In a country of 38 million, there are fewer than 10,000 Jews, most of whom are in their eighties. Yet this fact hasn't diminished the public debate concerning whether or not public officials ought to be required to reveal their Jewish ancestry. Scrawled across Jewish monuments, graffiti to discredit popular Polish figures make false claims that they are secret Jews.[29]

The eighty thousand Jews in Hungary have similarly experienced a revival of anti-Semitic sentiment, even as they benefit from a rising tide of democracy. The demolition of the Soviet Union has allowed a degree of Jewish practice in Hungary unthinkable under the communist order. Hungary has resumed relations with Israel. The central synagogue in Budapest is now filled to capacity on religious holidays. An official memorial to the country's Holocaust victims was dedicated. And the first Jewish secular school is in full operation.[30]

Because some Jews held party positions under the communist system, the new Hungarian version of anti-Semitism is being merged with anticommunism. During the national election in 1990, for example, Miklos Tamas, an important member of the Hungarian parliament, was singled out for harassment. Although Tamas's political party is avowedly anticommunist, it appeals to a broad constituency including many intellectuals, former communists, and Jews. A practicing Protestant whose mother was Jewish, Tamas received at least thirty anti-Semitic death threats by mail and telephone. In one letter, the anonymous bigot wrote, "The place for the Jews is Israel; the place for Dr. Tamas is the cemetery."

During the election campaign, one Hungarian political party sought to exploit anti-Semitism by making veiled references in its radio broadcasts to the "dwarfish minority" that was stealing Hungarian culture from its people. In an article published in the Hungarian socialist press, Jews were told that they must limit their presence in visible occupations—for example, radio, TV, and newspapers—in order to ensure that anti-Semitism would not increase. Socialist columnist Gyorgy Domokos wrote, "They must be careful that the number of Jews does not dominate."[31]

Paul Bookbinder, professor of history at the University of Massachusetts in Boston, suggests that the old Soviet regime—by means of police state tactics and extremely tight controls—had long suppressed overt expressions of anti-Semitism. According to Bookbinder, "Anti-Semitism had no place officially in communist ideology and, in fact, was specifically opposed by early creators of the communist movement. From 1919 through the 1930s, anti-Semitism was against the law in the Soviet Union, and people were prosecuted for distributing anti-Semitic propaganda or committing acts of violence against Jews."[32]

Bookbinder contends that the Russian government was generally passive in its reaction to bigotry. If it seldom singled out Jews for harassment, the Soviet system did even less to attack the centuries-old underlying roots of anti-Semitism. Under communism, bigotry lay dormant but never disappeared, and it festered among many elements of the population. In the wake of the disintegration of the Soviet Union, eastern Europeans were free for the first time since the Russian Revolution to express openly their beliefs and feelings about many things. Thus, when the tight controls were lifted, anti-Semitism burst loose with a vengeance.

To some extent, violence directed against newcomers may reflect an enduring mixture of such irrational factors as racism, ethnocentrism, and xenophobia. Regardless of the state of the economy at any given point in history, certain members of society—especially those who can trace their own ancestry in a country back several generations—are bound to be offended by, and seek to remove, the strange customs, rituals, and appearance of "inferior outsiders."

At the same time, however, antiimmigrant and anti-Semitic violence also may have a more "rational" political and economic basis. During periods of economic retrenchment, it sends a powerful message to foreigners and minorities from those who seek to reduce competition for jobs. Hate violence says to everyone and anyone who might consider emigrating for the sake of a better standard of living: "Your kind is not welcome in *our* country. Don't bother to come. If you do, the same thing will happen to *you.*" And to minorities, it says loud and clear: "Go back where you came from . . . or else."

As a form of collective scapegoating, hate violence serves a purpose for the rulers of a nation as well. Sociologist Lewis Coser once referred to this phenomenon as a "safety valve." He suggested that when times are bad, hostility that might otherwise be directed at the leaders of a society—its king, president, prime minister, senators, and so on—is instead aimed squarely at its marginal members, those located along the bottom-most rungs of the socioeconomic ladder. By focusing blame on the "outsiders," the rulers of a society are able to preserve their positions of power, even if their policies and programs are in fact responsible for pervasive economic hardships.

twelve

POLICE RESPONSE: TRAINING, CULTURAL SENSITIVITY, INTERNAL MONITORING, AND TAKING A HARD LINE AGAINST HATE CRIMES

A swastika is spray-painted on a synagogue; a rock is hurled through the window of a Black family that recently moved into an all-White neighborhood; a man perceived to be gay is assaulted, an Arab convenience store owner finds his front window smashed and a note telling him to go back to his own country. When a hate crime occurs, the local police department is generally the first governmental agency to be notified. The victims of the hate crime, most often members of a minority group, call the police because they are afraid and because they hope that local law enforcement officials can do something to prevent future threats to their well-being. The police, on the other hand, often find themselves in an awkward position. In some minority communities, *they* are perceived not as allies or protectors, but as major violators of civil rights; in other communities the police are viewed simply as outsiders by local leaders who wish to handle all problems internally.

Not without some justification, the minority community across the United States has long viewed the police as oppressors. During the era of Jim Crow, it was the local police who enforced the rigid segregation laws in the south, who prevented Blacks from sitting at "Whites only" lunch counters or riding in the "Whites only" front section of the bus. In the north, the police also played a major role in supporting segregation, if not as openly as in the south. Apparently in the interest of keeping the peace, they enforced unwritten rules of conduct that kept Black youths out of White neighborhoods, except in the role of servants. Of course, the police never attempted to keep White shopkeepers from doing business in Black neighborhoods. Most importantly, the preferred method of enforcing this segregation on the minority community was through the use of violence. Black youngsters who "didn't understand" were frequently taken to the local police station and "taught a lesson," a lesson often driven home by a beating. The attitude of local law enforcement officials during this period of oppression may best be summed up in the words of a White local sheriff who, in the film documentary *Eye on the Prize*, spoke about violence toward a member of the Black community: "Son, it's mind over matter. I don't mind and you don't matter."

Minority hostility toward the police peaked during the mid–1960s, when a number of cities erupted in violence. In August 1965, a White California patrol officer stopped a young Black motorist for an equipment problem in the Watts section of Los Angeles. The young man appeared to be drunk, and the officer arrested him. Jaded by years of police hostility toward the Black community, Black onlookers misperceived this incident as biased. When the police left the scene, members of the crowd began throwing rocks at cars and setting them on fire. A few White drivers were pulled from their automobiles and beaten. Before the force of the riot was blunted thirty-six hours later, there had been thirty-four deaths, hundreds more injured, $35 million in property damage, and four thousand arrests.[1]

The disorder in Watts marked the beginning of a period of burning and looting that swept across the country. By the end of 1967, riots had ignited in many urban minority neighborhoods including Jersey City, Atlanta, Philadelphia, Los Angeles, Cleveland, Newark, Boston, and Detroit. The majority of these violent outbursts were ignited by police incidents, frequently routine arrests of Blacks for minor offenses by White police officers. In July 1967, for example, the police in Newark arrested a Black cab driver whose license had been revoked for several previous accidents. At 9:30 P.M., residents of a high-rise public housing project watched as the cab driver was dragged kicking and screaming from a police car into the front door of the police station across the street. Rumors spread quickly that he had been a victim of police brutality and that he was either injured or dead. Hundreds of people gathered in front of the station house to protest. By midnight, the crowd grew unruly. Several Molotov cocktails were thrown at the station. When the police attempted to disperse the crowd, hundreds rampaged through the streets, breaking the windows of shops and stores and looting their contents. The Newark riots resulted in twenty-three deaths and $10 million in property damage.

As a result of this wave of urban unrest, President Lyndon Johnson formed the National Advisory Commission on Civil Disorders to study the causes of violence in the major cities and to make recommendations for changes that would reduce the likelihood that such violence would recur. The commission confirmed that one major factor contributing to urban violence was the deep hostility between the police and inner-city residents.

An important area of tension between the police and the minority community has been police use of disproportionate deadly force under questionable circumstances. Serving as a catalyst to unprecedented rioting on the streets of Los Angeles, the case of Rodney King is only one highly publicized example. On March 3, 1991, the twenty-five-year-old Black motorist was stopped by Los Angeles police officers, taken from his car, and beaten. A two-minute videotape secretly shot by an amateur photographer showed King lying on the ground as officers took turns swinging their nightsticks at him and kicking him in the head. King sustained extensive injuries including skull fractures, a broken cheekbone, a shattered eye socket, and a broken leg. The videotape depicted the beating by four officers and, even more shocking, between ten and twenty officers who stood by and made no attempt to stop the violence.

Though the officers who participated in Rodney King's beating were later acquitted in a criminal trial, the Christopher Commission, an independent panel headed by former Undersecretary of State Warren Christopher, determined that racism and excessive force were a major problem within the Los Angeles police department. Some officers in patrol cars, the commission discovered, sent racist and sexist messages over police computers to describe their encounters with Black residents: for example, "Don't cry Buckwheat, or is it Willie Lunch Meat" and "Sounds like monkey-slapping time." In an exchange made the same evening King was stopped, two of the officers later indicted for the beating of the Black motorist sent a message referring to a domestic argument in a Black household as "right out of 'Gorillas in the Mist.'"[2]

In another well-known case, in August 1997 New York City police officer Justin Volpe beat and sodomized Abner Louima in the bathroom of a New York City precinct house. Officer Volpe and his partner had been called to a disturbance at a local Haitian club. Upon arriving, they stopped and questioned Louima. When they decided to arrest him, the officers allege that Louima punched officer Volpe and tore his shirt. The suspect was then driven to a deserted location and beaten by Volpe who wanted to teach him never again to hit a police officer. Unfortunately, Officer Volpe was not yet finished. He and his partner then brought Louima into the men's room of the precinct house, where they inserted a wooden stick into his rectum, tearing his colon and causing massive internal injuries. Doctors who treated Louima were totally amazed that he did not die from loss of blood. After initially denying that this attack happened, Volpe finally pled guilty and was sentenced to thirty years for the beating and torture. In July 2001 the city of New York agreed to an $8.75 million settlement with Louima.

In the aftermath of the beating of Abner Louima, "New York's finest" was not able to avoid the controversy surrounding excessive force. In February 1999, the street crime unit of the New York City police department encountered a twenty-four-year old West African man, Amadou Diallo, who was coming home late at night. When the officers called for him to stop, Diallo made the fatal mistake of reaching for his wallet to show his identification, which would prove the fact that he was trying to enter his own apartment. Operating under false assumptions, the officers thought that he was reaching for a gun. In response, the police fired forty-one shots at Diallo, hitting him nineteen times and killing him.

Clearly charges of racism and excessive violence in police response have not been confined to Los Angeles and New York City. In Toronto, the local police slaying of a young Black Canadian man, Raymond Lawrence, precipitated a spree of window smashing and looting.[3] Lawrence was shot twice in the chest by a White police officer after a lengthy chase through the downtown area of Toronto. According to police reports, the twenty-two-year-old Black man had first threatened the officer with a knife so that the policeman had no choice but to protect himself; Black leaders argued instead that excessive and unnecessary force was used. What began as a protest against racism was transformed quickly into a riot. Four hundred young people, Black and White, paraded down the city's main thoroughfare, breaking hundreds of store windows and snatching merchandise.

Similarly, in Vineland, New Jersey, scores of Black and Latino protesters engaged in a night of rioting and looting after a local Black man was fatally shot by a White police officer who attempted to arrest him on outstanding warrants for possession of a handgun and assault. The twenty-four-year-old shooting victim, Samuel Williams, had tried to outrun the officer on foot but was chased down in a gravel pit. According to the police, Williams still refused to surrender, instead attacking the officer with a heavy metal bar. At this point, the policeman fired his weapon and Williams dropped to the ground.[4] Critics argued that excessive force had been used and pointed out that only one member of the one hundred–member Vineland police force was Black.[5] In February 2002, seven police officers from the Montgomery, Alabama, police department resigned, and four officers went on administrative leave after allegations that they participated in a pattern of excessive force, including assault and the use of mace. In each case the victim of brutality was Black.[6] In Teaneck, New Jersey, a sixteen-year-old Black youth was shot to death by a White policeman, touching off a candlelight vigil and a night of violence involving local teenagers who charged police harassment. Two police officers had responded to a 911 call that reported that a youth holding a handgun was seen hanging out with his friends in a schoolyard in a predominantly Black section of the town. When the police arrived on the scene and attempted to search him, the teenager suddenly bolted by running down a driveway behind the school and hopping a hedge. One of the policemen shot him in the back.[7] In Long Beach, California, a Black civil rights advocate claimed that a White officer beat him and then slammed his head through a window in a routine traffic stop. Adding to the credibility of the victim's account, the entire encounter was secretly recorded by a local television news team and played on national television.[8]

A number of studies have documented the discriminatory use of deadly force against minorities, both nationally and in selected cities. A national review of citizens killed by police from 1965 through 1969 found that 42 percent were Black, 13 percent Latino, and 2 percent Asian or Native American, numbers much higher than would be expected by either population rates or arrest rates.[9] In Miami, a study of citizens killed by police between 1956 and 1983 revealed that the majority of the victims were Black, at a time when the Black population of Miami never exceeded 20 percent.[10] Racism and violence have historically combined to produce feelings of distrust and suspicion of the police on the part of the minority community. These perceptions, in turn, may prevent victims of bias-motivated violence from coming forward to report these crimes.

Because the police themselves are already suspected of being prejudiced, it is essential that police departments develop policies and procedures for handling bias-motivated violence as part of an overall effort to be responsive to victims of hate crimes. Unfortunately, however, most police agencies around the country do not treat hate crimes as seriously as they should. A recent survey of police chiefs reported in 2000 by the Center for Criminal Justice Research for the Justice Department concluded that the majority of police chiefs across America felt that many hate crime victims do not report the incidents because they distrust the police. It is important to note that these comments came from police leaders themselves. The study also concluded that most American police agencies still do not include hate crime training as a normal part of their recruiting or in-service training programs, since they believe that hate crimes are not a problem in their communities.

In contrast, progressive police departments across the United States, although few in number, have recognized the harm that hate crimes can cause in their communities. These departments have taken a number of steps to improve the identification and investigation of hate offenses. Indeed, some have developed a specific departmental policy for handling all hate crimes that are reported to them, have assigned specialized units to investigate these crimes, and have developed training programs for all officers in techniques for the proper identification of hate crimes.

In departments that have developed hate crime investigation policies, their procedures specify the steps that must be taken by all police personnel under their jurisdiction whenever a possible bias-motivated crime is committed. The key elements of such policies include designating who within the police department should be notified and when. They require that officers complete and maintain certain records and outline procedures to be followed with the victim.

In the Baltimore County police department, for example, the official hate crime policy requires that the responding officers notify their immediate supervisor first and their second-level supervisor before the end of the shift. This policy also requires that a formal police report be filled out in all cases that could be bias motivated. This report must be reviewed by the supervisor and forwarded to the hate crime investigating unit of the department. In most police departments with such a policy, the initial incident report must be submitted by the responding officer within twenty-four hours of receiving the call from the victim. Finally, these policies require that a supervisor contact the victim, in person, shortly after the incident occurred. The supervisor is required to take all precautions necessary to protect the victim from further harassment.

Hate crime policies are important to the extent that they send a strong message both to the victim and to the officers in the department. By requiring that a report be written and a supervisor play a personal role, the department gives notice that these are indeed serious crimes and are to be treated as a high priority. Many departments, however, still do not have a formal policy in place. A recent national survey by the Bureau of Justice Statistics found that only 45 percent of the departments across the country had a hate crime policy in place.[11] In addition, by requiring a supervisor to contact the victim to follow up on the investigation, the department communicates to the victim that it understands that these crimes are serious and that the local police cares about the victims and the difficulties that they may be experiencing. Again, very few departments designate any special procedures for their supervisors to follow while handling hate crimes.[12]

As with all governmental policies, a hate crime procedure is only as good as the department's overall commitment to fighting hate crimes. If a department develops a hate crime policy but does not take steps to ensure that it is implemented in good faith, the policy will be meaning-less. To date, most police agencies have not adopted a hate crime pol-icy. As more police departments develop such formal procedures, it will be up to community residents to ensure that they are being fully imple-mented.

An analysis by the Uniform Crime Reporting (UCR) section of the FBI concluded that the most successful strategy for investigating a hate crime is to employ what the FBI calls a two-tier investigation process.[13] This procedure involves two levels of response by the local police de-partment to a crime that may be motivated by prejudice. The first re-sponse is by the officer who receives the initial call for assistance from the victim; the second or follow-up response comes from a specialized unit or officer who has responsibility for investigating all hate crimes in that particular jurisdiction and has been trained to properly identify them. The FBI now recommends this two-tier response strategy to all law enforcement agencies, regardless of their size, for investigating any crime occurring in their jurisdiction that may be motivated by bias or bigotry. Even in smaller departments where hate crimes are fairly rare, it is important to have a designated hate crime officer, even if this offi-cer has additional responsibilities.

In departments that do not have such a specialized unit or officer, the victims of bias-motivated violence are too often overlooked when they ask police for help. Previous research in Boston indicates that nonspecialized officers, for a number of reasons, fail to properly iden-tify hate crimes. Some blunder because of their own bigotry, others be-cause they are not trained to ask the appropriate questions. Inexperienced and untrained officers, for example, may not think to ask the Black family that has just had a rock thrown through its window if it has also been the recipient of any bigoted threats or racial slurs. In Boston, a group of officers refused to identify certain offenses as hate crimes because they felt it was in the victim's best interest not to do so. As one officer explained it, "I know we have a strong case of assault here, but if I bring up civil rights the case will get bogged down and we might lose it because it is harder to prove a hate crime."[14] Actually, one accusation does not preclude another. Trained officers would under-stand that both charges—assault *and* a civil rights violation—could be brought, leaving the court with the responsibility for determining the guilt on both counts.

One type of evidence that should be collected but frequently is missed is the offender's use of language. Language is the most frequent indicator of bias motivation in hate crime cases. In order for a prosecutor to convince a jury that the incident was motivated by bias, the exact language used by the offenders must be included in the original police report. Sometimes officers are reluctant to include certain racial slurs in their formal written report. One Massachusetts police officer wrote when describing an attack on a Black man, "During the course of the attack the perpetrators called the victim the 'N' word." This may seem like a small error, but it hampers the prosecutor's case. Once the officers are told that it is acceptable, in fact important, to record the exact language used in the attack, they do so.

In addition to specialized units, *all* officers must be trained in the proper methods of identifying hate crimes. The failure of an officer to properly identify an incident as hate motivated sometimes results in escalated violence and additional harm to the victim. Say, for example, that someone slashes the tires on an automobile belonging to an Asian family that recently moved into an all-White neighborhood and the police treat it as a "prank" that doesn't warrant investigation. Because the police don't know to ask whether there have been prior incidents of harassment, the offender might easily be convinced that the police will look the other way. This belief may "empower" the offender to escalate the violence against the victim, under the assumption that "the police don't care about those people any more than I do."

A number of model hate crime training programs are already in place across the country. Three of the best-known are the FBI's Hate Crime Training program, the Anti-Defamation League's Training for Law Enforcement and the National Hate Crime Prevention Center's Hate Crime Training for Law Enforcement. The curriculum and target audiences for these training programs are very similar. All are directed at local police officers and first-line supervisors who may come in contact with victims of hate violence. And all include sessions aimed at understanding prejudice and increasing police awareness of the cultural differences within the minority populations of the local community.

Most training programs begin with a session that attempts to explain to the officers how prejudiced attitudes are formed, how stereotypes are used to bolster prejudice, and how prejudiced attitudes and discriminatory actions are interrelated. These sessions are frequently taught by a member of a local advocacy organization or a local university professor, and are in many cases the first time the officers, many of whom lack any postsecondary education, have been exposed to formal instruction in the socio- and psychodynamics of prejudice and discrimination.

Such training programs also deal with cultural differences; specifically, different traditions and beliefs shared by the minorities who live in the local area. In these sessions, such differences are discussed, often by members of the minority community. In one program, for example, members of the Southeast Asian community presented problems they had encountered in interacting with the police in the past. One common complaint was based on a cultural difference in expressing deference and honesty. Strictly as a sign of respect, a particular Southeast Asian victim of violence—while in the process of reporting a hate crime—may refuse to look the police officer directly in the eye. Drawing on American cultural norms, traditional police investigation manuals cite a victim's inability to look an officer in the eye as an indicator that the victim may not be telling the truth. The officer in question therefore assumed that the Asian victim might have lied. Once this cultural difference was explained to police officers, they understood that the Southeast Asian victim they interviewed had attempted to show the officer respect and turned out to be telling the truth.

Another problem in dealing with the Asian community arises from the vastly different nature of the criminal justice system in their country of origin. As some Asian hate crime victims have explained, when the police in Cambodia or Vietnam came calling, it was invariably to report bad news. In addition, corruption was rampant in some Southeast Asian countries, where offenders routinely escaped punishment by paying off local officials. When Asian victims see the American system of bail, where money is exchanged to guarantee the defendant's return to court, they frequently think that they are again witnessing the corruption encountered in their homeland, where the police sided with the offender. As a result, many Asian victims are reluctant to assist the police in their investigation of hate crimes, believing the police corrupt.

In a recent training another example of potential cultural conflict came to light. Apparently in Cameroon the common practice of responding to a traffic stop is to leave your vehicle and go to the officer. This is a sign of respect, not defiance. In addition, many people from Cameroon carry their wallet in their sock. A number of potentially dangerous incidents have occurred in which immigrants from Cameroon were stopped by the police in the United States. Rather than wait for the officer to approach, they got out of their car and, while walking back to the cruiser, reached into their sock for their wallet and license. Police in the United States are likely to interpret this behavior as threatening and may pull their gun or worse. But once police are informed about this cultural practice among Cameroon immigrants, they may be relieved to have a better understanding of what they saw as a dangerous situation.

A number of training sessions bring victims of hate crimes to meet the officers. Having victims of bias-motivated violence speak to the officers about the impact of the crime on their lives can be a powerful technique in helping police understand the importance of the role they play in protecting hate crime victims. At the Anti-Defamation League, for example, a panel of victims relate the experiences they have had during their victimization and subsequently when they sought the assistance of the police. Retired Deputy Superintendent Bill Johnston, commander of the Boston police hate crime unit, believes that this component is essential: "We may not be able to change an officer's bias in the course of a single training session. Our experiences would suggest that these individuals got into policing to help people who were victims of crime; and if you can show them that hate crime victims need their help, that might make the difference the next time a victim comes forward."

Identifying a hate crime is an issue that all hate crime training sessions for police must tackle. Traditionally, many hate crimes have gone uninvestigated, simply because the police officer responding to the crime did not think of bias as a possible motive for the incident. In learning how to identify a hate crime, the police must understand that the victim is not always a reliable indicator of whether or not any particular offense is motivated by bigotry. Discussions with victims have indicated that many of them look for reasons other than their group membership to explain their victimization. These victims feel particularly vulnerable because they carry the cause of their victimization around with them wherever they go. If people are attacked because they are Black or Asian, then there is nothing they can do to reduce the likelihood of an attack happening again. Whatever they do and however they behave, they will always be Black or Asian. Training sessions stress that the investigation by the hate crime unit or officer should determine whether a crime is in fact motivated by bias.

The FBI training sessions list a number of indicators that responding officers should consider in determining whether or not an incident is bias motivated. These factors by themselves do not indicate that any given episode was a hate offense, only that additional investigation may be necessary. For example,

- that the offender and the victim were of different racial, religious, ethnic/national origin, or sexual orientation groups.
- that bias-related oral comments, written statements, or gestures were made by the offender, which indicate his/her bias.
- that bias-related drawings, markings, symbols, or graffiti were left at the crime scene.
- that the victim is a member of a racial, religious, ethnic/national origin or sexual orientation group that is overwhelmingly outnumbered by members of another group in the neighborhood where the victim lives and the incident took place.
- that the victim was visiting a neighborhood where other hate crimes had taken place or where tensions are high against his/her group.
- that a substantial number of people in the community where the crime occurred perceived that the incident was motivated by bias.
- that the incident coincided with a holiday relating to or a date of particular significance to, a racial, religious, or ethnic/national origin group.
- that the offender was previously involved in a similar hate crime or is a member of a hate group.[15]

The final sessions of most hate crime training programs for police generally include strategies of how to investigate this type of offense. These sessions stress that most of the victims of hate crimes do not know the identity of their attackers. At least in this respect, therefore, hate crimes differ from many other crimes of violence in which there is a prior relationship between offender and victim.

Training sessions need to make police officers aware that the motivation for all hate offenses is not the same and that the investigation will differ depending on the type of hate crime being probed. If, for example, investigating officers suspect that a thrill hate crime has been committed, they should anticipate that the perpetrators are *likely* to be a group of males in their teens or early twenties probably without a criminal record who live some distance from the immediate crime scene. If, however, the police suspect that the hate crime is defensive, they might instead anticipate that the offenders are *likely* to be young adults who live or work close to the crime scene—for example, in the same neighborhood or company as the victim. Also, the police should recognize that the offender's bigotry may be widely shared by other residents of the neighborhood (or by co-workers), many of whom may see the victim as threatening their property values or their chances of being promoted. Thus information about the circumstances of the crime may be unusually difficult to obtain by normal interviewing procedures. Finally, if the police encounter what they believe to be a mission hate crime, they should anticipate that members of organized hate groups—for example, White Aryan Resistance, the Klan or a local skinhead group—may be involved, or the offender may have a history of severe mental illness and may very well consider taking his own life.

The most essential lesson for police officers is that in order to be effective, they must put increased effort into hate crime investigations.[16] If the police are to resolve these incidents by arresting the offenders, they will need to conduct a complete investigation, such as is done in a homicide or a rape, and they will need the continued support of the victim. This latter element, continued victim support, is frequently a major stumbling block in hate crime investigations. Research in Boston indicates that many victims ultimately withdrew their cooperation during the course of the police investigation.[17] Some misunderstood the way the American criminal justice system operates; others were reacting to threats from the offenders or from the offenders' friends. Therefore, the police are encouraged to offer victims substantial support to increase the likelihood of their continued participation in the case. This support could include giving a precinct phone number to the victim in case of any further incidents, placing the victim's home on a regular patrol route, and stopping by the victim's home once a week to update him or her on the progress of the case.

Recognizing that many members of the minority community distrust or fear the police, some local police agencies have begun to work with existing advocacy organizations in their communities to present programs that emphasize the rights of minority citizens and the steps that the police can take to protect these rights. This lack of prior contact has been particularly troubling in the aftermath of the September 11 attack on America. As already noted, Middle Eastern residents in many communities around the country were subjected to a great deal of harassment and violence. When the local police attempted to react to these incidents, it became clear that there were very few existing partnerships between the police and Arab religious or community leaders.

The Japanese American Citizens League has outlined a series of strategies that can be effective in community outreach programs generally.[18] The league suggests that such programs should distribute pamphlets or educational videos that explain to community members what their rights are and define the police role in guaranteeing these rights. The police should also organize community forums in the minority neighborhood to explain what they will do for victims of hate-inspired violence. All too often, the police hold a program on the rights of citizens at police headquarters and then complain when attendance is low. If the police want these programs to work, they must go to the neighborhoods where victims live in order to make clear to potential victims that they are committed to protecting victims' rights. Other outreach components recommended by the league include civil rights programs at local schools. The Boston police department currently presents to all public school fifth graders a program in which a hate crime investigating officer discusses the constitutional rights of the students and their families. A final suggestion from the Japanese American Citizens League for outreach activities is to have police representatives participate in the ethnic or religious celebrations of local minority groups. This is a particularly useful approach because the police and minority group members have an opportunity to see each other enjoying themselves, something that rarely, if ever, happens in the course of normal interaction between the two groups.

It is particularly important that the police reach out to members of the gay and lesbian community. Because many victims of gay bashing have not revealed their gay lifestyle to their friends and family, they are extremely reluctant to come forward and report violence to the police. In addition, the police have traditionally been major violators of the civil rights of gay and lesbian victims. One gay victim of a hate crime in a Massachusetts suburb who was dressed in drag when he was attacked was forced to wait in a cell before being sent to a hospital, while the officers who were out on patrol got a chance to come in to the station and "take a peek." In order for gay and lesbian victims to feel comfortable enough to approach officials, the police must first go to members of the gay and lesbian community to explain that they will no longer condone offensive conduct and to discuss what protection the police can provide. Gay hate crime victims have long been among the most difficult groups for the police to understand. Possibly because the stereotype of the gay man is antithetical to the macho image that many police officials project, the latter have trouble dealing with the gay community.

One final component in an integrated approach for police to deal with hate crimes is a continued commitment to affirmative action programs. The single most significant policy the police can adopt over the long term to combat hate crimes is to bring in to their ranks more women and minority officers. It is generally more difficult to harbor prejudice against individuals who are different when you find yourself working side by side with them *toward a common goal*. This is not to say that today's affirmative action programs are working well or are without costs. It is, however, clearly in the long-term interest of all police agencies to represent the communities they serve more adequately than they presently do.

A Department of Labor study found that police agencies were doing better in bringing in minority employees than the civilian labor force in general. In fact, 12.6 percent of the police forces are Black compared to 11.3 percent of the labor force nationally and 12 percent of the population.[19] In addition, the diversity within police agencies has increased rapidly in recent years with the percentage of Black officers growing from 9.5 percent in 1983 to 12.6 percent in 2001 and the percentage of female officers rising from 5.7 percent in 1983 to 14.1 percent in 2001.[20]

Bringing minority officers into the force has an additional benefit, according to some research. An analysis of the 1981 Miami riot found that Black officers felt far less alienated from the minority community than their fellow White or Latino officers.[21] If the police departments are to be believed when they say they want to help victims of bias motivated violence, their staff must be representative of all the groups found in their local community. In Boston a recent survey of community leaders suggested that having police who reflected the diversity of the community increased the community's trust in the police overall.[25] The presence of Black police officers at the scene of an arrest of a Black suspect may help to defuse the charge of racism that frequently precipitates an angry response from community members.

Frequently scared and angry, the victims of hate crimes are typically in need of help. The first official agency that they are likely to contact is the local police. In the past, the police have too often regarded such calls for help from members of their community as mere nuisances to be disposed of with the least possible effort or to be ignored altogether. Some police responded out of bigotry; others lacked knowledge or sensitivity. In addition, the appropriate organizational supports for dealing with hate offenses were often missing from police procedures.

To an increasing extent, however, police departments around the country have enlarged and modified their procedures for dealing with hate crimes. In response to a growing demand for their services, some police agencies have provided training in the area of hate crimes and have charged particular members of their staff with the specialized role of responding to hate offenses. Moreover, as a result of affirmative action legislation, larger numbers of minorities and women have been hired by police departments in many jurisdictions.

Conflict between the police and minorities will probably never be eliminated, but it can be reduced to a considerable extent. Although still far from ideal, the part played by police officers in responding to hate crimes has improved over the past few years. It is true that many police agencies continue to ignore attacks motivated by bias or perhaps even play an obstructionist role. But increasing numbers of police departments have chosen to move in another direction—they have risen to the challenge posed by a rising tide of hate crimes around the nation. We hope to see much more of the same in the years to come, when it will be sorely needed.

thirteen

PUBLIC POLICY AND THE LAW: HOW HATE CRIMES ARE PROSECUTED AND INTERPRETED

When the police are fortunate enough to make an arrest in a hate crime case, the next decision is how to charge the offender. This judgment is most often made by the prosecutor with jurisdiction over the crime: the U.S. attorney for violations of federal law and the local prosecutor for violations of state law. The decision about which criminal violation to charge can drastically affect the processing of a case by increasing the potential penalties and thus raising the stakes for the offender. An offender who is facing an enhanced penalty because his breaking of a window was motivated by hate is more likely to obtain an attorney and refuse to plead guilty, thus causing the local prosecutor significantly more work. The decision to charge a crime as a hate offense will also raise the interest of community leaders and the media. For example, if a fight occurs between two groups of high school–age youths in a local community, the crime—assault—is generally not considered newsworthy. If, however, the two groups are from different races, one White and the other Black, the decision about whether to charge the crime as a hate offense is news and will involve not only the prosecutor and the victim but also the mayor and the local office of the NAACP and other area human rights groups as well. What is more, the crime will likely be reported as the lead story on the eleven o'clock news.

Legislation intended to punish acts of hate violence can be either federal (dealing with violations of constitutional rights) or state (resulting from violations of a particular state law). Conducted by the

National Institute Against Prejudice and Violence in Baltimore, an analysis of laws dealing with bias-motivated violence concluded that there are four main categories of federal remedies for crimes motivated by bigotry.[1] The first federal statute regulating bias-motivated behavior was passed by the U.S. Congress and forbids conspiracies intended to interfere with an individual's enjoyment of his or her civil rights. This statute has been used, for example, in cases where a group of White neighbors conspired together to prevent a Black family from moving into their community.

One such case happened in an apartment complex during the summer of 1989 in Coon Rapids, Minnesota. On the morning of August 11, several White residents of the complex, a group of close friends and neighbors, gathered as they often did at a picnic table outside the home of Bruce Roy Lee. Over beer and pretzels, they discussed what ought to be done about fighting that had recently erupted between Black and White children in the apartment complex. At about three o'-clock in the afternoon, one of the residents, Werner Jahr, mentioned that he had read an article recently about the Ku Klux Klan's methods of dealing with Blacks who live where they are not wanted. Just as the Klan would have a cross burning, so, he said, should the White residents of their apartment complex. Bruce Roy Lee took his neighbor's advice to heart. At about ten o'clock that night, he put on dark clothes and crept out to a small hill about four hundred feet from the apartment complex. There, he placed a wooden cross that he had fashioned earlier in the day and set it ablaze.

Although Lee was upset that his cross burned only for a few minutes, it stayed lit long enough to be seen by its intended victims, the Wilsons, a Black family that lived in the apartment above Lee's. Telling her husband, "I hope they don't come up here and burn us up," Mrs. Wilson became extremely agitated and upset.

Lee later talked about the incident with a neighbor, to whom he explained that he felt compelled to take a stand. From his point of view, the cross burning was a warning "that would get rid of some of the bad Blacks that were there. They would take the message seriously and leave."[2] After a thorough police investigation, however, the Wilsons remained in their apartment. Both Lee and Jahr were arrested and eventually convicted in federal court of conspiracy to deny civil rights.

Responding to a series of violent attacks on civil rights workers in the South, the second federal statute, "Forcible Interference with Civil Rights," was enacted in 1968.[3] This statute prohibits individuals from interfering with anyone who is exercising his or her constitutionally guaranteed rights and has been used to prosecute individuals who by force or threat of force interfere with such public rights as enrolling in a public school or eating in a public restaurant.

Known as "Deprivation of Civil Rights Under Cover of Law," the third federal statute concerns actions committed by public officials—most often the police—who intend to deprive an individual of his or her constitutional rights. It is this statute that the U.S. attorney in Los Angeles County employed to prosecute the police officers who beat Black motorist Rodney King. These officers were acquitted of assault charges in California state court, after the trial had been moved to the predominantly White community of Simi Valley. Following their acquittal on state charges, however, the accused officers were then indicted by a grand jury in federal court, not for assault but for violating the civil rights of Rodney King while the officers were acting under the "color of law."

The final federal civil rights statute, "Willful Interference with Civil Rights Under the Fair Housing Act," prohibits any interference with an individual's right to buy, rent, or live in his or her home. This act has been applied in cases of firebombing and shots being fired into a home where these actions were motivated by prejudice.

Although such federal statutes seem to cover a broad range of behavior motivated by bigotry, they are rarely applied. A study by the Southern Poverty Law Center found that between 1987 and 1989, the entire U.S. Department of Justice had prosecuted only thirty-one federal cases of racial violence, most of which involved housing discrimination.[4]

One reason for the small number of federal hate crime prosecutions is that, in practice, the federal remedies are extremely limited. They only protect citizens who are threatened or attacked while they are exercising a federally protected right, such as buying a home, renting an apartment, eating in a public restaurant, or riding on public transportation. Unfortunately, many of the activities that victims are engaged in when they are attacked are not included among these federally protected rights.

An additional limitation of federal statutes at present concerns the variety of groups protected by the remedy. Most federal statutes apply only to actions motivated by racial or religious prejudice, thus excluding from protection a number of victim groups, including those who are attacked because they are perceived to be gay or lesbian.

As noted earlier, the U.S. Supreme Court has ruled on the constitutionality of one type of hate crime legislation. On June 22, 1992, the Court struck down a St. Paul, Minnesota, hate crime ordinance on the grounds that it singled out certain topics of expression for prohibition while leaving other topics of expression legal.

Two years earlier, a Black couple from St. Paul, Russell and Laura Jones, awoke to discover that someone had burned a two-foot cross in the front yard of the single-family home they had recently purchased. Within a few weeks of the cross burning, authorities in St. Paul charged two White teenage boys, one of whom lived across the street from the Joneses, in connection with the incident. According to the police, one of the boys had asked a group of his friends "if they wanted to cause some skinhead trouble" and "burn some niggers." He explained that "lighting a cross has been passed down [as a tradition]. If it's lit in somebody's yard, they're doing something you don't like or that you want stopped—like living in your neighborhood."[5]

One of the defendants pleaded guilty and received a sentence of thirty days in jail. The second defendant pleaded not guilty and then challenged the St. Paul statute under which he had been charged as being unconstitutionally broad. This statute provides that

> Whoever places on public or private property a symbol, object, appellation, characterization or graffiti, including but not limited to a burning cross or Nazi swastika, which one knows or has reasonable ground to know arouses anger, alarm, or resentment in others on the basis of race, color, creed, religion, or gender, commits disorderly conduct and shall be guilty of a misdemeanor.

The court agreed with the defendant and dismissed the complaint against him, saying that the St. Paul statute was overly broad and could infringe on free speech rights. The state then appealed the ruling to the Minnesota State Supreme Court, which reversed the lower court decision. The State Supreme Court ruled instead that the statute in question may have been constructed in an overly broad fashion, but that a narrow interpretation was still possible. It recommended that such a narrow interpretation be applied in the St. Paul case as follows:

> *Although the St. Paul Ordinance could have been more carefully drafted, it can be interpreted so as to reach only those expressions of hatred and resorts to bias motivated personal abuse that the first amendment does not protect.*[6]

The Minnesota cross-burning case didn't end at the state level. The decision was appealed to the U.S. Supreme Court, which accepted the case for its 1992 term. As already noted, the Court decided that the Minnesota statute was unconstitutional because it protected only a limited set of intolerant expression; for example, actions intended to arouse anger, alarm, or resentment based on sexual orientation were not covered by the ordinance.[7]

The Supreme Court decision suggested as well that existing vandalism and malicious destruction of property statutes provided enough protection for the Jones family, making the Minnesota ordinance unnecessary. Unfortunately, this ruling fails to recognize that crimes motivated by bias differ considerably from other offenses in terms of their impact on the victim as well as the community.

The Supreme Court decision notwithstanding, the St. Paul cross-burning episode emphasizes the need to recognize the particularly harassing nature of hate crimes. Like acts of terrorism, they send a message not only to the particular victims of an incident, but to all members of the victims' group and in fact to all minority groups who live or work in the area. To burn garbage in a neighbor's front yard may involve vandalism, trespassing, or both. But burning a cross is much worse: its symbolic association in the past with organized hate gives it the status of a widely recognized sign of violence and brutality—an intention to do harm to its victims. In response to the St. Paul incident, Russell Jones told his wife, "We are being told we had better get out of here or something bad is going to happen." This is precisely the message that the teenagers who burned the cross were attempting to send.

The Court's decision applies only to the St. Paul ordinance, which has been declared null and void. It is not at all clear, however, in which direction the Supreme Court will proceed in the future. The Minnesota statute was widely believed to be unconstitutional because it was too broad. In fact, a number of Supreme Court justices who concurred in the judgment argued that the overly broad nature of the statute, and not its selectivity, should have been the basis for striking it down. In this view, the St. Paul statute could have been invoked to prohibit a broad range of activities historically protected by our First Amendment right to free speech. However, the majority on the Court chose to challenge the law based on the fact that it singled out some minority groups for protection and not others. In the future, if the same standard should be applied to other types of hate crime legislation, many other state and federal statutes will be in jeopardy. More recently, courts in Maryland, New Jersey, and South Carolina have struck down state cross-burning statutes, whereas courts in California, Florida, Virginia, and Washington have upheld theirs.[8]

The largest number of criminal prosecutions by far occur at the state level. According to Bureau of Justice statistics, only 4 percent of all offenders convicted and sentenced to prison in 2000 came from the federal court system.[9] Similarly, most hate crime prosecutions occur at the state rather than the federal level. More progressive and dynamic than its federal counterpart, state legislation has been changing at almost monthly intervals in response to a new realization of the harm these crimes can cause in a community. According to a review of hate crime statutes by the Anti-Defamation League of B'nai B'rith, forty-nine states currently have some sort of hate crime legislation; only Wyoming does not.

The most common type of hate crime statute in place at the state level deals with institutional vandalism. Such laws prohibit vandalism and defacement of a variety of locations and institutions, including houses of worship, cemeteries, schools, public monuments, and community centers.

The following cases are examples of the crimes prohibited by institutional vandalism statutes:

- At the University of Mississippi, a building that was to house the first African-American fraternity was destroyed by arson.
- In Dayton, Ohio, two individuals threatened to shoot worshipers at a local Islamic Center. Later that night, several windows at the mosque were broken.[10]

- In San Francisco, the front windows of four Arab-American-owned food stores were smashed. The vandals hurled flashlight batteries and a fire extinguisher through the plate glass window.[11]
- In Denver, Colorado, gunshots were fired at a grocery store owned by a Libyan-American. Previously, someone threw a box through the store window. The owner has since taken down the Arabic sign and a sign that says "Middle East Grocery Store."[12]
- The home of a Black family in Bucks County, Pennsylvania, twice was firebombed. The second bombing destroyed everything the family owned; they barely escaped with their lives. The bombings were preceded by vandalism and harassment incidents.[13]
- A Catholic church, a Catholic cemetery, and three homes of Catholic families were vandalized in Corry, Pennsylvania, and more anti-Catholic vandalism incidents were reported in the town.[14]

Institutional vandalism statutes are in place in thirty-six of the forty-nine states with some form of hate crime legislation. There is a broad range of penalties attached to these statutes, with some states designating such crimes as misdemeanors and several others designating them as felonies.

Another common type of state hate crime statute across the country cover "bias-motivated violence and intimidation." These laws, in effect in forty-one states, make it illegal to intimidate, harass, trespass on the property of, or assault an individual because of that person's race, religion, national origin, or (in several states) sexual orientation.

These statutes are intended to prohibit the most violent hate crimes, which include the following examples:

- In Temperance, Michigan, after an African-American family received numerous threatening telephone calls, their thirteen-year-old son was chased down the road by White youths wielding car jacks, and their nine-year-old daughter was chased into a ditch by a car also driven by White youths.[15]
- An African-American woman was injured as she and her two children fled the path of a pickup truck in Taylorsville, North Carolina. Three White males in the truck yelled racial slurs and

swerved the truck toward the family. On the third pass, the truck cut off the woman's path of escape and then left the scene when another vehicle approached. The woman fell twice, sustaining injuries to her elbow that required surgery to reset the bone and repair arteries.[16]

- An African-American man was killed in Halifax, North Carolina, after being terrorized with a six-foot long boa constrictor, beaten with a stick, punched and stabbed by a White male and female.[17]
- In the Crown Heights section of Brooklyn, following the death of a young Black child and the murder of a twenty-nine-year-old Jewish scholar, a series of incidents occurred, including the following series of attacks on Jewish residents:
- Two men received serious slash wounds. Another man beaten by a crowd of youths suffered a broken collarbone and a concussion.[18]
- Another man was pulled from his car and beaten; another car was surrounded by a mob that smashed the windshield with a concrete block, injuring one passenger.[19]
- Another individual was severely slashed in the face with a broken bottle, requiring reconstructive surgery.[20]
- In Denver, Colorado, an Arab student leaving a store was beaten up because of his appearance. As a result he dropped out of school and returned home to the United Arab Emirates.[21]
- In Philadelphia, a mob of nearly one hundred Whites gathered at the home of the Williams/Bloxom family in November. The Black family had moved into a White neighborhood. The family left Philadelphia, and one month later four White arsonists destroyed their vacant home.[22]
- In Washington State, a Black teacher in Federal Way reported that, over a period of four years, he received 150 hand-delivered racist notes, his classroom was vandalized twice, and he received two fake bombs through the mail.[23]

Recent developments in intimidation laws are occurring on two fronts; first, in states that are passing such statutes for the first time and, second, in states with existing intimidation statutes that are attaching sentence enhancements—additions to the potential sentences that can be applied to certain specific cases—to their existing penalties. Previously employed in cases of gun crime and crimes committed by "career criminals," sentence enhancement statutes work by allowing the sentencing judge to increase the penalty that he or she would impose under specified conditions. In Michigan's firearm enhancement statute, for example, if a felony is committed with a gun, the judge is allowed to increase the penalty by up to two additional years. In Oregon, if intimidation is motivated by prejudice or bigotry, the severity of the offense is increased from a class B to a class A misdemeanor.

In most cases the passage of hate crime legislation comes only after a long battle over the issue of which groups deserve protection as victims of civil rights violations. The most recent instance of a sentence enhancement was the James Byrd Hate Crime Act signed into law by Texas Governor Rick Perry on May 11, 2001. Earlier versions of this law had been proposed in the Texas legislature for each of three previous years and had failed. Interestingly, the reason provided for not passing the law previously included the fact that the statute offered protection for gay and lesbian citizens. In addition, some argued that hate crimes were no different from other crimes and should not have additional penalties. This second reason was given by Governor George W. Bush when he opposed the bill. It took a national outcry from citizens after one of the most heinous hate crimes ever committed, the dragging death of James Byrd, to convince the Texas legislature to pass this hate crime law.[24]

An additional characteristic of enhancement statutes is that the legislation frequently specifies that the additional penalty cannot be served until the original sentence has been completed. These "on and after" provisions effectively guarantee that the offender will actually serve additional time for violating the sentence enhancement provision.

New Jersey has a typical enhancement provision. In its sentencing structure, crimes are grouped together by degree: first degree crimes, second degree crimes, and so on. But if a crime is bias motivated, the next-highest level sentencing provision becomes available to the judge. For example, if a fourth degree crime is committed and it is determined that the crime was motivated by bigotry, a judge may sentence the crime as if it were a third degree offense.

Most states that employ bias-motivated violence and intimidation statutes cover hate crimes based on religion, race, or ethnicity. At present, fewer than half of the states with such statutes extend their protection to victims of violence based on their sexual orientation. More specifically, only twenty-seven states include violence against individuals perceived to be gay or lesbian under their bias violence and intimidation laws.[25]

An increasing number of states are extending the protection of these statutes to individuals attacked on the basis of their gender. Twenty states now offer such protection, and a number of others are considering expanding the scope of their statutes to include gender hate offenses. Senator Joseph Biden, who chaired the proceedings investigating Anita Hill's allegations against Clarence Thomas, has also held U.S. Senate hearings to consider the use of hate crime statutes as a further protection for female victims of violence. Other groups specified in the legislation in various states include attacks against disabled individuals, attacks based on political affiliation, and attacks on members of labor unions.

A third category of state statutes prohibits interference with religious worship. Such laws, in place in twenty-one states, make it punishable to disrupt an ongoing religious service or to steal a scroll, a religious vestment, or other object normally used in a religious service.

Crimes covered by such statutes include the following:

- The New Bethel African Methodist Episcopal Church in Alton, Illinois, was repeatedly burned down by arsonists.[26]
- Two synagogues in Dayton, Ohio, were desecrated with spray-painted swastikas.[27]
- A Frederica, Delaware store being converted into a church by a Puerto Rican group was damaged by fire believed to be arson. A few days afterward, the words "KKK, We're going to burn it down, be careful" were spray-painted on the storefront.[28]
- In Spokane, Washington, the Christ Holy Sanctified Church was bombed. In the wreckage, literature from the Aryan Nations was found.[29]

Sixteen states have statutes that make it a criminal offense to burn a cross or other religious symbols. These laws differ according to whether the cross is burned on public or private property. In some states, a cross may be burned on private property with the owner's permission. In these states, it is permissible to burn a cross on your own property or on a neighbor's property if you have that neighbor's permission. These states view burning a cross as a protected First Amendment right of free speech. And our present Supreme Court agrees.

Cross-burning statutes developed as one of a series of measures designed to disrupt Ku Klux Klan activities. For the members of this organized hate group, the burning cross has served two purposes: (1) to send a message to the members of a minority family (most often a Black family) that they were not wanted in a town or neighborhood and (2) to be used as a ceremonial initiation as part of a ritual of violence, just prior to a Klan-committed lynching. As a result, the burning cross continues to strike fear in the hearts of many minority victims. It was, in many instances, a sign that an innocent Black man was about to be murdered. Many fear that it still is.

In general, cross-burning statutes are designed to counteract situations like the following:

- A six-foot cross was burned in the backyard of an African-American man and his three young children in Temperance, Michigan, after he received numerous threatening telephone calls.[30]
- In Gastonia, North Carolina, a wooden cross was wrapped with rags, laid on the hatchback window of an African-American family's car, and ignited. The burning cross destroyed the car at the family's home in a mostly White neighborhood into which the family had recently moved.[31]
- A cross was burned at the Carr home in Daytona Beach, Florida. The Carrs were the only Black family in the neighborhood.[32]
- A cross was burned at St. Mary's Abbey in Wrentham, Rhode Island. On the next night, forty windows were smashed at a Cumberland school, which also was vandalized with anti-Semitic graffiti.[33]
- In Grand Prairie, Texas, when a Buddhist temple was established, men dressed in KKK-type robes or army fatigues harassed the worshipers by burning a cross in full view of them.[34]

With the single exception of Minnesota, no state cross-burning statutes have yet been invalidated by the recent U.S. Supreme Court decision concerning the St. Paul ordinance. According to the Court's reasoning in that case, however, these statutes would seem to be in the most serious jeopardy of all hate crime legislation. If the logic in the Minnesota case is applied to cross-burning state statutes, only the few laws that do not list a particular set of "protected groups" (e.g., Blacks) will withstand constitutional scrutiny. Because the vast majority of state cross-burning statutes do identify a set of protected victims, they are potentially vulnerable to future challenges.

In many southern states, another type of anti-Klan statute prohibits wearing hoods, masks, and disguises. On the books in fourteen states, such laws seek to limit the activities of the Klan by requiring that members of organized hate groups not hide from prosecution behind their hoods. (This discussion of hate crime statutes and legal decisions presents an overview of important issues. For a more in-depth discussion, please see the excellent work by Frederick Lawrence and Brian Levin.)

In theory, hate crime statutes provide a legal remedy for victims of bias-motivated violence. For such laws to be constructive, however, prosecutors must effectively charge defendants, juries must convict them, and judges must sentence offenders to an appropriate punishment. Little systematic research has been done on how hate crime cases have been processed through the courts. Unfortunately, according to research that does exist, the present system for processing hate crime cases frequently breaks down. The arrestees may not be charged under hate crime statutes and, even when they are, may never be convicted in a court of law. Moreover, when the prosecution obtains a conviction, judges often do not know what to do with the offenders. Should they serve additional time? Provide restitution to the victims? Be forced to take appropriate courses? Or what?

A study that addressed court processing of hate violence reviewed 452 hate crimes that had been reported to the Boston police between 1983 and 1987.[35] Following cases through the criminal justice system to their final resolution, the researchers obtained results indicating that few cases ever got to court and fewer still were sentenced to a prison term.

From the sample of 452 cases reported to the police, sixty cases resulted in arrest (some of these remained under active investigation at the time of the report), representing an arrest rate of 15.4 percent. It should be noted that the Community Disorders Unit of the Boston police department has been cited as a national model of hate crime investigations, and arrest rates elsewhere are frequently lower.

Of the sixty cases that ended in arrest, thirty-eight resulted in formal charges being filed. Several of the twenty-two cases not charged were dropped by the prosecutor's office because it felt the evidence was insufficient to sustain a conviction as a hate crime. Several other cases were diverted by the prosecutor's office, by means of an agreement with the offender that he or she would do a certain amount of community service or attend a particular program.

Of the thirty-eight cases formally charged in court, thirty were convicted, a rate slightly lower than in other comparable cases. Finally, of those thirty convictions, only five cases resulted in an individual being sentenced to a term of incarceration. The Boston experience seems to demonstrate that hate crime offenders are very unlikely to face punishment. Out of 452 incidents over a five-year period, only five individuals went to jail!

One reason for the low probability of punishing hate crime offenders is the tendency for prosecutors to look for the perfect case when a new statute is enacted. Specifically, they seek an incident in which clear references about the motivation for the crime are made in front of reliable witnesses, and the offender has previously engaged in a pattern of bias-motivated violence. Even prosecutors who are strongly committed to eliminating hate violence frequently fear that if they lose the first case brought under a new statute they will render the law ineffective for future prosecutions. In an effort to prevent losing the first case, then, a prosecutor may reject a series of cases because they are not strong enough to guarantee a conviction. During this transitional period, a large number of victims who have good but not the strongest cases may be turned away. In Massachusetts, where a state civil rights act was passed in 1979, the first case brought under the statute occurred more than one year later. Moreover, as recently as the year 2001, police officers charged with investigating hate crimes in one Southern California county refused to bring any hate crime cases to court because the prosecutor had not accepted a single hate crime case for the past four years.

The same sort of reluctance to prosecute can develop when a statute is applied in a new way to a previously unprotected group. In a number of states, for example, prosecutors are presently looking to extend the protection of hate crime legislation to women who are attacked because of their gender. Not unlike their response in the case of new statutes, many of these prosecutors seek the perfect case of gender bias, one they are sure they can win. This leaves women whose cases are not "perfect"—where there are no eyewitnesses to the crime and the offender doesn't make his motivation clear—without the protection of hate crime legislation.

One of the most common misconceptions about hate crimes is their frequency. A comparison of the incidence of reported crime from various jurisdictions reveals that hate offenses are relatively rare. In New York City during 2000, for example, there were 400 hate crimes (referred to as bias crimes in New York City),[36] while at the same time there were 673 homicides, 1,630 forcible rapes, 40,880 aggravated assaults, and 32,562 robberies.[37] In fact, hate offenses made up only 0.005 percent of the personal crimes of violence that were reported to the New York City police department in 2000. In Boston, a similar pattern emerges. In 2000, there were 177 hate crimes,[38] compared to 39 homicides, 325 rapes, 4,507 aggravated assaults, and 2,451 robberies.[39] The proportion of all crimes of violence reported to the Boston police accounted for by hate crimes was much higher than in New York City but remained a relatively low 2 percent of the total.

Looking at the situation on a state level, we see a similar pattern. In Florida during 2000, 269 hate crimes were reported to the police,[40] compared to 127,991 crimes of violence. Thus hate offenses composed merely 0.002 percent of all violent crime.

We make this point to demonstrate an additional problem in the prosecution of hate crimes—how unusual it is for a particular prosecutor or judge ever to see a bias-motivated offense. The small number of reported crimes is exacerbated by a low arrest rate as well. Because most hate crimes are committed by offenders who are strangers to their victims,[41] these are among the most difficult crimes for the police to solve. The arrest rate for bias crimes in New York City was 23.9 percent.[42] In Boston, it was 21 percent.[43] Over a twelve-month period, this resulted in 261 individuals being arrested in New York City and 62 in Boston. Thus, when a judge is deciding on the appropriate sentence for a hate crime offender, he or she probably has little prior experience on which to base a decision. Facing uncommon territory, aware that America's prisons are dangerously overcrowded, and facing a controversial case, judges may decide to take the easy route—give the offender probation and let the probation officer decide what to do with him.

Sentencing decisions in hate crime cases are frequently influenced by media attention, though this has not always been true. During the early part of the century, Black rape victims in southern states were ignored by the public, the police, and the courts. By contrast, a crime that is motivated by bigotry is currently considered "big news." Local as well as national media frequently follow all aspects of a hate crime case. Even the demonstrations and rallies convened by hate organizations are often deemed newsworthy. On August 16, 1992, for example, a KKK rally in the streets of Janesville, Wisconsin—a blue-collar town of some 60,000 near the Illinois border—attracted no more than one hundred White power advocates and a similar number of anti-Klan counterdemonstrators. But local television stations and newspapers from both Milwaukee and Madison were interested enough to send reporters to the scene. On the national level, Geraldo Rivera was there as well. When Geraldo punched a Klansman who harassed and assaulted him, virtually every TV station around the country aired the tape. So did CNN and *Entertainment Tonight.* Even the *National Enquirer* ran a cover story. According to *Geraldo* producer Bill Lancaster, "the hate groups represented at the rally in Janesville usually don't get along. The significance of this meeting was that they set aside their differences, in order to unite in a common cause: an ethnic cleansing of America."

By placing an incident like a Klan rally in the spotlight, the media may influence the decisions of judges and prosecutors who are sensitive to public opinion. A local prosecutor may think twice about the adverse publicity he will surely receive in deciding to drop the charges. A judge who comes up for reelection may feel pressured to impose a severe sentence, so as to avoid being attacked as "insensitive." The net effect is to push for treating hate offenses in a more serious manner, so that more severe sanctions are applied.

Media attention may also have educated a growing number of people about the occurrence and character of hate crimes. Currently, one of the most common hate crime laws consists of statutes requiring the collection of data about hate-motivated incidents. According to the Anti-Defamation League, as of 1991, twenty-one states had data collection statutes in place.

During the spring of 1990, in an attempt to remedy the problem of inconsistent reporting by individual states and to provide higher quality national data on hate crimes, the U.S. Congress passed and President Bush signed into law the Hate Crime Statistics Act. Supported by a bipartisan coalition in Congress, this law calls on the U.S. attorney general to acquire data "about crimes that manifest evidence of prejudice based on race, religion, sexual orientation, or ethnicity, including where appropriate the crimes of murder, nonnegligent manslaughter, forcible rape, aggravated assault, simple assault, intimidation, arson, and destruction, damage or vandalism of property." The act also requires that the attorney general publish an annual summary of the data acquired under the provisions of the act.

The Hate Crime Statistics Act does not criminalize any bias-motivated behavior or increase penalties for such offenses. It requires only that the attorney general obtain data on crimes motivated by bigotry. From the point of view of a number of the advocacy groups that sponsored the legislation, the goal of the act was to set the stage for beefing up both state and federal legislation by collecting more and better information on bias-motivated activity across the United States.

Before passage of the Hate Crime Statistics Act, there was no national public data source on the extent or characteristics of hate crimes. The two major national crime data collection sources, the FBI Uniform Crime Report and the Bureau of Justice Statistics National Crime Survey, did not include hate crimes among the criminal incidents on which they collected information.

Some private organizations have collected hate crime information in past years and continue to do so. Nationally, the Anti-Defamation League has conducted the *Audit of Anti-Semitic Incidents* since 1979, in which it records information on all anti-Semitic attacks and vandalism reported to regional ADL offices. In addition, the National Gay and Lesbian Task Force Policy Institute has issued an annual national report since 1985, *Anti-Gay/Lesbian Violence, Victimization, and Defamation*, detailing instances of antigay violence in major U.S. cities. A third organization, the Southern Poverty Law Center in Montgomery, Alabama, has collected information on the activities of organized hate groups and reported this information in its publication *Intelligence Report*.

Before the passage of the Hate Crime Statistics Act, these alternative sources of information on bias-motivated violence constituted the only national reservoir of information on hate crimes. Their effectiveness was limited by the fact that each group collected information only on a particular area of bias-motivated violence; for example, the ADL collects information only on anti-Semitic incidents, whereas the Gay and Lesbian Task Force collects information exclusively on antigay/lesbian violence.

A second limitation involves the consistency and reliability of the data across groups. Each organization has its own particular data collection regulations and procedures that do not necessarily conform with those of the other organizations. As a result, there are significant areas of inconsistency when information from different sources is compared. For example, the National Gay and Lesbian Task Force accepts reports of antigay hate crimes from anonymous sources while the ADL does not.

The Hate Crime Statistics Act sought to reduce issues related to coverage, consistency, and reliability, publicly collecting all hate crime information in a single format by a single agency: the Uniform Crime Reporting Section of the Federal Bureau of Investigation. The U.S. attorney general designated the FBI as the agency responsible for collecting hate crime data and, following the model in effect in the Uniform Crime Reports, the local police agencies as the data providers.

The FBI was a controversial choice as the federal agency designated to implement a civil rights act. After all, it was pointed out, the FBI itself has been associated in the past with major violations of civil rights. As recently as 1991, for example, the agency came under fire for discriminatory treatment of its Hispanic agents, a charge that culminated in a class action lawsuit. Despite its checkered history with respect to civil rights, however, two years after the passage of the act, members of the FBI directed to implement it have received high praise for their efforts from advocacy groups such as the NAACP, the ADL, and the Gay and Lesbian Task Force.

In August 1992, Senator Paul Simon of the Senate Judiciary Committee held hearings on the implementation of the Hate Crime Statistics Act. As the original sponsor of the legislation in the Senate, Simon wished to learn how the national data collection effort was going. He was told by a number of witnesses that the implementation was going well but that the undertaking was more complicated than originally anticipated and thus would take longer to complete. Because the Hate Crime Statistics Act did not require local police agencies to submit their hate crime data, many agencies were slow to comply. The two major reasons for this reluctance were budgetary constraints and a lack of awareness about hate crimes in general. It should be noted that no funds were provided by the Hate Crime Statistics Act to either the FBI or local police agencies.

Although the FBI couldn't do anything about the financial burden on the local police, it attempted to increase awareness of hate crimes in law enforcement. In training sessions for representatives of all fifty states and the two hundred largest U.S. cities, FBI staffers taught how to identify, investigate, and report hate crimes. Trainers also sought to sensitize police officials to the importance of taking seriously all hate crimes in their community. Senator Simon's committee was surprised to learn that increased awareness on the part of local police as a result of FBI training, rather than the actual collection of data about hate crimes, has been the most significant contribution of the Hate Crime Statistics Act.

A study of the implementation of the Hate Crime Statistics Act during its first ten years by McDevitt et al. found that significant problems with the collection of hate crime statistics still exist. This study discovered that although many law enforcement agencies nominally participate in hate crime data collection, the vast majority of agencies have never reported a hate crime in their jurisdiction. A review of the reporting practices revealed that only 18 percent of the agencies "participating" in the Hate Crime Statistics Act reported that a hate crime had occurred in their jurisdiction during the previous year. Although it may be true that many small communities do not have a hate crime in a given year, the FBI report included many large cities and entire states that reported no hate crimes in the previous year. The report recommends additional training and auditing of agencies where hate crimes might be expected but are not reported.

An additional debate has developed around the need for legislation pertaining to hate crime. A number of critics have suggested that legislation based on a perception of increasing rates of hate violence is misguided. James Jacobs at NYU and his associates have recently argued that those who suggest that hate offenses have recently increased are creating a "social construction" lacking any basis in reality. They suggest that journalists, politicians, and academics all agree that the incidence of hate crimes is "at an all-time high," ignoring a history of institutionalized slavery and genocide and undeterred by a total absence of any reliable evidence. In the view of Jacobs and his colleagues, academics have constructed "an unprecedented hate crime epidemic."

The social constructionist perspective has been extremely valuable in shedding light on exaggerated claims in such areas as missing children, serial murder, and drug abuse. For decades, sociologists have suggested that what becomes regarded as a social problem need not actually be true. People talk about it, believe the allegation, and then cover it on television and radio and in the press. When a significant number of people do this—especially people who are organized and have influence, we have something we call a social problem.

Jacobs and his associates deserve credit for sensitizing us once again to the possibility that our estimates of trends in hate crimes have been out of proportion to the changing reality. Few would deny that the measurement of hate crimes has been plagued with difficulties. For example, because legal definitions are in flux and additional law enforcement agencies are constantly being added to those who report to the FBI, the national data from one year to the next are frequently difficult if not impossible to compare. In addition, as Jacobs points out, much of the data collected on an annual basis have been reported by advocacy groups such as the Anti-Defamation League and the Gay and Lesbian Alliance, making them subject to the criticism that such organizations have a vested interest in generating inflated figures.

Despite such limitations, it may still be possible to gain some perspective as to changes in the prevalence of hate crimes over time. Based on data collected by various advocacy groups such as the ADL, the Southern Poverty Law Center, and the Gay and Lesbian Alliance, it is likely that hate crimes increased throughout the decade of the 1980s and into the early years of the 1990s.

Why should we believe it, you ask. Well, first, this conclusion agrees with evidence gathered by independent research organizations concerning hate incidents generally. The National Institute Against Prejudice and Violence in Baltimore found, for example, a dramatic upsurge in 1989 in racial and anti-Semitic incidents on college campuses around the country. At the same time, sociologist Gary Spencer reported a growth of JAP (Jewish-American princess) baiting on his campus, Syracuse University, as well as on other campuses around the country.[44] Spencer's observations coincided with those of a professor of English whose 1990 research suggested that a new form of "attack comedy" aimed at the most downtrodden and least fortunate members of our society was on the rise.[45] Finally, antigovernment militias and survivalists—groups almost totally unheard of before 1980— made their presence increasingly known throughout the 1980s and into the 1990s. Although many militia members disavow any connection with hatemongers, there is at least some overlap between militia groups and White supremacists.

Certainly, reports of ethnic violence lend support to the suggestion that hate crimes have been on the rise. Reports of escalating violence in the early 1990s directed against Jews and immigrant groups remain essentially undisputed for many European countries, including France, Germany, England, Poland, Italy, Russia, and Hungary. In these nations, there were dramatic increases in violent skinhead and neo-Nazi demonstrations or in the prevalence of political bigotry.

A second factor in evaluating the validity of the argument that hate crimes are on the increase involves the issue of research bias. All data about social and political phenomena are collected by either individuals or organizations consisting of human beings who come to the research situation with their own personal biases and preconceptions. Feminist methodology wisely requires that the researcher make explicit the details of his or her biography, so that the reader can place into proper perspective the results of any study. Every individual who does research, whether or not holding membership in any particular advocacy group, can be regarded as an advocate for some cause or set of values, regardless of whether he or she exercises bias in reporting a set of findings. The value-free position clearly does not apply to the selection of a topic for research, especially in the area of social and behavioral science; it probably does not apply, at least completely, to the interpretation of results as well. As a result, it often becomes possible to predict the position taken by many social scientists, based simply on an examination of the patterns present in their previous work. Some researchers always seem to take a conservative position; others take a liberal stance, and so on. If there is a social construction among those who have observed an increase in hate crimes, then there may also be a social construction among those who deny it. Forces of resistance around the country have recently mobilized against those who seek to protect hate crime victims, and it's not just one law professor at NYU. Recently numerous columns in major newspapers and magazines, book-length critiques, and National Public Radio editorials have proposed banishing hate crime laws to the junk heap of defective and irrelevant legislation.

Yet very few conclusions based on social science research are as clear-cut as we would like to believe. For example, although incredible amounts of evidence point to the harmful nature of violent television programming on children, there are observers who deny that television violence is the least bit harmful. Those who are eager to criticize researchers who have argued that hate crimes are on the rise must be careful not to expect more rigorous evidence from their ideological opponents than they expect of themselves. Indeed, it is naive to believe that any body of research is without major flaws; all of our research findings in criminology have been derived from less-than-perfect empirical studies. Sadly, we are left to live with the ambiguities because the only alternative is to abandon the scientific method (a position that has become increasingly popular, at least in some circles).

Reports of increased hate offenses are supported also by studies that show intergroup hostility escalating as a result of increasing integroup contact, especially in the form of competition.[46] and, at the psychological level, frustration leading to displaced aggression.[47] Whether or not economically based, growing threats to the advantaged majority group since the early 1980s may have inspired a rising tide of hate incidents directed against members of challenging groups. Over this period, there have been dramatic increases in interfaith and interrace dating and marriage, migration (especially from Latin America and Asia), newly integrated neighborhoods, schools, college dormitories, and workplaces, and gay men and lesbians coming out (and, in many cases, organizing on behalf of their shared interests).

As indicated earlier, in connection with defensive hate offenses, Donald Green and his associates have shown that hate crimes occur most frequently in "defended" White neighborhoods—predominantly White areas that have experienced an in-migration of minorities.

Research conducted by the *Chicago Reporter*[48] suggests similarly that Chicago-area suburbs with growing minority populations have recently experienced increasing numbers of hate offenses against Blacks and Latinos. In many previously all-White suburban communities, minorities have reached a critical mass, causing White residents to feel threatened by the influx of newcomers. This seems to be the point at which hate crimes escalate.

If these results make sense and can be generalized, they suggest that the impact of a growing minority presence on hate crimes has a limited lifespan. As the increase in newcomers becomes more and more threatening—as it seems to have done in the early 1980s, hate crimes rise. These are the defensive hate crimes designed to discourage outsiders from moving into the community. At some point, the opposition sort of gives up—those who hate Jews or Blacks or Asians either move to some other neighborhood or resign themselves to a fate that they now feel incapable of changing. And hate attacks subside.

As for the contention that advocacy groups inflate their estimates of hate crimes, it is interesting to note that the ADL recently reported *decreases* in skinhead activity and in the overall level of anti-Semitic incidents. Their more recent conclusions concerning the downward trend in hate offenses is consistent with evidence collected by the FBI indicating that serious crime in general has declined since 1992.

Regardless of the reality, the question of whether hate crimes have been increasing or decreasing overall may not be very useful. Hate crimes are relatively rare and often result from a particular incident or a set of conditions in a local area. We have seen increases in hate crimes in local communities as a result of court orders to desegregate public housing (Boston), after a highly publicized death (Howard Beach, N.Y.), or in response to some large-scale external situation (attacks on Arab-Americans after the attacks of September 11, 2001). In addition, demographic shifts within a metropolitan region can cause hate crime incidents to rise and fall. In the Chicago area, many suburban communities in which the proportion of Black and Latino residents has recently increased now have higher hate crime rates than the city of Chicago.[49] The harsh reality is that hate crimes have existed for as long as recorded history and they continue to exist today. Whether the number of hate crimes is increasing or stabilizing, hate crimes are still occurring and victims are being harmed by individuals who perceived of them as inferior. This supports the need for legislation so that agencies of the criminal justice system will have tools to assist these particular crime victims when they ask for help.

Throughout the country, laws are being modified and local prosecutors and judges are becoming more responsive to the victims of hate violence. Yet, in terms of embracing all victims of bias-motivated crime and providing appropriate sentencing, change continues to be very slow and uneven. Some groups in need of protection, for example, women and gays, are still left out of state statutes, and offenders are too often permitted to go free with a slap on the wrist. Most frightening is the potential retreat by the Supreme Court from its role as a protector of civil rights. Government officials, advocacy groups, and citizens themselves must keep the pressure on legislatures and courts to prevent a withdrawal from the goal of protecting all victims of hate crimes everywhere.

fourteen

PREVENTION: STOPPING THE CRIMES AND OFFENDERS IN THEIR TRACKS

Local officials and community residents around the country are just beginning to view hate crimes as serious offenses that can tear a community apart, pitting neighbor against neighbor in acts of vandalism and violence. Moreover, as we have seen, hate crimes often have a profound impact on their victims, making them feel fearful and vulnerable. Public officials are consequently being encouraged by local residents and advocacy groups to take a strong public stand against all crimes motivated by bigotry as part of a response to prevent future hate crimes. State legislatures, as noted previously, have also responded by passing laws that increase the penalties for crimes that are bias motivated.

In more and more communities, once a hate crime is committed, citizens are coming forth to pressure local police to make an arrest, local prosecutors to get a conviction, and local judges to sentence the offenders harshly. This pressure on local law enforcement to deal with hate crimes is generated from communities that realize the severity of these offenses and their impact on victims. But there is often a more practical reason as well. Citizens are becoming increasingly aware that there may be significant negative economic repercussions on communities that are labeled as racist. In one small bedroom community west of Boston, for example, a police officer arrested a Black man for suspicious activity. It was later learned that the man was waiting for his daughter, who was late leaving a sleep-over party at the home of her girlfriend. In a successful lawsuit, the court awarded him $600,000 in damages, which the town was forced to pay.

For reasons both moral and practical, local law enforcement personnel in a number of communities are intent on communicating a strong message that hate crimes will not be tolerated. Yet they do not always carry through on their intention. Although hate crimes often have severe consequences, they are not typically committed by the most seasoned offenders. The first characteristic that distinguishes hate crime offenders from other serious offenders is their age. Most research to date indicates that the vast majority of perpetrators are very young males, often juveniles. Several studies have uncovered this characteristic of offenders, including a report by the Massachusetts Hate Crime Task Force which revealed that in 2000 nearly half of all hate crimes committed in Massachusetts (45 percent) were committed by offenders under twenty-one years of age.[1] An earlier Anti-Defamation League report similarly found that 70 percent to 80 percent of the offenders in anti-Semitic hate crimes are under twenty-one. A large proportion were much younger.[2]

A second characteristic of the hate crime offenders that mediates against harsh sentencing is the lack of a long history of prior criminal activity. Most prosecutors and judges believe that youthful first- or second-time offenders charged with almost any crime should be given another chance. The fear of labeling and stigmatizing a basically good youth "who just made a mistake" leads many in the criminal justice system to look for alternatives to incarceration for first- or second-time offenders.

The present level of overcrowding in our jails and prisons is another factor in judges' decisions regarding incarceration of these youths. The U.S. prison population is at an all-time high. As of December 31, 2001 (the most current statistics available), the prison population equaled 1,381,892, up by more than 50 percent since 1990.[3] At the end of 2001 the state prison facilities were operating at 15 percent above capacity while the federal system was operating at 31 percent above its rated capacity.[4] This trend places additional pressure on judges to use incarceration as a sanction for the most dangerous offenders.

A fourth factor leading judges to consider alternative sentences is the group nature of hate crimes. Research indicates that most crimes motivated by bias are committed by groups of offenders, not single individuals acting alone. Although a judge may want to impose a harsh sentence in order to send the community a message, hate incidents frequently involve a "ringleader" and two or more youths who are present at the scene but do not play an active part in committing the crime. A judge may believe that incarceration is the appropriate sentence for the "ringleader" but not for the others involved, especially for those who did not participate actively in the attack.

A case that typifies the difficulty of this decision is the Rodney King beating in Los Angeles. Much of America saw the videotape depicting four Los Angeles police officers beating King senseless while twenty-one officers stood by and observed. The Los Angeles police department took action against the four officers who actually engaged in the beating by firing them. But the department decided to take no action against the officers who watched, even though they did nothing to stop King's victimization.

Prosecutors who are responsible for charging and judges who are responsible for sentencing often find themselves in a difficult position. Although many may want to send a strong message that bias-motivated violence will not be tolerated, they are faced with other considerations—overcrowded courts and prisons as well as the youth and inexperience of many hate crime offenders—which undercut the call for the harshest sentences.

It is helpful to note that all hate crime offenders do not share the same level of culpability or blameworthiness for the crime. There are four different levels of responsibility in many hate crimes, and understanding them will help elucidate the decisions rendered by prosecutors and judges.

The first and most culpable level of hate crime offenders is the *leader*—that person whose idea it is to engage in the violence. He (the vast majority are young men) might be the first to strike the victim in an attack or may the first to use a weapon such as a baseball bat. Often no hate crime would have taken place without the active encouragement and inspiration of the leader. From the criminal justice system's point of view, this is the most culpable offender and should thus be subject to the harshest punishment.

The second category of offender is the offender whom political scientist Meredith Watts refers to as the *fellow traveler*. This person might never had committed the hate crime if it weren't for the encouragement of the leader but joined in once the attack was under way. Fellow travelers bear almost as much culpability as the leader, and their level of punishment should be related to the level of involvement in the crime.

The third category of offender is the *unwilling participant*. This category of offender does not condone the act of violence and does not participate in the attack except by his presence. The unwilling participant is often involved by virtue of a relationship with someone else in the group, possibly a girlfriend or a brother; they are much less culpable than the prior two groups, yet they do bear some responsibility because they did not attempt to intervene to protect the victim.

The final group of participants in hate crimes are *heroes*. These are the rarest of all hate crime participants, individuals who actively attempt to intervene to stop a hate crime from occurring. Heroes risk losing their friends and being the victims of physical violence, but they nonetheless step forward to attempt to stop the hate crime and protect the victim.

We offer these categories of culpability as a guide to prosecutors and judges facing the difficult decisions of what to do when faced with a group of hate crime offenders who play different roles in the same actual crime.

Judges have expressed another concern about imprisonment: the increasing presence of gangs behind bars. In prisons around the country, gangs have formed primarily along racial and ethnic lines. They often espouse racist beliefs and maintain connections with organized hate groups outside of the prison. Such gangs have become so prevalent that, according to the U.S. Circuit Court of Appeals in Illinois, 90 percent of the inmates in one state prison are gang members. Although little information has been collected about the extent of gang involvement nationally, correctional administrators often cite the activities of gangs as a major cause of inmate violence.

One of the most popular gangs in American prisons is the Mexican Mafia, a group of Chicano inmates from Los Angeles that formed in the late 1960s in San Quentin. A Chicano gang, La Nuestra Familia, is a chief rival of the Mexican Mafia, but its members are mainly from Texas or areas of California outside of Los Angeles. For Black inmates, there is the Black Guerrilla Family and for White inmates, the Aryan Brotherhood.

Prison gangs like the Mexican Mafia, La Nuestra Familia, the Black Guerrilla Family, and Aryan Brotherhood offer their members protection from antagonistic inmates and a certain amount of prestige within the prison. For hate crime offenders in particular, protection may be essential. After all, many of them have been incarcerated for assaulting individuals from the same racial groups as large numbers of their fellow inmates.

Because gangs are typically organized along racial or ethnic lines and often espouse racist beliefs, their members tend to develop or intensify biased feelings toward other races or ethnic groups. Once judges realize this, they may resist sending young hate crime offenders to prison—an environment that all too often intensifies prejudiced feelings and beliefs. A young White man serving time for committing a hate crime against Blacks will be recruited by gangs like the Aryan Brotherhood who'll regard him as a prime candidate for membership. On his part, the hate crime offender will be drawn to White supremacist gangs for protection. As much as he may be admired and respected by the Aryan Brotherhood, he will be despised and threatened by the Black and Latino gangs. It should come as no surprise, therefore, that hate crime offenders may be released from prison having more profoundly bigoted attitudes than the ones they held when they committed the original offense. In one of the most heinous hate crimes in this country's history—the dragging death of James Byrd, a Black resident of Jasper, Texas—the attackers had adopted their racist beliefs after becoming members of the Aryan Brotherhood while in a Texas prison for having committed minor offenses.

The reticence of some judges to imprison hate crime offenders is therefore not without some basis in reality. Rather than rehabilitate, the prison experience may instead harden the views of hatemongers and bigots. Moreover, after being released, they may become even more zealous about expressing their hatred in violence. According to Daniel Weiss, a counseling psychologist at the Massachusetts State Prison at Cedar Junction, an inmate who serves time for a racially inspired crime wears a symbolic badge that shows in dramatic fashion that "the man" is after him. He means that *he* was "a victim of the system, that he was down for the cause. After all, he was willing to serve time for his beliefs. As a result, the hate crime offender is likely to become a legendary figure so long as he remains behind bars."[5]

Judges have attempted to resolve this problem by employing a form of "alternative sentences." Initially, some judges assigned book reports as a part of the sentence to certain youths convicted of bias-motivated crime. In the case of an anti-Semitic attack, for example, a teenage offender might be required to read a book that describes the atrocities of the Holocaust. The hope, of course, is that exposure to such information will increase the youthful perpetrator's sensitivity to the horror and revulsion that the swastika represents to the Jewish community.

Although appealing in theory, the educational approach has limited effectiveness. First, there is a paucity of effective reading materials designed to counteract hatred, especially materials geared to the reading level of youthful offenders. Consequently, sentenced youths frequently return to the courtroom with a book they cannot read or understand and ask the judge to suggest something more appropriate. Most judges are simply not aware of age-suitable reading alternatives.

A second problem with this approach has been its lack of control; in some cases, the parents or friend of an offender actually writes the book report for the student. This becomes apparent in certain cases when the judge asks the youth to describe what he or she has learned from the book and the student can't recall anything contained in it. A final problem faced by judges employing this approach is based on what to do when presented with a bad or inaccurate book report. Several judges received reports that they felt were unsatisfactory due to the grammar, the conclusions, or both. In at least one case, a judge received a summary of a book that suggested that the Holocaust was a hoax, a finding with which the offender wholeheartedly agreed. In such instances, judges are faced with a very real problem: Do they incarcerate a youth basically for writing a bad book report? Many judges therefore find this approach unsatisfactory.

In dealing with first-time youthful hate crime offenders, some judges have chosen a community service sentence. Through volunteer service at a local advocacy organization, offenders learn about the community they have harmed while repaying some of the damage they have caused. One common example of this kind of sentence consists of six month's probation including, as a condition of probation, that the offenders provide one hundred hours of community service to a local advocacy group such as the office of the Anti-Defamation League of B'nai B'rith (ADL).

Like book reports, the community service option appears to be a creative approach until it is examined closely. In one case, a Massachusetts judge was faced with two youths convicted of defacing a Jewish temple with Nazi swastikas. The offenders had no prior criminal history but were loosely tied to a local skinhead group. The judge believed that if these youth could understand the harm they had caused, they might be deterred from future racist and anti-Semitic activity. He therefore required the offenders to work with a group whose main function is to fight anti-Semitism, the ADL. Specifically, they were sentenced to perform one hundred hours of community service at its New England office.

The judge didn't know much about the ADL except that it was a strong force against bigotry in the community. He reasoned that this would be the kind of group that might be able to teach offenders the harm of anti-Semitic crime. Unfortunately, the local ADL office was not, at that time, providing service to the court on an ongoing basis and had not been notified that it was to play a role in the sentence that had been imposed.

Without warning, therefore, two anti-Semitic skinheads simply showed up at the local ADL office one day reporting that a judge had sent them to do community service and asking for an assignment. Their presence caused a great deal of consternation among the ADL staff, who had no programming in place to deal with convicted offenders and were not at all accustomed to having skinheads in their offices.

In this case, the situation was resolved successfully when the local director of the ADL's World of Difference Program, a bias sensitivity program for school-age children with a record of success, decided to develop a program for these and other youths. Still, when local advocacy organizations are asked without warning or financial support to develop new programs for hate crime offenders, they typically cannot be counted on to provide an effective form of community service.

A major limitation of the community service sentencing approach is its lack of formal treatment programs. Having a location for the assignment of offenders is one thing; putting together an effective program to reduce hatred is quite another. Having an offender paint the exterior of a synagogue that he has defaced might return something to the community he has harmed, but it is questionable that this activity alone would teach the offender why what he did was wrong. To do that, he would need a program that effectively addressed his misconceptions.

Programs to combat hate can be seen as either preventative of rehabilitative. Prevention programs are intended to increase awareness of the dangers posed by hate crimes and thus stop hate violence before it occurs, while prevention programs are specifically intended to alter the behavior of offenders in order to deter future acts of violence.

There are many strong prevention programs across the country, some of which are directed at schoolteachers. The World of Difference Program, mentioned above, sponsored by the Anti-Defamation League, has trained more than 300,000 teachers across the country in skills necessary to identify and combat acts motivated by hate in their schools.

The Teaching Tolerance Program offered by the Southern Poverty Law Center has trained thousands of teachers over the past ten years. The goals of this program are to foster equity, respect, and understanding in the classroom and beyond.

Facing History and Ourselves is another program aimed at middle school and high school history and social studies teachers. This curriculum uses the Holocaust to teach about the dangers of bigotry generally. A highlight of this program is a section focusing on the positive and negative roles bystanders can play in hate crimes.

Several rehabilitative programs have been developed and implemented across the country specifically to deal with hate offenders. The first large-scale program is the STOP Program of the Montgomery County, Maryland, Office of Human Relations. Begun in July 1982, STOP was established as a juvenile diversion program, or an alternative to formal court processing for youth arrested for hate crimes.

STOP involves six sessions, including one entrance interview, one exit interview, and four two-and-a-half-hour sessions. In addition, the participants are required to do forty hours of community service. All sessions are conducted by staff from the Human Rights Commission in conjunction with members of local teen organizations who act as positive teen role models. The curriculum includes discussions about the basis of prejudice and racism, the role of organized hate groups, the impact of bias-motivated violence on victims, and the legal ramifications of perpetrating hate crimes.[6]

In Massachusetts, a partnership involving the Anti-Defamation League, the Attorney General's Office, Harvard University, and Northeastern University has come together to design and implement a program for hate crime offenders. Like STOP, the Massachusetts Youth Diversion and Community Service program was designed to provide a sentencing alternative for youths convicted of such crimes. It is a sixteen-week program that begins with a needs assessment to identify the major psychological, educational, and vocational needs of each offender. Like STOP, the Youth Diversion Program educates the offenders through sessions that deal with the impact of hate crimes on the victims, the cultural differences between groups, and the legal implications of actions motivated by bigotry. This program also includes a component of required service to a local minority community program. Unlike many other similar efforts tried elsewhere, the community service component of the Youth Diversion Program is planned ahead of time and included as part of the overall educational experience of the offender.

Under the direction of the state attorney general's office, an alternative sentencing program for youthful hate crime offenders has been developed for implementation in all counties in the state of New Jersey. Similar to the Massachusetts program, the New Jersey approach combines a psychological assessment with an agenda consisting of community service and sessions to increase awareness of cultural differences. Statewide in scope and sponsored by a public agency, the attorney general's office, the New Jersey program has become the most extensive effort at hate crime offender rehabilitation to date.

After reviewing the curricula from these and other hate crime offender rehabilitation programs, we believe that a model hate crime offender treatment or rehabilitation program must include the following elements: assessment, discussion of impact on victims, cultural awareness, restitution/community service, delineation of legal consequences, participation in a major cultural event, and aftercare.

Initially, all offenders should go through an assessment designed by trained professionals (e.g., psychologists, sociologists, and clinical social workers) of their attitude toward minorities in general and their previous experience with violence. This assessment should identify the

extent of the offender's commitment to racist/antiethnic or homophobic philosophy and should allow the program's staff to distinguish thrill
hate offenders from their more committed reactive and mission counterparts.

In addition, a number of officials who deal extensively with these offenders believe that many come from homes where violence is commonplace. As Deputy Superintendent Bill Johnston suggests, "These
kids come from homes filled with violence. The first time they see a
person attacked because they are different is when they see their father
hit their mother."[7] To the extent that violent behavior is generalized
from home experience to the streets, any effective treatment program
must also uncover and deal with a history of family violence, when it
exists.

A model hate crime offender program should also explain to offenders
how their actions have harmed the victim. To many hate crime offenders,
the victims of hate crimes are "different" in the most negative sense; that is,
they are regarded as not quite human. It is therefore important in treatment
programs to seek to reverse dehumanization of the victims by having the
offenders meet their victims and see, in unequivocal terms, just how much
pain and suffering they have caused *another human being*. For this purpose,
it may be helpful to have victims tell their own story.

Most hate crime offenders uncritically accept a number of false stereotypes concerning the behavior of minorities. Offender programs should attempt to identify and confront these misconceptions. In addition, such programs should seek to promote cultural diversity by identifying and
emphasizing the positive contributions made by the members of different
minority groups.

Another dimension of a model program involves the offender giving
something back to the minority community. This restitution/community
service component should be tied to the harm caused to the victim and not
simply be dirty work that no one else wants to do. Ideally, offenders should
feel good about the service they provide and should be thanked for their efforts. In this way, the offenders will not wind up resenting their experience
and may instead use it to feel closer to the minority group whose members
they have harmed. One strategy that can be useful in making the victim
seem more of a real person is to have offenders participate in a major cultural event in the victim's community.

Additionally, a model program should have a session describing the legal consequences of bias-motivated crime. Many youths who engage in this type of behavior believe that they are immune from serious penalties because public authorities share their biased feelings. This perception should be challenged by indicating what legal consequences could result from continued bias-motivated behavior. The presentation of actual case studies where offenders were sentenced to time in prison for bias-motivated property crimes, for example, has proven to be a useful technique for beginning a discussion.

The final component of a model hate crime offender treatment program is an aftercare plan. Developed jointly by the offender and the program staff, aftercare would provide continuing support to each offender on an "as needed" basis. The plan would allow the offender to come back to the program for support and to continue to deal with issues not resolved by the basic program.

In addition, any offender treatment program should have an ongoing evaluation component. Too many programs begin with a series of concepts that have worked in other contexts but have not been tested in the area of hate crimes. An evaluation component can determine to what extent this assumption is warranted and whether portions of the program should be adjusted.

Conducted by either outsiders or project staff, the goal of any evaluation procedure is to improve the program. As one possibility, at a minimum of every six months, the full staff should spend a day discussing the successes and failures of their program. From their meeting together, they should then adopt changes in the program to deal more effectively with the failures they might have experienced. At the same time, they should set goals for the next six months. Through a process of periodic evaluation, the program is less likely to become "stale" as it continues to make changes as its clients change.

It should be recognized that model programs are best viewed as dynamic, in constant flux as new and more accurate information is reviewed and incorporated into programmatic thinking. One fundamental premise of a model program should be that next year's program will be different—better—in some respects than this year's effort. Having an ongoing evaluation process and an openness to change is the only means for assuring that progress will be made.

We emphasize that treating hate crime offenders through the criminal justice system has at least two possible consequences, potentially at odds with each other. On the one hand, a strong prison sentence sends a signal to would-be hatemongers everywhere that their violation of the law will simply not be tolerated—that they too can expect to receive more than a mere slap on the wrist if they similarly express their bigotry in an illegal manner. In other words, a severe sentence may deter future hate offenses. On the other hand, a lengthy prison sentence—especially in response to a thrill hate offense—may actually harden and reinforce the bigoted attitudes of the youngster who serves time. If prison is a "school for crime," it is surely a crash course in expressing hatred through violence.

Experts on the issue of hate violence have suggested that some hatemongers may watch what happens in an initial hate crime before deciding to take part in the violence. But when judges are facing certain hate crime offenders, they find themselves in a difficult situation. They may want to communicate a strong message, but the offenders—especially in the case of thrill hate crimes or those we regard as unwilling participants—may be first-time offenders who have no strong commitment to violence motivated by bigotry. This type of offender is not typically incarcerated in our present system.

Judges often have only two real options: either to incarcerate the offender once he has been convicted or to put the offender on probation. Probation is often perceived by the general public as little more than a minor nuisance, and a judge may fear the reaction of members of the victim's community to this perceived light treatment. What appears to be lacking in certain hate crime cases, if not in the correctional system generally, is some sanction between prison and probation. To be effective, such a program would allow the offender to remain living at home while he participates in an ongoing educational program and, at the same time, works to compensate (in money, service, or both) either the victim or the victim's community.

In our view, tough sentencing is absolutely essential for protecting members of society against hate crime perpetrators who have demonstrated repeatedly that they are beyond rehabilitation and represent a danger to society. At the other end of the spectrum, however, creative alternative sentencing is crucial for responding to young first-time offenders who may have been influenced not only by their youth but also by their friends' bigotry and may be capable of making profound reforms. Intermediate sentences—less than prison but more than probation—are necessary for assuring that hate crimes are treated more seriously than ordinary offenses. However, many hatemongers can be rehabilitated—if they are fortunate enough to benefit from a serious but humane and imaginative approach to criminality.

fifteen

COMMUNITY RESPONSE: FIGHTING HATE CRIMES ONE NEIGHBORHOOD AT A TIME

Russell and Laura Jones awoke with a start. It was 2:30 A.M., and the sound of loud voices outside was unmistakable. By the time the couple checked their children and got to the living room window, the voices had gone, but not the two-foot cross burning on their front lawn.

In March 1990, less than three months earlier, the Joneses had moved from the inner city to their "dream house," a hundred-year-old four-bedroom home in a predominantly White middle-income section of East St. Paul. Their five children would benefit most from the move, they had reasoned—the youngsters would see no more crack houses and violence on the block, only safety, security, and tranquillity.

Shortly after moving in, however, disturbing things began to happen. First, the tires on their family car were slashed. A few days later, the windshield of their car was found shattered. Most troubling, a local teenager called their nine-year-old son a "nigger," and, for the first time, Laura Jones was forced to explain to her child the meaning of racism and bigotry.

One of the most difficult issues for the victims of hate crimes is wondering how widespread the bigotry is. How many of the other people on the block want them to leave the neighborhood? How many other students on campus resent their presence? How many other teenagers in town will impress their friends with their bigoted behavior? Victims often want to believe that the hate crime against them was the deviant behavior of a few "screwed-up kids," a small number of "bigots," but they also fear that these actions reflect the sentiments of the masses.

After the cross-burning incident in St. Paul, the local community came together to send a message of support for the Jones family. Some neighbors brought over pies and cakes. A number of them called to express their outrage and to confirm to Russell and Laura Jones that they did not share, but instead abhorred, the racist attitudes of the defendants. According to Laura Jones, this outpouring of support and encouragement from members of the White community "made the family feel more comfortable." It also sent a broader message to potential hate crime offenders everywhere—a message of racial tolerance and acceptance that directly contradicted the intolerant message that the offenders had sought to communicate.

Unfortunately, communicating a message after a hate crime is committed doesn't always have an ameliorative effect. On the contrary, the community reaction is often defensive and retaliatory. In response to the torture of Abner Louima by Officer Justin Volpe in the bathroom of a New York police department station, angry protesters, mostly Black, paraded through the streets of the predominantly White neighborhoods where the hate crime had occurred. Led by Black activists like the Reverend Al Sharpton, large numbers of outsiders marched to dramatize the wrongdoing perpetrated against members of their group.

The accusatory tone of such parades, marches, and demonstrations can have the effect of dividing groups even more against one another. When people of color march through a White neighborhood, they are usually perceived, correctly or not, as indicting the entire community of racism. Moreover, the presence of marchers is taken as additional evidence that "outsiders" are intruding on the neighborhood. In many cases, the demonstration brings out even more intense and dangerous expressions of racism on the part of community members who "stand accused" of crimes they did not personally commit, or perhaps even condone. After the murder of Yusef Hawkins in Bensonhurst, for example, marchers were met by hordes of angry spectators shouting racial slurs and throwing watermelons. After a racial incident in Canarsie, spectators from the community yelled racial epithets at marchers. In addition, a group of White teenagers held up a watermelon as they drove in the back of a pickup truck painted with racist sayings.

If it is less effective for Blacks to demonstrate in protest after a Black is victimized in a brutal crime of hate, what should be done? Clearly, hate crimes cannot go unchallenged. The community reaction to the cross burning in St. Paul gives us a significant clue.

As divisive as his reaction may be, Sharpton fills a vacuum in community response that ought to be filled by the grassroots opposition of Whites. During the 1960s, Whites and Blacks joined together in marches, demonstrations, and protests, creating the civil rights movement. In the same way, after the murder of James Byrd, the indignant residents of Jasper, Texas, themselves should have marched through *their* streets, in unified opposition to racial bigotry, preferably alongside Blacks. Although some White members of these communities did take action, more Whites should have sent cards to the family of the victim; more of them should have baked pies and cakes; larger numbers should have taken the initiative to assure the victim's family that they oppose violence, that they celebrate diversity, and that they will not tolerate further acts of racism in their neighborhood. Likewise, when gay University of Wyoming student Matthew Shepherd was brutally left to die in the desert, the straight residents of Laramie should have filled the streets to express their anger and indignation.

We must understand that in every community, there will be local residents holding a wide range of views on this issue. Some will regret that the hate incident ever happened and may be willing to go out of their way to support the victim, even at some risk to their image among neighbors or to their personal safety. Others will sympathize with the offenders and wholeheartedly support their intentions. But the largest group of residents will be indifferent; they simply want to go on with their lives as if nothing happened. The relative size of each group will differ depending on the community. In neighborhoods where the group supporting the offender is especially large, change will be most difficult to achieve. In a number of communities interracial, interethnic, and inter-religious groups have been formed to respond to incidents if they occur and, more importantly, to prevent these incidents from occurring in the first place. In Cook County, Illinois, the prosecutor's office has organized the Hate Crime Prosecution Council. This broad-based council works on planning and public policy development and helps craft prevention strategies that counter hate citywide.

The Los Angeles Human Relations Council has been working on the issue of hate crime prevention involving a broad-based grassroots coalition for more than twenty years. This group represents a coalition of more than seventy law enforcement and community organizations. The group meets monthly to monitor the problem areas in the county and has created a crisis response team to respond to hate crimes when they occur. A large number of local human relations commissions have begun to develop these broad-based coalitions to respond to hate violence.

In Massachusetts both the governor and the attorney general have established hate crime task forces. Backed by the power of the state's political leadership, both task forces have a broad-based and overlapping membership. Members of these task forces have done significant programming in schools across the commonwealth.

We believe that the goal of any effective community response must be to identify local residents who support the victim and work with them to promote more widespread acceptance of this view among their fellow community members. Those who are perceived to be outsiders can hardly expect to be effective as agents of change. But insiders—friends and neighbors—can really make a difference at the informal level, especially if they are observed putting themselves on the line on behalf of the hate crime victim.

One example of this can be seen in Boston. After the court-ordered desegregation of the housing developments in South Boston, several White residents of the developments formed a group to offer protection and support for the first Black families that first moved into the previously all-White housing development. As Deputy Superintendent William Johnston, commander of Boston Hate Crime unit, said at the time, "Without the courageous efforts of those well-meaning residents by standing up to their bigoted neighbors the violence faced by these Black families would be much worse."[1]

One important factor in the community response to a hate crime is the role played by local advocacy groups—organizations that represent the interests of a specific minority group and attempt to influence public policy regarding issues of interest to its members. Advocacy groups include such national organizations as the Anti-Defamation League of B'nai B'rith (ADL), the National Association for the Advancement of

Colored People (NAACP), the Gay and Lesbian Task Force, and the Pacific Asian Legal Society. At the local level, advocacy groups may include local chapters of these and other national organizations as well as other groups, including local human relations councils and equal opportunity councils.

One limitation on groups at the local level is that although some do exist in most communities, not all the minority groups in a particular community are represented by an advocacy group. For example, a neighborhood may have a very active office of the NAACP, but there may be no local group dealing specifically with the problems faced by gay and lesbian residents.

Such local advocacy groups can, however, play a significant role in responding to hate crimes. Initially, the group can provide support for the hate crime victim. As we have emphasized, victims of bias-motivated violence generally feel extremely vulnerable. The local advocacy group can support victims by letting them know that they are not alone and by assisting the victims in their contacts with the police, the courts, and the media. In some communities, local advocacy groups act as a liaison between the victim and the police and court officials. These advocates explain each step of the process to the victim and, if necessary, accompany the victim to the police station and to court.

Local advocacy groups can also follow up on incidents by visiting the police, who may be ambivalent about how to respond to allegations of bias-motivated violence. A call or visit from a local advocacy group might convince the police that a crime is heinous and should be investigated seriously. One follow-up strategy employed by the New England regional office of the ADL to sensitize local police to the hate crime problem is to send them a hate crime report, describing each anti-Semitic incident reported to the ADL office from their jurisdiction. In addition to working closely with police, advocacy groups can follow up with the local prosecutor's office and the local courts to ensure that once an arrest has been made, the case proceeds swiftly to trial.

Another role advocacy groups can play is to support the police by participating in hate crime training programs. In this way, such groups can directly educate police officers who will be dealing with issues of bigotry. An important consequence of this collaboration in training, as we have noted, is that members of the local police department and members of local advocacy groups will get to know each other and develop informal communication links that can be mutually beneficial should a major incident occur.

Again the ADL has been at the forefront of supporting law enforcement training. From speaking at academy and in-service training to offering workshops on organized hate group activity, the ADL has developed closer links to law enforcement.

Advocacy groups can also be helpful in collecting and reporting hate crime statistics. Many local organizations offer assistance to victims in completing police department paperwork—a service that can lead to improved data on bias-motivated violence provided to the police. In two states, Maryland and Massachusetts, advocacy groups have their own separate hate crime reporting system. Local advocacy groups collect information on bias incidents: bias-motivated actions that do not rise to the level of a crime. For example, a racial slur shouted from a moving car could be reported as a hate incident, though it may not qualify as a criminal act. These statistics serve as an early warning system to alert local officials and local community task forces of potential hot spots of racial tension.

Another important function of advocacy groups is supporting government agencies that are effectively responding to hate crimes. Particularly in the area of data collection, the agencies that are doing a good job are often severely criticized for their efforts. For example, Boston has been called the hate crime capital of America because a large number of hate crimes are reported there each year. This label is misleading. The large number of hate offenses reported is in part the result of advocacy groups and the police working together to encourage victims to come forward and report crimes motivated by bias. One pivotal function that local advocacy groups in Boston play is to stand with the police when it releases the hate crime statistics each year and explain to the local media how an increase in numbers of hate crimes may be a positive result of programs to encourage victim reporting.

Local advocacy organizations can also serve a more targeted response to bias-motivated crime. In 1990, for example, the Anti-Defamation League of B'nai B'rith initiated two programs of education, A Campus of Difference and A Workplace of Difference, designed to reduce prejudice. Both programs—one for colleges and the other for corporations and government agencies—were modeled after ADL's earlier educational and media initiative, A World of Difference, under whose auspices teachers in cities across the country were trained to increase their students' awareness of cultural diversity. Workshops in both of these programs are designed to encourage participants to discuss openly issues related to prejudice, discrimination, and diversity.[2]

But local advocacy groups are not enough. The response to hate crimes can only be effective if it also receives the inspiration and blessing of community leaders who represent a broad range of constituents, not just those in the victim group. In their public proclamations as well as their behavior, therefore, presidents, governors, mayors, and other government officials must make it known, in the most unequivocal terms possible, that hate crimes are evil, immoral, and unacceptable—that they simply will not be tolerated in any form. It is not enough for members of the affected group to respond to hate crimes. When an attack is directed against Blacks, White leaders must respond. When the crime is against gays, mainstream leaders must react, and so on.

A swift and solid response to an offense will most effectively minimize the potential for future hate attacks. After the September 11 attack on America, President George W. Bush made an unprecedented appeal for tolerance. On September 17, only days after the collapse of New York City's Twin Towers, Bush went to the Islamic Center in Washington, D.C., and appealed to the American people for understanding and tolerance. He emphasized that "these acts of violence against innocents violates the fundamental tenants of the Islamic faith and it is important for my fellow Americans to understand that." This and subsequent statements from the president and his staff have been viewed as partially responsible for a significant decrease in anti-Arab violence following the initial spate of attacks.

Another example of the power of leadership occurred in Hull, Massachusetts, a small coastal community located some eight miles from downtown Boston. Government officials in this suburban town voted to replace the floor tiles in its town hall that had offended Jewish residents. The floor in question consisted of inlaid tiles bearing swastikas. It had been laid many years before the Nazis came to power and the figures actually represented an American Indian symbol of peace and good fortune. The leadership of the town of Hull could easily have become defensive and recalcitrant in reacting to offended Jews in the area. Instead, the floor was covered. In so doing, the community defused a potential crisis. It sent a message of acceptance and respect to its few Jewish residents as well as any residents who might have considered committing anti-Semitic acts.[3]

Another case of appropriate response on the part of community leadership occurred in Wellesley, Massachusetts. In 1990, this affluent community was charged with racism and bigotry after an incident in which a Black Celtics basketball rookie, new to the town as well as the team, was humiliated by local police in what turned out to be a case of mistaken identity. Actually, this was not the first time that Wellesley residents had been accused of bigotry. As mentioned earlier, two young men were convicted in October 1989 of perpetrating hate crimes against Blacks and Jews in the town by spray-painting racist and anti-Semitic graffiti on driveways and sidewalks. The residents of Wellesley could have easily turned their backs on both occurrences, taking a position of resentment and denial. Instead, eight hundred Wellesley residents, most of whom were White, gathered for a candlelight march and rally against racism and anti-Semitism. More importantly, political leaders including Senator John Kerry and Representative Barney Frank provided muscle by showing up to voice their support.

Reactions in the aftermath of campus hate incidents can also be tempered by enlightened community leadership. On February 27, 2000, four Asian students were attacked by three White students on the campus of the State University of New York in Binghamton. The most seriously injured of the victims suffered brain damage and internal bleeding. The president of the university responded with a strongly worded letter condemning all forms of bigotry and violence. Moreover, the Asian student union sponsored a campuswide rally in which more than four hundred students of all races and ethnic groups gathered to show their solidarity with the victims and to denounce hatred and bigotry on campus.

In the fall of 1989, the members of a fraternity at the University of Vermont, on discovering that one of their pledges was a homosexual, informed the student that he was no longer welcome to become a brother. After finding that the fraternity had discriminated based on sexual orientation, a student judicial board on campus ordered the fraternity to apologize to the gay student, refund his pledge fee, and hold in-house educational programs about homosexuality. A rally and march on campus against hate attracted some four hundred students and local residents, including the mayor of Burlington, Vermont. He later asked the board of aldermen in his town to amend its housing discrimination codes so that college fraternities would be legally prohibited from discriminating on the basis of sexual orientation.[4]

In another racial incident on campus, hundreds of students at Brandeis University conducted a weeklong boycott of their college bookstore, after thirty Black students accused its managers with having singled them out, based entirely on their race, for scrutiny and treating them all like potential shoplifters. More than seven hundred students, most of whom were White, signed a pledge saying that they would not buy from the bookstore until its managers had been fired. In response, the bookstore agreed to replace the managers, institute a new system for handling complaints, make a conscientious effort to hire more Black students, and implement a training program for the purpose of increasing racial sensitivity among its employees.[5]

What happens when leadership is slow in responding to incidents of hate? Orleans, France, is a town of eighty-eight thousand people located 110 kilometers south of Paris. In May 1969, students at Orleans high school began spreading stories that two women in town had disappeared while shopping at a local boutique owned and operated by a Jewish couple. According to the story circulated among students at the school, the victims had been trying on clothes in a dressing room when they were given injections of an unknown drug that rendered them unconscious. They were then imprisoned in the basement while waiting to be sold into slavery.

After a few weeks, versions of the same story began to circulate outside of the high school in families, offices, and factories as well. The newer versions were more elaborate than the old. The number of abductions increased from two to sixty. The number of shops responsible for the crimes increased from one to an entire network of half a dozen stores in town, most of which were owned by Jews.

At this point, parents and teachers warned the teenage girls in Orleans to avoid the boutiques named in the rumor until the matter had been totally cleared. There were also anti-Semitic allegations specifically targeting Jewish shopkeepers as the culprits. No kidnappings had actually been reported to the police and none was reported in the local newspaper. Yet the victim count continued to increase and the story became even more complex and dangerous. By the end, the residents of Orleans were convinced that the police and press had been bribed into inaction and that a conspiracy of silence was in effect. An angry crowd formed in front of the shops named in the story in order to prevent customers from entering them.

Why had these totally unfounded stories about Jewish shopkeepers become a focal point of panic among the people of Orleans? They had been allowed to grow and flourish by the failure of local leadership in politics, the police, and the press to take a definite stand in condemning the falsehoods. Only when the entire affair had mushroomed into near disaster did town authorities finally step in. When they did—by reassuring the townspeople, discrediting the rumormongers, and writing articles about the false reports in local newspapers—all traces of the false accusations quickly evaporated.[6]

In communities across the country, government leaders must have the courage to take strong positions against acts of bigotry. In the climate of hate so prevalent in our country, however, they cannot count on receiving the support and encouragement of all their constituents. Today we hear a great deal about the insidious prevalence of political correctness (PC). But where does a preference for tolerance and liberalism exist aside from college faculty members or ACLU attorneys? Certainly, tolerance for diversity does not exist to any great extent among those college students who feel squeezed by the growing presence of cultural diversity on campus. Nor does it exist among employees who fear they might lose promotions, raises, or possibly jobs to "outsiders."

All too often, national and state leaders who hope to maintain the loyalty and respect of their mainstream constituents feel pressured to pander to the insecurities of the masses. The more they gripe about "welfare parasites," "reverse discrimination," and "femi-nazis," the louder the applause they receive from their constituents. At the same time, some leaders are able to rise to the challenge and take a strong stand against bigotry. In the long run, they may save us from even more bloodshed and violence.

sixteen

REVISITING HATE CRIMES

As bad as race relations in the United States may be, Americans have since the 1950s at least moved in the direction of making some effort, through public policy, to reduce inequality and increase opportunities for people of color, women, the disabled, gay men, and lesbians. Various federal initiatives including the 1964 Civil Rights Act and, more recently, the Americans with Disabilities Act have carried our society further toward the goal of protecting the rights all of our citizens.

Data on public acceptance of such policies and programs have been mixed, however. In fact, public opinion survey reports and hate crime data are apparently at odds. When Americans are asked about their acceptance of racial integration in schools, neighborhoods, and friendship circles, large numbers of them express tolerance for diversity, at least on an abstract level. Yet almost every advocacy organization reports that hate crimes have not abated, and in some communities they are on the rise.

It may well be that our relative tolerance for diversity as an abstract principle, to some degree, has set the stage, during the past few years, for the rise of hate crimes in the United States. To the extent that our policies have indeed worked, we have moved away from questions of what ought to be done in principle and instead have created concrete challenges and threats to the traditionally advantaged position of White males. We have therefore unwittingly provided the breeding ground for growing resentment. In light of the very real possibility of an approaching era of economic stagnation, if not decline, hate crimes may become a more common way for some people to express their resentment.

During the past twenty years, more and more gays have come out of the closet, have demonstrated loudly for equality of opportunity, and have openly expressed their affection for members of the same sex. During the same period, people of color and women have made their growing presence felt in companies and colleges that formerly were reserved almost exclusively for White males. At the same time, emigrants into the United States from Latin America, eastern Europe, and Asia have arrived in almost record numbers. More recently, as America embarks on its long-term war on terrorism, more and more American citizens are going to be profiled as having the characteristics of those we identify as terrorists. A climate of tolerance and inclusion, beginning in the late 1960s, has created more and more *challenges* to the status quo and thus more opportunities for outsiders to be victimized. On college campuses, Blacks and Whites interact where they previously had not; on the job, women and men work more closely together, increasingly in positions of equality or near equality.

As a consequence, hate crimes are occurring in every region of the nation, including the Deep South. For example, the Grand Dragon of the Tennessee White Knights of the Ku Klux Klan pleaded guilty to shooting into a Nashville synagogue in order to intimidate the Jewish congregation.[1] In Louisiana, a federal grand jury indicted five Ku Klux Klan members for civil rights violations arising from cross burnings at schools, a court house, the home of a Black family, a church, and an apartment building.[2]

At the same time, it should be noted that fewer of the hate offenses described in this book have taken place in southern states than in any other region of the nation, at least during the past few years. Statistical evidence supports this contention. In both Florida and Oklahoma, states in which hate crimes are reported by police jurisdictions, relatively few such offenses have come to the attention of the police.

The reasons for the relative paucity of hate crimes in southern states remain a matter of conjecture. Perhaps victims fail to report such offenses out of fear that they will not receive support from official sources or even be further intimidated by them. Maybe southerners, recognizing the legacy of slavery as an institution, are more sensitive than other

Americans to the plight of minorities living in their region. Or perhaps people of color in the South no longer challenge the status quo, at least not to the extent that they are doing in other parts of the country. Millions of southern Black Americans, over the past few decades, have relocated to northeastern and western states for the sake of opportunity. Although some have found what they set out to secure for themselves, many others have uncovered more stubborn obstacles in their path.

During the 1950s and 1960s, at a time of rapid change in the South, violence in the region often occurred in response to Blacks demanding their civil rights. As the new millennium begins, however, the major battleground for equality may have moved out of the South into communities like Jasper, Texas, Laramie, Wyoming, New York City, Dubuque, and Los Angeles—localities in which hate crimes continue to plague many victims.

Public policy aimed at reducing racial inequity has too often been driven by fear and anxiety rather than a genuine desire to do the right thing for those members of our society who are caught in the hideous grip of bigotry and inequality. The result has been a "patchwork policy" without long-term advantage. After the urban riots of the 1960s, for example, welfare expenditures were for a time increased in order to stem the tide of urban unrest and disorder. Similarly, in the aftermath of the Los Angeles riots in 1992, proposals for enhancing the quality of inner-city life were introduced with fanfare and publicly debated anew, but few effective measures ever saw the light of day. We typically respond to soaring crime rates by advocating law and order policies such as the death penalty or longer prison sentences. The rush to develop programs to increase understanding of and support for victims of anti-Arab violence after the attacks of September 11 has begun to slow as these attacks fall from the daily headlines.

In a sense, the hatemonger often uses the same logic as our political leaders. The perpetrator *fears* the encroachment of Blacks, gays, or Asians; and he acts, often in an impulsive and ineffectual manner, to remedy what he sees as an intolerable situation. The hate crime offender actually commits an act of terrorism by sending a message to *all* members of his victim's group. If successful, he reduces the immediate threat that he feels coming from those who are different. His hate crime represents a short-term response to profound feelings of powerlessness and despair that can hardly be eliminated by engaging in an act of violence.

Hate offenses work against the long-term interests of the perpetrators by protecting the true sources of their everyday problems and placing the blame on innocent targets at the margins of society. Hate crimes function to maintain the status quo; they protect the leaders—the people in charge, the men and women who are responsible for making important decisions at the highest levels of society. Blame tends to move away from the top, minimizing the possibility that profound changes could ever occur. For example, a disgruntled teenager who, out of a sense of personal frustration, spray-paints homophobic slurs on a government building may temporarily experience some psychological satisfaction, but he comes no closer to succeeding in school or on the job.

In 1830 the largest number of newcomers to the United States were Irish; in 1890 they were German. In 1900 they were Italian; then they were Canadian. During the 1980s, four out of five immigrants came from Asia, Latin America, and the Caribbean. By 2002 the newcomers were arriving in great numbers from Mexico, the Philippines, Vietnam, China and Taiwan, South Korea, and India. Smaller numbers entered from the Dominican Republic, El Salvador, Jamaica, Haiti, and Iran.

The foreign-born population of the United States is currently more than 14 million, by far the largest in the world. Moreover, we are presently in the midst of the second largest wave of immigration in U.S. history. Between 1980 and 2000, more than 11 million newcomers, for political as well as economic reasons, pulled up their roots and left their homelands to begin new lives in the United States. There will be more newcomers in America in the years to come than we have witnessed in more than a century; the overwhelming majority are Asians, Latinos, and Blacks—very few are White.

The continuing influx of newcomers into the United States will have profound implications for the future of intergroup relations. Within a decade or so, multiculturalism will have become a focal point of social change. Indeed, within the lifetime of most Americans living today, the White Anglo-Saxon majority will have become a statistical minority. In many cities across the country this demographic transformation has already occurred.

In the years ahead, people of color—Asians, Latinos, and Blacks— will increasingly challenge the traditional power structure for jobs, status, and power, demanding to share the wealth of the nation. At the same time, gays, women, and people with disabilities will continue to seek equality of opportunity. In our postindustrial society, there is likely to be growing conflict among groups for scarce economic resources. Prejudice and violence may escalate to levels that endanger each one of us.

By randomly examining hate confrontations occurring in the recent past, we may be able to catch a glimpse of what crises lie ahead should we fail to improve the climate of intolerance in the United States. In April 1992, on the campus of Olivet College in Michigan, Black and White students engaged in what one Black sophomore called "a civil war on this campus."There were rumors about groups of Black men attacking White females, confrontations in which racial epithets were exchanged, allegations of Ku Klux Klan intervention, death threats recorded on a telephone answering machine, and a fire set in a dormitory where many of the Black students lived. Fearing for their personal safety, many of the Black students packed their bags and abandoned the campus.[3]

In February 1990, some six hundred Blacks marched through the streets of Selma, Alabama, to protest the decision of the school committee's White majority to fire the town's first Black school superintendent. One side claimed personal incompetence; the other charged racism. Black members of the school board walked out; Black students boycotted classes while their parents picketed the schools. Angry White parents urged officials to end"mob rule"by ejecting the demonstrators from the school.[4]

At New York's City College (CUNY) recently, a Black historian blamed"rich Jews"for the African slave trade and for a"conspiracy"to defame Black Americans through their stereotyped portrayal in Hollywood motion pictures. Down the hall, another CUNY professor, this one White, suggested that Blacks were intellectually inferior to Whites.[5]

The violent reaction of inner-city Blacks in Los Angeles to a not-guilty verdict in the April 1992 trial of police officers responsible for Rodney King's beating provides frightening testimony as to the possibility of extreme forms of racial turmoil. In all likelihood, King had been the victim of a hate crime—police brutality. Unfortunately, the rioters in Los Angeles perpetrated their own hate crimes. A truck driver was pulled from his truck and nearly killed simply because he was White. Stores were looted and burned because their proprietors were Koreans or Whites. Hoping to protect their property, Black shopkeepers in inner-city Los Angeles displayed signs reading "Black Owner." After all the fires were finally extinguished and most of the smoke had cleared, more than fifty people had lost their lives and thousands more had been injured.

At a time when affirmative action programs are finally making some difference in the lives of women and minorities, we simply cannot afford to abandon our national commitment to eliminating racial and gender inequities. Nor can we afford to back away from our promise to provide equal access to Americans with disabilities. But we must also be prepared to redesign our policies and programs for implementing change, so that they are consistent with the political and economic climate of our times. Otherwise, no one will enjoy the privilege of a safe and prosperous environment.

During the 1960s, Americans enjoyed a period of unparalleled prosperity and economic growth. Hence, many supported affirmative action programs. After all, if you believe that the "pie" is getting larger, you are more willing to reserve a slice for someone without a piece. In the postindustrial era of the new millennium, however, the pie no longer appears to be growing—if anything, it seems to be shrinking. Compared with the stock market of 1990s, the market of the new millennium seems less reliable, making the promise of capitalism less broad based and everyone's future a little less secure. Millions of Americans who might have supported affirmative action policies twenty-five years ago now think about holding on to a slice of the pie for themselves and their own families.

To respond to the increased presence of hatemongers in our society, we need effective hate crime legislation, at least in the short term. Statutes that increase the penalties for committing a hate crime, for example, provide the weapons necessary to keep hardened recidivists behind bars and away from their potential victims. Creative alternative sentences must also be available to reach youthful hate crime offenders *long before* they have become hardened recidivists. At the same time, we emphasize that the criminal justice system—even when it operates at maximum effectiveness—is limited in its ability to stem the rising tide of bigotry and bloodshed. Solutions that work will require that our leaders lay the groundwork by long-term planning to reduce both intolerance and resentment.

Wherever possible, we need more programs and policies that help vulnerable groups without being specifically created for them. Rather than base all affirmative action policies solely on race or gender, we might develop programs and policies of affirmative action to reduce poverty—based, for example, on the neighborhood in which a person lives or the economic condition of a family. Such programs would disproportionately benefit people of color and women, who have been historically disadvantaged, without singling them out; and they might well generate less resentment from Americans who have become self-defensive in attitude. Focusing more directly on poverty, we would hope to counteract the perceived inequity in policies that aid racial minorities regardless of income or assets. Struggling to send their own children to college, for example, many middle-class Americans conjure up an image of affirmative action that seems as extreme as it is unfair. They ask, "Why should the son of a successful Black doctor receive preferential treatment from college admissions over the son of an unemployed White laborer?" Or "Why should a Latino candidate for admission qualify before a comparable White student with a higher SAT score?"

Colleges and universities located in the urban core provide a case in point. Such institutions of higher learning are increasingly being regarded by residents of surrounding neighborhoods as symbols of disenfranchisement rather than hope. To reverse this trend, institutions of higher learning must change their image from that of exclusivity to access. These institutions must look beyond simple measures such as SAT scores and determine which students if provided reasonable levels of support could succeed at their institutions.

Many private universities have long maintained scholarship programs for students with financial need. In many cases, aid has been targeted specifically at students representing racial and ethnic minorities. Though effective, such programs are increasingly under attack. Moreover, they often fail to address the particular needs of lower-income families in the neighborhoods in which colleges are located.

James Fox and one of the authors of this volume, Jack Levin, have urged schools to take steps to recruit larger numbers of disadvantaged students specifically from surrounding inner-city neighborhoods. Some colleges—Brown University, Northeastern University, University of Pennsylvania—have already directed their scholarship aid in this direction.[6] In addition, they have sought to contribute the academic support needed—extra help through in-school mentoring as well as after-school and summer tutoring—in order to give underrepresented youngsters a real chance to compete for a place in an appropriate institution of higher learning.

Aside from the obvious advantage of providing assistance for students almost literally in a college's backyard, targeting aid by residence rather than race has considerable potential as a more acceptable general model. It illustrates a program that affects a particular group—in this case, people of color—without being specifically for them. Blacks, Latinos, and Asians tend to be clustered in lower-income urban centers and would therefore disproportionately benefit from residence-based scholarship aid. In one Northeastern University program, for example, the population of the targeted school is 58 percent Latino and 35 percent Black, with the remaining 6 percent divided evenly between Asians and Whites.

Minority recipients of such residence-based financial assistance would, at the same time, be less likely to be stigmatized by such programs. Because scholarship aid is potentially available without regard to race, religion, or national origin, no one group would likely be singled out as recipients of special treatment. Aside from shared residence, the common denominator is shared poverty. As a result, resentment toward minority populations would, we hope, be minimized.

Some universities have directed their aid to students in neighborhood schools by offering full scholarships to sixth graders who later graduate from high school and qualify for college admission. Initial evaluations of such programs reveal less success than had been hoped for. The carrot of a free college education motivates some students to study hard, distance themselves from debilitating peer influences, and take education seriously even at bad schools. But many others have fallen out of these programs, defeated by personal and family problems that are simply too great to overcome. For such programs to fully reach their potential, universities will have to intervene earlier and more effectively in the educational experiences of disadvantaged students.

One final suggestion for reducing hate crimes in our society is in order. We are convinced of the effectiveness of *coalitions* against bigotry. At the beginning of the twentieth century, labor unions developed out of a temporary alliance of newcomers who put aside their vast differences to join together for the sake of a common objective—higher pay and better working conditions. In the 1940s and 1950s, the civil rights movement began as a coalition of Blacks and Whites, many of whom were Jewish, who regarded bigotry as a common enemy deserving of a united response. In the 1960s, a coalition of women and Blacks successfully lobbied for affirmative action legislation at the federal level, a goal that neither group would in all likelihood have achieved by itself.[7]

Coalitions against hate have worked just as effectively to discourage organized hate groups. In August 2001, a few weeks before the attack on the Twin Towers and the Pentagon, the National Alliance, a White supremacist group out of West Virginia, dumped racist and anti-Semitic leaflets on lawns across the town of Sharon, Massachusetts. In response, several hundred Sharon residents came together to participate in a candlelight vigil against hate. Local leaders also held a day-long meeting in which they addressed the issue of bigotry and sought to find an appropriate long-term response. Many concerned Sharonites placed candles in their windows.

The National Alliance counted on its late-night distribution of flyers in Sharon to provoke widespread anxiety and division. But this hate group never counted on local residents to respond by coming together in a broad-based coalition of Muslims, Christians, and Jews, of Whites, Blacks, Asians, and Latinos, and by acquiring the strong backing of the board of selectmen, state representatives, the school committee, district attorney's office, local police, recreation department, Sharon Clergy Council, Islamic Center of New England, Office of the Superintendent of Schools, Gay/Straight Student Alliance, the Council on Aging, Sharon's Community Youth Coalition, ADL, and many Christian clergy and congregations in town.

The response by members of the Sharon community could serve as a model for how to respond to hate incidents in general. Where residents let the small incidents pass without response, hate can escalate into ever more serious offenses. Interpreting silence as support and encouragement, hatemongers are likely to take their tactics to a more dangerous level, stopping only when they have achieved their intended purpose.

The college campus is, in many respects, a microcosm of the larger society in which we live. Much of what works on campus can also be generalized to everyday life on the job and in the neighborhood. In addition to organizations that exclusively service the needs of a particular group of minority college students, campuses need a balance of more cooperative organizations and activities in which diverse members of the student body come together to achieve a common goal. The campus is a highly competitive social environment, much like its counterpart in the business world. Students often see one another as rivals for scarce resources. Only if they are interdependent—forced to rely on one another for the fulfillment of their important goals—will they begin to recognize their commonalities as targets of bigotry. Of course, they compete for better grades, good letters of reference, social relationships, and ultimately career opportunities. At the same time, there are many curricular and extra-curricular areas in which cooperation is desirable, if not necessary.

An interesting example of coalition politics on a college campus is provided by student reactions to Louis Farrakhan from the Nation of Islam—a Black Muslim sect—at Trinity College in Hartford, Connecticut. Sponsored by an organization of Black students on campus, the speaker was accused by some Trinity students of making statements that violated the college's recently established racial-harassment policy.

Outside the lecture hall, representatives from a number of different student groups handed out flyers containing the allegedly racist and anti-Semitic remarks of the speaker. Among those protesting the Black Muslim speaker were students from Hillel (a Jewish organization), Lavoz Latina, a Latino organization, College Democrats, and College Republicans.

Their actions paid off, at least in the short term. Trinity's president sent a letter inviting students to attend a campuswide discussion of bigotry. More than four hundred students of diverse ethnic backgrounds attended, providing an opportunity for them to share their viewpoints and pressure college administrators into considering alternative speakers on future occasions.[8] Coalitions can also initiate positive actions, instead of merely responding to negative actions, on their own behalf. Across the country, groups and organizations of students at major universities are coming together—women and men, Whites, Blacks, and Asians, Christians, Muslims, and Jews, straights and gays, Latinos and Anglos, able-bodied and students with disabilities—to celebrate the diversity of humankind by holding lectures, food fairs, and music festivals that highlight the strengths of *all* the cultures they represent. As separate factions, such groups are often viewed as little more than a thorn in the side of campus bigotry. Together, however, they represent a powerful force to be reckoned with by anyone who is intolerant of differences.

NOTES

CHAPTER 1

1. Charles Hynes, speech to the annual meeting of the Anti-Defamation League, Boston, October 11, 1989.
2. American-Arab Anti-Discrimination Committee, *Report on Anti-Arab Hate Crimes,* 1991.
3. Center For Democratic Renewal, *They Don't All Wear Whites Sheets: A Chronology of Racist and Far Right Violence—1980–1986* (Atlanta: Center for Democratic Renewal, 1987).
4. Center For Democratic Renewal, *They Don't All Wear Sheets.*
5. Richard Severo, "Former Klansman Indicted in Bombing of Synagogue," *New York Times,* March 8, 1984, p. 18.
6. Center For Democratic Renewal, *They Don't All Wear Sheets.*
7. Jack McDevitt, "Character of Civil Rights Violations in Boston Massachusetts, 1983–1989" (paper presented at the American Society of Criminology annual meeting, Reno, 1990).
8. McDevitt, "Character of Civil Rights Violations."
9. George Hacket, "Women Under Assault," *Newsweek,* July 16, 1990, pp. 23–24.
10. Lieutenant William Johnston, Boston Police Department, interview, September 1991.

CHAPTER 2

1. Alison Lurie, *The Language of Clothes* (New York: Random House, 1981), p. 70.

2. Lurie, *Language of Clothes*, p. 81.

3. Lurie, *Language of Clothes*, p. 81.

4. Jack Levin and William C. Levin, *The Functions of Discrimination and Prejudice* (New York: Harper and Row, 1982); Jack Levin, William C. Levin, and Arnold Arluke, "Powerful Elders" (paper presented at the annual meeting of the American Sociological Association, Pittsburgh, 1992); Nel Noddings, *Women and Evil* (Berkeley: University of California Press, 1989); Sam Keen, *Faces of the Enemy* (San Francisco: Harper and Row, 1986); Jack Levin, *The Violence of Hate* (Boston: Allyn and Bacon, 2002).

5. Elinor Langer, "The American Neo-Nazi Movement Today," *The Nation*, July 16–23, 1990, pp. 82–107.

6. Noddings, *Women and Evil*; Sam Keen, *Faces of the Enemy* (San Francisco: Harper and Row, 1986).

7. Lynne Duke, "Race Relations Are Worsening," in *Racism in America: Opposing Viewpoints* (San Diego: Greenhaven, 1991), pp. 17–20; Levin, *Violence of Hate*

8. Thea Lee, "Racism Is a Serious Problem for Asian Americans," in *Racism in America: Opposing Viewpoints* (San Diego: Greenhaven, 1991), pp. 38–45; Louis Harris, *Survey of Intergroup Relations in the United States* (New York: National Conference for Community and Justice, 2000).

9. Lee, "Racism Is a Serious Problem," pp. 38–45.

10. Richard D. Mohr, "Anti-Gay Stereotypes," in *Gays/Justice: A Study of Ethics, Society and Law* (New York: Columbia University Press), pp. 21–27.

11. Levin and Levin, *Functions of Discrimination and Prejudice.*; Levin, *The Violence of Hate*, (Boston: Allyn & Bacon).

CHAPTER 3

1. Jeffrey H. Goldstein and Paul E. McGhee, *The Psychology of Humor* (New York: Academic Press, 1972).

2. Marvin R. Koller, *Humor and Society: Explorations in the Sociology of Humor* (Houston: Cap and Gown, 1988).

3. John Leo, "Even Lenny Bruce Would Know Better," *U.S. News and World Report*, May 28, 1990, p. 21.

4. William Keough, *Punchlines* (New York: Paragon House, 1990), 194–197.

5. William Keough, *Punchlines*, 194–197.

6. Jerry Adler "The Rap Attitude," *Newsweek,* March 19, 1990, pp. 56–59.

7. Fred Bruning, "The Devilish Soul of Rock and Roll," *Macleans,* october 21, 1985, p. 13.

8. Jerry Adler, "The Rap Attitude," p. 59.

9. Brian D. Johnson, "Spanking New Madonna," *Maclean's,* June 18, 1990, pp. 48–50.

10. Andrew Cheung, "Racial Slurs by Sarah Silverman," 80–20 Initiative, July 2001, at www.80–20initiative.net.

11. Michele Greppi, "Rock Solid," *New York Post,* July 8, 1999, p. 82.

12. Michael Moynihan and Didrik Soderlind, *Lord of Chaos* (Venice, Calif.: Feral House, 1998).

13. Adler, "Rap Attitude," pp. 56–59.

14. R. Reese, "From the Fringe: Hip Hop Culture and Ethnic Relations" (paper presented at the Far West Popular Culture conference, Las Vegas, 1998).

15. Reese, "From the Fringe," p. 3.

16. Derrick Z. Jackson, "Unlikely Embrace," *Boston Globe,* February 14, 2001, p. 10.

17. Mary E. Ballard and Steven Coates, "The Immediate Effect of Heavy Metal and Rap Songs on the Mood of College Students," *Youth and Society,* December 1995, pp. 148–168.

18. Fred Bruning, "The Devilish Soul of Rock and Roll," *Maclean's,* October 21, 1985, p. 168.

19. Adler, "Rap Attitude," p. 56.

20. Ballard and Coates, "Immediate Effects," pp. 148–168.

21. Moynihan and Soderlind, *Lords of Chaos.*

22. ADL, "'HateCore' Music Label: Commercializing Hate," 2001.

23. ADL, "'HateCore' Music Label," 2001.

24. Special Edition, ADL Civil Rights Division, October 1987, p. 1.

25. *David Duke: A Bigot Goes to Baton Rouge,* Special Edition, Anti-Defamation League of B'nai B'rith—Civil Rights Division, March 1989, p. 2.

26. David Duke Web site, at www.duke.org.

27. William F. Buckley Jr., "In Search of Anti-Semitism," *National Review,* December 30, 1991, p. 32.

28. Eric Alterman, "The Pat and Abe Show," *The Nation,* November 5, 1990, pp. 517–520.

29. Richard Goldstein, "Celebrity Bigots," *Village Voice,* July 18, 2000, p. 37.

30. David Wild, "Who Is Howard Stern?" *Rolling Stone*, June 11, 1990, p. 87.

31. Edward Donnerstein, Daniel Linz, and Steven Penrod, *The Question of Pornography* (New York: Free Press, 1987).

32. Ni Yang and Daniel Linz, "Movie Ratings and the Content of Adult Videos: The Sex-Violence Ratio," *Journal of Communication*, Spring 1990; Donnerstein, Linz, and Penrod, *Question of Pornography*.

CHAPTER 4

1. Mark Pitcavage, "Ideology and Incompetency in the Courtroom," 2000, ADL Web site, at www.adl.org.

2. Julia Hatch and Angela Clinton, *Job Growth in the 1990s* (Washington, D.C.: Bureau of Labor Statistics, 2000).

3. Isaac Shapiro, Robert Greenstein, and Wendell Primus, *An Analysis of CBO Data* (Washington, D.C.: Center for Budget and Policy Priorities, 2001).

4. Phillips, *Wealth and Democracy*.

5. Lawrence Mishel and David Frankel, *The State of Working America* (Economic Policy Institute, 1990–1991).

6. S. Levitan, G. Mangum, and M. Pines, *A Proper Inheritance: Investing in the Self-Sufficiency of Poor Families* (Center for Social Policy Studies, George Washington University, 1989).

7. Samuel Halperin, *The Forgotten Half Revisited* (Washington, D.C.: AYPF, 2002.

8. See, for example, Mark A. Fossett and K. Jill Kiecolt, "The Relative Size of Minority Populations and White Racial Attitudes," *Social Science Quarterly*, December 1989, pp. 120–176; Thomas C. Wilson, "Interregional Migration and Racial Attitudes," *Social Forces*, September 1986, pp. 177–187.

9. Colleen Brush, "Report Indicates Rise in Antigay Violence," *Boston Globe*, January 29, 1992, p. 43.

10. Jack Douglas, *Deviance and Respectability* (New York: Basic, 1970).

11. Gavin McCormick, "Southern Poverty Law Center Co-founder Urges 'Justice for All.'" Associated Press, November 21, 2001, internet.

12. "Should Punishment Fit the Criminal?" *Newsweek*, June 13, 1983, p. 22; "It Isn't Fair," *Time*, November 14, 1983, p. 46.

13. Charles Leerhsen, "Busing the Prince of Love," *Newsweek*, November 19, 1990, p. 45; Larry Rohter, "Sect Leader Convicted on Conspiracy Charge," *New York Times*, May 28, 1992, p. A16.

14. David Ellis, "L.A. Lawless," *Time,* May 11, 1992.

15. Southern Poverty Law Center, *Hate Violence and White Supremacy: A Decade Review, 1980–1990,* Klanwatch Intelligence Report no. 47, December 1989, pp. 2–3.

CHAPTER 5

1. As quoted in David Gelman, "Going 'Wilding' in the City," *Newsweek,* May 8, 1989, p. 65.

2. Southern Poverty Law Center, "Hate Incidents," *Intelligence Report,* Winter 2002. Available online at splcenter.org.

3. SPLC, "Hate Incidents."

4. Lieutenant William Johnston, Boston Police Department, interview, September 1991.

5. James N. Baker, "Hatred in a Tolerant Town," *Newsweek,* October 1, 1990, p. 33.

6. Kevin Sullivan, "2 Arrested in 'Heinous' Racial Assault," *Washington Post,* March 4, 1992, p. A1.

7. Eric Pooley, "With Extreme Prejudice," *New York Times,* April 8, 1991, pp. 36–43.

8. "Gay-Bash Killing Testimony," *New York Newsday,* November 8, 1991, p. 6; Joseph P. Fried, "Queens Man Describes Hunt for a Victim, Then a Murder," *New York Times,* November 8, 1991, B1.

CHAPTER 6

1. Associated Press, "Man Who Says He was Angered by Sept. 11 Attack Convicted of Murder," June 25, 2002, internet.

2. Luz Delgato, "Black Family in North End is Met with Racism Graffiti," *Boston Globe,* July 31, 1992, p.17

3. Ronald Smothers, "Hate Crime Found Aimed at Blacks in White Areas," *New York Times,* April 28, 1990, p. 26.

4. Bill Stanton, *Klanwatch* (New York: Grove Weidenfeld, 1991).

5. *Extremism on the Right: A Handbook* (New York: Anti-Defamation League of B'nai B'rith, 1988).

6. Howard W. French, "Hatred and Social Isolation May Spur Acts of Racial Violence, Experts Say," *New York Times,* September 4, 1989, p. 30.

7. Ronald Powers, "Defendant Acquitted of Murder in '89 Racial Killing," *Boston Globe,* December 7, 1990, p. 13.

8. Rieder, *Canarsie.*

9. Rieder, *Canarsie*.

10. Greg Smith, "In Iowa, a Burning Hate," *Boston Globe*, November 23, 1991, p. 3.

11. "Wilder Says Racism Is on Rise in America," *Boston Globe*, November 25, 1991, p. 9.

12. Greg Smith, "In Iowa, a Burning Hate," *Boston Globe*, November 23, 1991, p. 3.

13. "Decade after All the Accusations, Dubuque Learned Its Lesson," *20/20*, March 21, 2002.

14. "Klan Leader Visits City Hit by Cross Burnings," *Boston Globe*, December 1, 1991, p. 27.

15. "Klan Leader Visits City," p. 27; "Cross Burnings Reported in Iowa," *Boston Globe*, November 17, 1991, p. 18; "Diversity in the Heartland,' *20/20*, December 14, 1991.

16. "Decade after All the Accusations."

17. Paul Murphy, "13 Charged with Indian Attacks," *India Abroad*, July 5, 1991, p. 29.

18. Connie Leslie, "We Shall Not Be Moved," *Newsweek*, December 12, 1988, p. 67.

CHAPTER 7

1. Stuart Wasserman, "After Carnage at California School, Curiosity, Questions, and Fears," *Boston Globe*, January 19, 1989, p. 1; "Five Children Killed as Gunman Attacks a California School," *New York Times*, January 18, 1989, p. 1; Robert Reinhold, "After Shooting, Horror but Few Answers," *New York Times*, January 19, 1989, p. B6.

CHAPTER 8

1. Nicholas Geranios, "Morris Dees Urges That Aryan Marches Be Ignored," Associated Press, April 4, 2001; Paul Nyden, "Dees Tells SVSC Audience About Battles Against Racism," *Charleston Gazette*, November 13, 2001.

2. Elinor Langer, "The American Neo-Nazi Movement Today," *The Nation*, July 16/23, 1990, pp. 87–103.

3. SPLC, "Metzger Warns of More Violence," *Klanwatch Intelligence Report*, June 1991, p. 1.

4. Ibid.

5. *Klanwatch Intelligence Report,* "12.5 Million Verdict Holds War Liable," no.53, December 1990, p. 2.

6. Richard A. Serrano, "Metzger Must Pay $5 Million in Rights Death," *Los Angeles Times,* October 23, 1990, p. 1.

7. "Metzger Warns of More Violence," p. 1.

8. *Neo Nazi Skinheads: A 1990 Status Report* (New York: Anti-Defamation League, 1990).

9. *Neo Nazi Skinheads.*

10. *Klanwatch Intelligence Report,* "A Year of WAR in the Courtroom," no. 54, February 1991.

11. Ronald Smothers, "Hate Groups Seen Growing as Neo-Nazis Draw Young," *New York Times,* February 19, 1992, p. A2.

12. Kathleen N. Blee, *Inside Organized Racism* (Berkeley: University of California, 2002).

13. See WCOC and National Alliance Web sites.

14. Kris Axtman, "Campus Labs Eyed after Anrhrax Scare," *Christian Science Monitor,* December 10, 2001, p. 1.

15. Klanwatch, "White Pride Worldwide," 2002, SPLC Web site, at splcenter.org.

16. Reprinted in Langer, "American Neo-Nazi Movement Today," p. 88.

17. "ADL Says 'Hate' Shows on Rise on Cable," *Boston Globe,* June 13, 1991, p. 88.

18. Douglas Belkin, "Anti-Semitic Beliefs Revealed in Death," *Boston Globe,* January 7, 2001, p. B7.

19. Robert Jackson, "Militia Movement 'a Shadow' of Past, Study Finds," *Los Angeles Times,* May 9, 2001, p. 20.

20. Langer, "American Neo-Nazi Movement Today."

21. "Hate Violence and White Supremecy, "*Klanwatch Intelligence Report,* no. 47, December 1989, p. 6.

22. *Extremism on the Right: A Handbook* (New York: Anti-Defamation League of B'nai B'rith, 1988), p. 106.

23. Linda Deutsch, "Man Gets Life for Calif. Hate Crime," Associated Press, March 27, 2001.

24. *Extremism on the Right,* p. 106.

25. "Hate Violence and White Supremacy," *Klanwatch Intelligence Report,* no. 47, December 1989, p.6.

26. *Extremism on the Right.*

CHAPTER 9

1. Frederick A. Hurst, *Report on University of Massachusetts Investigation* (Massachusetts Commission Against Discrimination, February 1987).

2. Hurst, *Report on University of Massachusetts Investigation.*

3. La Monica Everett-Haynes, "Hate Crimes Prompt Campus Campaign," *Arizona Daily Wildcat,* January 13, 2000.

4. Center for the Study of Sport in Society, *Youth Attitudes on Racism* (Northeastern University, October 1990).

5. Jean Merl, "Survey of Schools Finds Hate Crimes Widespread," *Los Angeles Times,* October 26, 1989, pp. A1, A43.

6. Shively et al., *Bias Crimes.*

7. Robert L. Gross, "Heavy Metal Music: A New Subculture in American Society," *Journal of Popular Culture,* 1990, pp. 119–130; Raschke, *Painted Black.* To be fair, it should be noted that the majority of heavy metal songs do not focus on violence. Sociologist Heather Walcutt content analyzed the lyrics from fifty top-selling heavy metal songs released between August 1991 and March 1992. She found that 20 percent of these songs contained violent or sexist lyrics (Heather Walcutt, "A Content Analysis of Heavy Metal Lyrics," unpublished manuscript, Northeastern University, Department of Sociology and Anthropology, 1992). Deena Weinstein, author of *Heavy Metal: A Cultural Sociology* (New York: Macmillan/Lexington, 1991), remarks that many critics of heavy metal give it a "maximally incompetent" reading. That is, "they have no sense of irony, take things at face value, take things literally, and therefore totally misinterpret the songs." As an example, she cites Ozzy Osbourne's "Suicide Solution," which some critics claim tells kids to commit suicide. But, according to Weinstein, "if you read the lyrics, listen to the song, or know who Ozzy Osborne is, it's a song denouncing alcoholism, a song of lament for a guy who drank himself to death." The problem, of course, is that many 12 and 13 year old kids are indeed "maximally incompetent" readers who take the lyrics of their favorite songs at face value.

8. *Neo Nazi Skinheads: A 1990 Status Report* (New York: Anti-Defamation League, 1990).

9. *Neo Nazi Skinheads.*

10. *Skinheads Target the Schools,* ADL Special Report, 1989.

11. *"Skinheads Target the Schools.*

12. "'JAP Baiting': When Sexism and Anti-Semitism Meet," *Special Edition of ADL Periodic Update,* October 1988.

13. Pete Hamill, "Black and Whites at Brown," *Esquire,* April 1990, pp. 67–68; Levine, "America's Youthful Bigots," pp. 59–60; Steele, "Recoloring of Campus Life," pp. 47–55; Ken Emerson, "Only Correct," *New Republic,* February 18, 1991, pp. 18–19; Howard J. Erhlich, *Campus Ethnoviolence and the Policy Options* (Baltimore: National Institute Against Prejudice and Violence, 1990); "Five Charged in Fatal Beating of Student," *The Enterprise,* August 19, 1992, p. 8.

14. "Bias Beating and a Death Shock a City," *New York Times,* August 23, 1992, p. 36.

15. Cited in Berrill, "Anti-Gay Violence and Victimization in the United States," *Journal of Interpersonal Violence* 5, no. 3 (1990).

16. Imtiyaz Deawala, "Graffiti Surfaces Near Harvard Dean's office," *Harvard Crimson,* January 12, 2000, internet.

17. Hamill, "Black and Whites at Brown," pp. 67–68.

18. *Extremism on the Right: A Handbook* (New York: Anti-Defamation League, 1988), p. 129.

19. Donald E. Muir, "'Whites' Fraternity and Sorority Attitudes Toward 'Blacks' on a Deep-South Campus," *Sociological Spectrum,* January-March 1991, pp. 93–103.

20. Andrew Merton, "Return to Brotherhood," *Ms.,* September 1985, pp. 60–65, 121–122.

21. "Anti-Homosexual T-Shirts Prompt Suspension of Syracuse Fraternity," *New York Times,* June 26, 1991, p. B4.

22. "5 Are Disciplined in Racial Prank at Fraternity," *New York Times,* October 22, 1989, p. 44.

23. Merton, "Return to Brotherhood," pp. 60–65, 121–122.

24. Hamill, "Black and Whites at Brown," p. 67.

CHAPTER 10

1. "Brooklyn Killing Reignites Strife," *Boston Globe,* February 8, 1992, p. 23; "Man Charged in Brooklyn Stabbing Death," *Boston Globe,* February 11, 1992, p. 60.

2. Debra Nussbaum Cohen and Jackie Rothenberg, "Blacks and Hasidic Jews Fighting in Brooklyn," *Jewish Advocate,* August 23–29, 1991, pp. 1, 25.

3. Adrian Walker, "Black Leader Defends Book Called Anti-Semitic," *Boston Globe,* July 27, 1992, pp. 1, 7.

4. Quoted in Walker, "Black Leader Defends Book," pp. 1, 7.

5. Paul Pringle, "While Tensions Sit Below Surface, California Becomes Minority Majority," *Charleston Gazette,* December 28, 2000, p. 4C.

6. Alex Prud'Homme, essay, *Time,* July 29, 1991, p. 15.

7. "More than 200 Arrested in Miami in 2nd Night of Racial Disturbances," *New York Times,* January 19, 1989, A1.

8. "Appeals Court Overturns Conviction of Miami Cop," *Jet,* July 22, 1991, p. 18.

9. James N. Baker, "Minority Against Minority," *Newsweek,* May 20, 1991, p. 28; "Congressional Probe Urged to Find Root of D.C. Rioting," *Jet,* May 27, 1991, p. 7.

10. Clarence Williams and Sylvia Moreno, "Chief Says Shooting Appears Justified," *Washington Post,* May 20, 2001, p. C1.

11. Linda Wheeler and Arthur Santana, "Shots Ring amid Crowd in Dupont," *Washington Post,* February 11, 2001, p. C1.

12. Jeffrey Gettleman, "Race-Related Brawl Erupts in Castaic Jail," *Los Angeles Times,* April 20, 2000, p. 3.

13. Mark Barabak, "Blacks See a Shrinking Political Role in California, *Los Angeles Times,* May 20, 2001, p. 1.

14. Muzafer Sherif et al., *Intergroup Conflict and Cooperation* (Norman: University of Oklahoma Press, 1961).

15. Quoted in Walker, "Black Leader Defends Book," pp. 1, 7.

CHAPTER 11

1. Harry C. Blaney, "Europe's Alarming Rise in Racism," *Toronto Star,* June 8, 2001, p. A15.

2. Denis Staunton, "Rise of Neo-Nazism Alarms Germany," *Manchester Guardian,* August 16, 2000, p. 4.

3. Judith Miller, "Strangers at the Gate," *New York Times Magazine,* September 15, 1991, pp. 33–37, 49, 80–81, 86.

4. Judith Miller, "Out of Hiding," *New York Times Magazine,* December 9, 1990, pp. 70–76.

5. "German Neo-Nazis Firebomb Foreigners' Housing," *New York Times,* August 26, 1992, p. A3; Jonathan Kaufman, "Attacks on Foreigners Daze Germany," *Boston Globe,* September 7, 1992, p. 2.

6. Staunton, "Rise of Neo-Nazism."

7. "German Mob Attacks Turkish Family's Home," Associated Press, October 30, 2000.

8. "Anti-Semitic Attacks Mar German Unity's 10th Anniversary," Deutsche Presse-Agentur, October 3, 2000.

9. "10,000 Demonstrate Against Extreme Right Violence," Agence France Presse, January 7, 2001.

10. Tony Paterson, "Violence Erupts in Berlin," *Ottawa Citizen,* December 2, 2001, p. A12.

11. "German Leftists Rally to Protest Hess Mourners," *Boston Globe*, August 16, 1992, p. 21.

12. Klanwatch, "The Ties That Bind," *Intelligence Report,* Fall 2001.

13. Allan Hall, "Shock as Half German Youth Back the Nazis," *Daily Mail,* February 8, 2001, p. 39.

14. Chris Wallace, *PrimeTime Live,* January 2, 1992.

15. Hall, "Shock."

16. Elizabeth Neuffer, "Killing Stirs Racism Fear in Marseilles," *Boston Globe,* March 5, 1995, p. 1.

17. Blaney, "Europe's Alarming Rise."

18. Youssef Ibrahim, "France Pushes Integration of Arab Immigrants," *New York Times,* December 7, 1989, p. A9.

19. Alan Riding, "Attacks on Jewish Graves Jolt France," *New York Times*, May 12, 1990, p. A3.

20. Julio Godoy, "Politics-France," Inter Press Service, January 22, 2002.

21. Alexander Stille, "Italy," *Atlantic,* February 1992, pp. 28–38.

22. Rigillo, "Anti-Semitic Attack in Italy Sparks Fears of Rise in Neo-Nazi Violence," Deutsche Press-Agentur, September 21, 2000.

23. Charles A. Radin, "Immigrants and Italians Face Strains," *Boston Globe*, February 26, 1992, pp. 1, 18.

24. Alison Mutler, "The Gypsy Minority," AP World Stream, September 10, 2001.

25. "African Pupils, Russian Police Clash," *Boston Globe*, August 13, 1992, p. 2.

26. Margaret Brearley, "The Persecution of Gypsies in Europe," *American Behavioral Scientist,* December 2001, pp. 588–599.

27. "ERRC Files Suit Against Slovakia," CTK News Agency, October 11, 2001.

28. Alan Lupo, "A Hatred That Endures," *Boston Globe*, February 22, 1992; Natan Sharansky, "The Greatest Exodus," *New York Times Magazine*, February 2, 1992, pp. 20–21, 46.

29. Stephen Engelberg, "Poland's Jewish Uproar, and with So Few Jews," *New York Times*, September 17, 1990, p. A6.

30. Miller, "Out of Hiding," pp. 70–76.

31. Quoted in Miller, "Out of Hiding," p. 74.

32. Paul Bookbinder, interview by author, August 26, 1992.

CHAPTER 12

1. *Report of the National Advisory Commission on Civil Disorders* (New York: Bantam, 1968).

2. James N. Baker, "Los Angeles Aftershocks," *Newsweek*, April 1, 1991, pp. 18–19; "Panel Probing L.A. Police Wants Chief to Resign; Cites Racism, Violence," *Jet*, July 29, 1991, p. 6; Seth Mydans, "Tape of Beating by Police Revives Charges of Racism," *New York Times*, March 7, 1991, p. A18.

3. "King Protest Turns Violent in Toronto," *Boston Globe*, May 5, 1992, p. 15.

4. Robert Hanley, "26 Arrested in Rampage in Jersey Town," *New York Times*, August 30, 1989, p. B1.

5. "Police Shooting Sparks Violence in New Jersey," *Jet*, September 18, 1989, p. 6.

6. Jannell McGraw, "Some Fear Pattern of Police Brutality," *Montgomery Advertiser*, July 30, 2000.

7. John Kifner, "Teaneck Youths Say BB Gun Was Waved Just Before Killing," *New York Times*, April 14, 1990, p. 1.

8. "Rights Advocate Maintains Police Beat Him in a 'Sting' He Arranged," *New York Times*, January 16, 1989, p. A11.

9. Arthur L. Kobler, "Police Homicide in a Democracy," *Journal of Social Issues*, Winter 1975, pp. 163–184.

10. *Miami Herald*, March 27 1983, p. 18A.

11. McDevitt, Balboni, and Bennett, *Improving the Quality and Accuracy of Bias Crime Statistics*.

12. McDevitt, Balboni, and Bennett, *Improving the Quality and Accuracy of Bias Crime Statistics*.

13. Federal Bureau of Investigation, *Training Guide for Hate Crime Data Collection* (U.S. Department of Justice, 1991). Developing and using a specialized unit or an officer to deal primarily or exclusively with hate

crimes offers a number of advantages for local police agencies. In smaller departments, one officer may be all that is necessary for the hate crime investigation unit. This person develops expertise in the phenomenon of hate crimes that can be applied to future investigations. For example, the hate crime officers may become sensitive to the anxieties that hate crime victims face—in particular, to the fear of retaliation from the offender or from the offender's friends. Once alerted to these very real fears, the officer can provide the victim with additional protection.

Affording the police more time to determine if an incident is actually hate motivated is a second advantage of a separate hate crime investigating unit. Turning the investigation over to a specialized unit with expertise in conducting hate crime investigations allows more time to be allocated to the investigation than would be available to the patrol officer who originally receives the call. Because these offenses are their primary responsibility, the hate crime officers can do a more complete inquiry, including canvassing a neighborhood for witnesses and interviewing the friends and family of potential suspects.

A third advantage of a specialized unit is that it offers a check against hate crimes being misclassified by the police during the initial investigation. Many specialized units have a policy of reviewing all incidents that might be bias motivated. In Boston's Community Disorders Unit, for example, the commanding officer reviews all interracial incident reports each day, whether bias is suspected or not. This procedure provides a check on cases that might be missed by the original responding officer. It affords a measure of accountability against bigoted officers who may feel that hate victims are not entitled to protection.

In Boston, for example, the policy works this way. For each case in which hate may be a motivation, the responding officer forwards a Boston police incident report form to the hate crime unit or officer. In addition, all incidents that involve interracial or interethnic crimes are forwarded to the unit as well. The descriptions of these incidents are reviewed by experienced hate crime investigators who, if they believe that bias or bigotry might be a motivation, can call the victim or the responding officer to begin an investigation.

A specialized unit also improves the likelihood that an arrest will result in a conviction by developing a relationship between the hate crime investigating officers and the local prosecutor's office. Hate crime cases are difficult to prosecute because the state has to prove the offender's intent in addition to elements of the crime that was charged. Specialized hate crime units learn from local prosecutors what types of evidence (e.g., witness testimony, use of defamatory language) are necessary to get a conviction. Once this is understood, the police can gear their investigation to collect the evidence that will be crucial to the case.

The existence of a specialized unit also promotes accountability in the police agency. Presently, in most police agencies throughout the United States, if a victim of hate violence who comes to the police is ignored, there is little that the victim or members of the local community can do. Even if they lodge a complaint with the police chief, the most victims can expect is an apology and a statement that the police will try to do a better job next time. Because the object of complaint was the action of a single officer, the police department in question may punish that officer but no department-wide changes will generally occur. By contrast, if there is a specialized unit or officer on staff, the victim and the community can point to a place where the department is not doing its job and can more forcefully demand system-wide changes.

Finally, the formation of a specialized unit continues to send the message that hate crimes are a priority with that particular police agency. As a result, victims may feel more secure, police may be more careful, and potential offenders may think twice before they break the law.

14. Jack McDevitt, "The Characteristics of Civil Rights Crimes in Boston, 1983–1987" (paper presented at the American Society of Criminology meeting, Boston, November 1989).

15. Federal Bureau of Investigation, *Training Guide for Hate Crime Data Collection* (U.S. Department of Justice, 1991).

16. McDevitt, "Characteristics of Civil Rights Crimes."

17. McDevitt, "Characteristics of Civil Rights Crimes."

18. Leslie Hatamiya, *Walk with Pride: Taking Steps to Address Anti-Asian Violence* (Japanese American Citizens League, August 1991).

19. Timothy Egan, "New Faces and New Roles for the Police," *New York Times,* April 25, 1991, p. A1.

20. Egan, "New Faces," p. A1.

21. Bruce True Berg and Marc Edmond Gertz, "Police Riots and Alienation," *Journal of Police Science and Administration* 12 (1984): 186–190.

22. Jack McDevitt, expert witness testimony in *Cotter v. Evans* (Boston, 2002).

CHAPTER 13

1. National Institute Against Prejudice and Violence, *Striking Back at Bigotry: Remedies Under Federal Law for Violence Motivated by Racial, Religious, and Ethnic Prejudice* (Washington, D.C.: NIAPV, 1986).

2. National Institute Against Prejudice and Violence, *Striking Back at Bigotry.*

3. National Institute Against Prejudice and Violence, *Striking Back at Bigotry.*

4. Southern Poverty Law Center, *Klanwatch Special Report Outlawing Hate Crime,* November 20, 1989, p. 4.

5. Dionne Jones, *Racially Motivated Violence: An Empirical Study of a Growing Social Problem,* National Urban League Report, May 1989.

6. Anti-Defamation League of B'nai B'rith, *Hate Crimes: ADL Blueprint for Action* (1997).

7. *R.A.V. v. St Paul,* 1992 WL 135564 (U.S).

8. Lyle Denniston, "Court to Rule on Legality of State Cross-Burning Bans," *Boston Globe,* May 29, 2002, p. A3.

9. Anti-Defamation League of B'nai B'rith, *Hate Crimes.*

10. Anti-Defamation League of B'nai B'rith, *Hate Crime Statutes: A 1991 Status Report* (1991).

11. National Institute Against Prejudice and Violence, *Striking Back at Bigotry.*

12. American-Arab Anti-Discrimination Committee, *1991 Report on Anti Arab Hate Crimes,* February 1992.

13. American-Arab Anti-Discrimination Committee, *1991 Report on Anti Arab Hate Crimes.*

14. American-Arab Anti-Discrimination Committee, *1991 Report on Anti Arab Hate Crimes.*

15. Center for Democratic Renewal, *They Don't All Wear Sheets: A Chronology of Racist and Far Right Violence, 1980–1986* (1987).

16. Center For Democratic Renewal, *They Don't All Wear Sheets.*

17. Center For Democratic Renewal, *They Don't All Wear Sheets.*

18. Center For Democratic Renewal, *They Don't All Wear Sheets.*

19. Center For Democratic Renewal, *They Don't All Wear Sheets.*

20. Anti-Defamation League of B'nai B'rith, *Hate Crime Statutes.*

21. Anti-Defamation League of B'nai B'rith, *Hate Crime Statutes.*

22. Anti-Defamation League of B'nai B'rith, *Hate Crime Statutes.*

23. Anti-Defamation League of B'nai B'rith, *Hate Crime Statutes.*

24. Dina Temple-Raston, *A Death in Texas* (New York: Henry Holt, 2002).

25. Council on Foreign Relations, *Hate Crimes* (Washington, D.C.: CFR, 2002).

26. Center For Democratic Renewal, *They Don't All Wear Sheets.*

27. Center For Democratic Renewal, *They Don't All Wear Sheets.*

28. Center For Democratic Renewal, *They Don't All Wear Sheets.*

29. Anti-Defamation League of B'nai B'rith, *Hate Crime Statutes.*

30. American-Arab Anti-Discrimination Committee, *1991 Report on Anti Arab Hate Crimes.*

31. United Press International, "Cross Burned at Black Man's Home," March 21, 1989, internet.

32. Center For Democratic Renewal, *They Don't All Wear Sheets.*

33. Center For Democratic Renewal, *They Don't All Wear Sheets.*

34. Center For Democratic Renewal, *They Don't All Wear Sheets.*

35. Jack McDevitt, "Characteristics of Civil Rights Violations in Boston, 1983–1987" (paper presented at American Society of Criminology meeting, Boston, 1989).

36. Federal Bureau of Investigation "Uniform Crime Reports: Hate Crime Statistics 2000," (FBI, 1991).

37. Federal Bureau of Investigation, *Crime in the United States, 1990* (FBI, August 1991).

38. Francis M. Roche, *Boston Police Department Community Disorders Unit Annual Report,* March 1992.

39. Federal Bureau on Investigation, *Crime in the United States,* 1990.

40. Fedural Bureau of Investigation, "Uinform Crime Reports: Hate Crime Statistics 2000," (FBI, 1991).

41. McDevitt, "Characteristics of Civil Rights Violations."

42. Wallace, Report of the Bias Incident Investigation Unit New Y ork City Police Department (February 1990), p.249

43. Roche, *Boston Police Department Community Disorders Unit Annual Report.*University Press, 1998).

45. William Keough, *Punchlines* (New York: Paragon House, 1990).

46. Muzafer Sherif and Carolyn Sherif, *Intergroup Conflict and Cooperation* (Norman: University of Oklahoma Press, 1961); Susan Olzak, "Poverty, Segregation, and Race Riots,"*American Sociological Review,* August 1996, pp. 590–613.

47. Carl Hovland and Robert Sears, "Minor Studies of Aggression," *Journal of Psychology,* Winter 1940, pp. 301–310.

48. Danielle Gordon and Natalie Pardo, "Hate Crime Strikes Changing Suburbs,"*Chicago Reporter,* September 1997, p. 1.

49. Danielle Gordon and Natalie Pardo, "Hate Crimes Strike Changing Suburbs,"*The Chicago Reporter* (September 1997), p.1.

CHAPTER 14

1. Michael Shively, Jack McDevitt, Shea Cronin, and Jennifer Balboni, *Crime in Massachusetts High Schools* (Boston: Center for Criminal Justice Policy Research, 2002).

2. Anti-Defamation League, *Audit of Anti-Semitic Incidents, 1991.*

3. Bureau of Justice Statistics, *Report to the Nation on Crime and Justice,* 2d ed., March 2002.

4. Bureau of Justice Statistics, *Report to the Nation.*

5. Dan Weiss, interview, Northeastern University, Boston, August 5, 1992.

6. Montgomery County Office of Human Relations, *Handling Hate Violence,* Resource Book ,1989.

7. Interview with Deputy Superintendent Bill Johnson (July 19, 1990).

CHAPTER 15

1. Deputy Superintendent William Johnston, Boston Police Department, interview, Northeastern University, February 13, 1994.

2. "ADL Finds Increase in Anti-Semitic Incidents During 1990,"*Jewish Life,* Spring 1991, p. 46.

3. "Massachusetts Town Votes to Remove Indian Swastikas," *New York Times,* January 14, 1990, p. 19.

4. "Fraternity Rebuff Stirs Whirlwind in Vermont,"*New York Times,* April 11, 1990, p. A17.

5. "Student Boycott Gains Staff Change at Bookstore," *New York Times,* February 25, 1990, Campus Life, pp. 44–45.

6. Edgar Morin, *Rumor in Orleans* (New York: Random House, 1971).

CHAPTER 16

1. "Klan Chief Pleads in Shooting Case," *Boston Globe,* April 12, 1992, p. 31.

2. "Five Louisiana Klansmen Are Indicted in Cross Burnings," *Boston Globe,* August 14, 1991, p. 8.

3. Lynne Duke, "How a Michigan Campus Erupted in Racial Strife," *Boston Globe,* April 14, 1992, p. 3.

4. Ronald Smothers, "25 Years Later, Racial Tensions Revive in Selma," *New York Times,* February 11, 1990, p. 30.

5. Lance Morrow, "The Provocative Professor," *Time,* August 26, 1991, pp. 19–20.

6. Jack Levin and James A. Fox, "Shooting at the Ivory Tower," *Boston Globe,* September 9, 1990, p. C20.

7. Jack Levin and William C. Levin, *The Functions of Discrimination and Prejudice* (New York: Harper and Row, 1982).

8. Jack McDevitt, "Black Talks Prompt Protest and Complaint," *New York Times,* December 10, 1989, Campus Life, p. 67.

BIBLIOGRAPHY

Abelmann, Nancy, and John Lie. *Blue Dreams: Korean Americans and the Los Angeles Riots.* Cambridge: Harvard University Press, 1995).

Adorno, Theodore, Else Frankel-Brunswick, Daniel J. Levinson, and Nevitt Sanford. *The Authoritarian Personality.* New York: Harper and Row, 1950.

Allport, Gordon W. *The Nature of Prejudice.* Reading, Mass.: Addison-Wesley, 1954.

Anti-Defamation League of B'nai B'rith. *An ADL Special Report: The KKK Today: A 1991 Status Report.* New York: Anti-Defamation League, 1991.

_____. *1989 Audit of Anti-Semitic Incidents.* New York: Anti-Defamation League, 1990.

_____. *1990 Audit of Anti-Semitic Incidents.* New York: Anti-Defamation League, 1991.

_____. *Combatting Bigotry on Campus.* New York: Anti-Defamation League, 1989.

_____. *Hate Crimes: Policies and Procedures for Law Enforcement Agencies.* New York: Anti-Defamation League, 1989.

_____. *Liberty Lobby: Network of Hate.* New York: Anti-Defamation League, 1990.

_____. *Louis Farrakhan: The Campaign to Manipulate Public Opinion: A Study in the Packaging of Bigotry.* New York: Anti-Defamation League, 1990.

_____. *Neo-Nazi Skinheads: A 1990 Status Report.* New York: Anti-Defamation League, 1990.

Berrill, Kevin. *Anti-Gay Violence: Causes, Consequences, Responses,* pp. 1–26. Washington, D.C.: National Gay and Lesbian Task Force. 1986.

Bettelheim, Bruno, and Morris Janowitz. *Social Change and Prejudice*. New York: Free Press, 1964.

Blackwell, James E. *The Black Community*. New York: Harper and Row, 1991.

Blauner, Bob. *Black Lives, White Lives: Three Decades of Race Relations in America*. Los Angeles: University of California Press, 1989.

Bureau of Justice Statistics. *Correctional Population of the United States, 2000*. Bureau of Justice Statistics Report, December 2001.

Clark, Floyd I. "Hate Violence in the United States." *F.B.I. Law Enforcement Bulletin* 60 (1991).

Clark, William. *The California Cauldron: Immigration and the Fortunes of Local Communities*. New Haven: Guilford, 1998.

Coates, James. *Armed and Dangerous*. New York: Noonday, 1987.

Cohen, David. *Chasing the Red, White, and Blue*. New York: Picador, 2001.

Comstock, Gary David. *Violence Against Lesbians and Gay Men*. New York: Columbia University Press, 1991.

Council on American Islamic Relations. *The Status of Muslim Civil Rights in the United States*. Washington, D.C.: CAIR, 2002.

Donnerstein, Edward, Daniel Linz, and Steven Penrod. *The Question of Pornography*. New York: Free Press, 1987.

Eagles, Charles W., ed. *The Civil Rights Movement in America*. Jackson: University Press of Mississippi, 1986.

Finn, Peter. "Bias Crime: Difficult of Define, Difficult to Prosecute." *Journal of Criminal Justice*, Summer 1988.

Finn, Peter, and Taylor McNeil. 1988. Bias *Crime and the Criminal Justice Response: A Summary Report Prepared for the National Criminal Justice Association*. Cambridge, Mass.: Abt Associates, 1988.

Fox, James Alan, and Jack Levin. *Overkill*. New York: Dell, 1996.

_____. *The Will to Kill* (Boston: Allyn and Bacon, 2001).

Garofalo, James. "Bias and Non-Bias Crimes in New York City: Preliminary Findings." Paper presented at the American Society of Criminology, Baltimore, 1990.

Governors Task Force on Civil Rights. *Report on Racial, Ethnic, and Religious Violence in California*. Sacramento: California Department of General Services, Office of State Printing, 1982.

Green, Donald, Dara Strolovitch, and Janelle Wong. *Defended Neighborhoods, Integration, and Hate Crime*. New Haven: Yale University Press, Institution for Social Policy Studies, 1967.

Hamm, Mark. *Hate Crime*. Cincinnati: Anderson, 1994.

Hatamiya, Leslie. *Walk with Pride: Taking Steps to Address Anti-Asian Violence.* Handbook prepared for Coro Foundation. San Francisco, 1991.

Herek, Gregory, and Kevin Berrill. *Primary and Secondary Victimization in Anti-Gay Hate Crimes: Official Response and Public Policy in Hate Crimes Confronting Violence Against Lesbians and Gay Men*. Newbury Park, Calif.: Sage, 1992.

Hodge, John L., Donald K Struckmann, and Lynn Dorland Trost. *Cultural Bases of Racism and Group Oppression*. Berkeley, Calif.: Two Riders, 1975.

Jacobs, James B., and Kimberly Potter. *Hate Crimes*. New York: Oxford University Press, 1998.

Jenkins, William D. *Steel Valley Klan*. Kent, Ohio: Kent State University Press, 1990.

Karl, Johnathon. *The Right to Bear Arms*. New York: HarperCollins, 1995.

Kerner, O. *The 1968 Report of the National Advisory Commission on Civil Disorders*. New York: Pantheon, 1968.

Kim, Kwang C. *Koreans in the Hood*. Baltimore: Johns Hopkins University Press, 1999.

Klanwatch. *Hate Violence and White Supremacy: A Decade Review, 1980–1990.* Klanwatch Intelligence Report, no. 47 Montgomery, Ala.: Southern Poverty Law Center, 1989.

_____. *Special Report: Outlawing Hate Crime*. Montgomery, Ala.: Southern Poverty Law Center, 1989.

LaFree, Gary. "Homicide: Cross-National Perspectives." *Studying and Preventing Homicide,* ed. M. Dwayne Smith and Margaret A. Zahn. Thousand Oaks, Calif.: Sage, 1999.

Lawrence, Frederick M. *Punishing Hate: Bias Crimes Under American Law*. Cambridge: Harvard University Press, 1999.

Leiberman, Michael. "The Hate Crime Statistics Act." *Anti-Defamation League of B'nai B'rith Bulletin,* May-June 1990, p. 1.

Levin, Brian. "Extremism and the Constitution." *American Behavioral Scientist.* December 2001, pp. 714–754.

Levin, Jack. *The Functions of Prejudice*. New York: Harper and Row, 1975.

Levin, Jack, and James Alan Fox. *Mass Murder: America's Growing Menace.* New York: Plenum, 1985.

Levin, Jack, and William C. Levin. *The Functions of Discrimination and Prejudice.* New York: Harper and Row, 1982.

Levin, Jack, and Alexander Thomas. "Racial Identity of Police and Perceptions of Police Brutality." *Justice Quarterly*. September 1997, pp. 276–283.

Massachusetts Executive Office of Public Safety. *Hate Crime in Massachusetts Preliminary Annual Report: January-December 1990*. Boston: Executive Office of Public Safety and Criminal History System Board, Crime Reporting Unit, 1990.

McDevitt, Jack. "The Study of the Character of Civil Rights Crimes in Massachusetts (1983–1978)." Paper presented at the American Society of Criminology Meeting, Reno, 1990.

_____. *The Study of the Implementation of the Massachusetts Civil Rights Act*. Boston: Northeastern University, Center for Applied Social Research, 1989.

McDevitt, Jack, Jen Balboni, and Susan Bennett. *Improving the Quality and Accuracy of Bias Crime Statistics*. Washington, D.C.: Bureau of Justice Statistics, 2000.

McDevitt, Jack, Jennifer Balboni, Luis Garcia, and Joann Gu. "Consequences for Victims: A Comparison of Bias- and Non-Bias Motivated Assaults." *American Behavioral Scientist*, December 2001, pp. 697–713.

National Gay and Lesbian Task Force. *Dealing with Violence: A Guide for Gay and Lesbian People*. Washington, D.C.: National Gay and Lesbian Task Force, 1986.

National Institute Against Prejudice and Violence. *Prejudice and Violence: An Annotated Bibliography of Selected Materials on Racial, Religious, and Ethnic Violence and Intimidation*. Baltimore: National Institute Against Prejudice and Violence, 1985.

National Organization of Black Law Enforcement Executives. *Final Report: Racial and Religious Violence: A Model Law Enforcement Response*. Washington, D.C.: National Organization of Black Law Enforcement Executives, 1985.

Newman, Katherine S. *Falling from Grace: The Experience of Downward Mobility in the American Middle Class*. New York: Free Press, 1988.

Padgett, George. "Radically Motivated State Enforcement and Federal Civil Rights Remedies." *Journal of Law and Criminology* 75 (1986): 103–138.

Phillips, Kevin. *Wealth and Democracy*. New York: Broadway Books, 2002.

Raschke, Carl A. *Painted Black*. New York: Harper, 1990.

Rieder, Jonathan. *Canarsie*. Cambridge: Harvard University Press, 1985.

Schuman, Howard, and Charlotte Steeh, Lawrence Bobo, and Maria Kryson. *Racial Attitudes in America*. Cambridge: Harvard University Press, 1997.

Shively, Michael, Jack McDevitt, Shea Cronin, and Jon Balboni. *Bias Crimes in Massachusetts High Schools*. Boston: Center for Criminal Justice Policy Research, 2002.

Sigelman, Lee, and Susan Welch. *Black Americans' Views of Racial Inequality.* Cambridge: Cambridge University Press, 1991.

Sniderman, Paul M., and Michael Gary Hegen. *Race and Inequality: A Study in American Values.* Chatham, N.J.: Chatham House, 1985.

Southern Poverty Law Center. "The Roots of Hate." *Intelligence Report,* Spring 2002, pp. 58–60.

Sparks, Richard F. *Research on Victims of Crime: Accomplishment, Issues, and New Directions.* Crime and Delinquency Issues: A Monograph Series. Rockville, Md.: National Institute of Mental Health Center for Studies of Crime and Delinquency, 1982.

Tafoya, William. "Rioting in the Streets: Deja Vu." Nancy Taylor, ed., *Bias Crime: The Law Enforcement Response.* Chicago: Office of International Criminal Justice, 1991.

Tobin, Gary A., and Sharon L. Sassler. *Jewish Perceptions of Anti-Semitism.* New York: Plenum, 1988.

U.S. Department of Justice. *Hate Crime Collection Guidelines.* Washington, D.C.: Federal Bureau of Investigation, 1991

_____. *Measuring Crime.* Washington, D.C.: Bureau of Justice Statistics, 1981.

_____. *Training Guide for Hate Crime Data Collection.* Washington, D.C.: Federal Bureau of Investigation, 1991.

_____. *Uniform Crime Reporting National Indicent-Based Reporting System.* Vol. 1, *Data Collection Guidelines.* Washington, D.C.: Federal Bureau of Investigation, 1988.

Ward, Benjamin. "Hate Crimes: The Police Response in New York City." *Police Chief* 53 (1986): 46–47.

Watts, Meredith W. "Aggressive Youth Cultures and Hate Crime." *American Behavioral Scientist.* December 2001, pp. 600–615.

Weiss, Joan, Howard Ehrlich, and Barbara Larcom. "Ethnoviolence at Work." *Journal of Intergroup Relations.* Winter 1991–1992, pp. 21–33.

Weiss, Joan C., and Paul H. Ephross. "Group Work Approaches to 'Hate Violence' Incidents." *Social Work* 31 (1989): 19.

Wexler, Chuck. 1986. "When Law and Order Works: Boston's Innovative Approach to the Problem of Racial Violence." *Crime and Delinquency* 32 (1986): 205–223.

Wilson, William Julius, ed. "The Ghetto Underclass: Social Science Perspectives." *Annual of the American Academy of Political and Social Science* 501 (1989).

INDEX